CASH IN A FLASH

ALSO BY MARK VICTOR HANSEN AND ROBERT G. ALLEN

Cracking the Millionaire Code
The One Minute Millionaire

CASH
IN A
FLASH

FAST MONEY IN SLOW TIMES

MARK VICTOR HANSEN
AND ROBERT G. ALLEN

HARMONY BOOKS

NEW YORK

Grateful acknowledgment is made to the following for permission
to reprint previously published material:

Nahmod Music Co.: "Sacred Love," by Daniel Nahmod, copyright © Nahmod
Music Co. (ASCAP). Reprinted by permission of Daniel Nahmod.

Tulshi Sen: Excerpt from *Ancient Secrets of Success for Today's World*
by Tulshi Sen, published by Omnilux Communications, Inc, 2006.
Reprinted by permission of the author.

James Skinner, Mark Victor Hansen, and Roice Kruger: Text from the book
The Devil Only Knows One Word . . . BUT! by James Skinner, Mark Victor Hansen,
and Roice Kruger. Reprinted by permission of the authors.

Library of Congress Cataloging-in-Publication Data is available upon request.

ISBN 978-0-307-45330-3

Printed in the United States of America

Design by Helene Berinsky

Illustrations and diagrams by Chaz DeSimone, chazdesimone.com
Hummingbird illustrations by Cash Donovan

10 9 8 7 6 5 4 3 2 1

First Edition

We want this book to tenfold you

CONTENTS

FORWARD

Most books begin with a foreword—a short introductory essay preceding the text of a book. This book begins instead with a forward—a look into your future.

Imagine how you'll feel as you finish reading the last page of this book. If your finances are in fairly good shape now, within ninety days you could be on your way to financial freedom. If your finances are upside down now, as is the case for millions of people during these uncertain economic times, you'll have a plan to turn them right side up and put your money worries behind you forever—assuming you simply follow the plan. How does that feel?

Now, zip forward three months as you successfully complete your ninety-day adventure. You've learned how to play the money game. The burdens of your financial insecurities are lightening. Extra streams of income are now pouring into your life—small streams of cash that immediately give moisture to parched areas of your financial landscape. Winter is over. Spring has arrived. The fruits of a bountiful money harvest are imminent.

Move forward to this time next year. Memories of credit card debt and financial pressures are receding into the past. That was the old you. The lifestyle of the new you has stabilized, with increasing signs of abundance. Pools of prosperity are showing up everywhere—growing bank accounts, stock portfolios, and equities.

You pinch yourself. Are you dreaming? Is this for real?

Yes, it is.

Within five years, you can hardly remember why you used to have concerns about your finances. Increasingly, you've become a magnet for wealth. You reside in an oasis of opportunity. You live in a new home in a better neighborhood and your new neighbors greet you with respect. Your old clique of family and friends is still wondering how you did it. You smile inwardly. If they only knew how simple it was.

Simple, yes.

But easy? No.

Those first ninety days were not easy. It takes time to learn good habits and jettison bad ones. However, from your vantage point now—your new way of seeing—you realize it was worth it. You wonder why more people don't do what's necessary to enjoy a prosperous lifestyle.

Looking into the distant future, you picture how your new money habits have begun to positively affect your family, your friends, and everyone you meet. Your children and their children's children now have access to the finest education. You have the freedom to pursue your passions. You can see yourself being generous with your overflowing wealth. Magnanimous. Philanthropic. From this position, it's only natural for you to want to help others.

The nicest part of all of this is the confidence you feel. You feel more awake than you have ever felt before. Indeed, you feel blessed. You know that in today's uncertain climate, you could lose it all. But since you've learned how to launch new streams of cash, you'd just start over and create it all again. Knowing this, you have a sense of peace and inner security.

BUT WAIT . . .

This is not the future. This is today. You're back here. In the present. With more debt than you might like and less freedom than you probably hoped for at this time in your life.

The pressures of your current life are crowding in on you. They are so real. The dreams of the abundant future can appear to be so far off. So distant. The chasm that separates these two existences can sometimes seem so wide. So deep. So seemingly impassable.

This book is the bridge across that chasm . . . one step at a time.

So today. Right now. This moment. Take a deep breath.

The lifestyle you experience today has been cooking for a long, long time. You might be financially comfortable. You might be financially strapped. What recipe did you use to get here? Who wrote that recipe? Who taught it to you? How did you learn it?

Did anyone ever sit down with you and teach you how to cook a delicious life? A life filled with cash, abundance, happiness, freedom, and joy?

If your life is not as rich and satisfying as you'd like, it's time to learn a better recipe.

RECIPE FOR A RICHER LIFE: THE FASTEST WAY TO CASH

Suppose there was a recipe book for a successful life. What kind of recipes would you find in it? Is there a secret recipe for happiness in your relationships? Is there a special recipe for peace and inner joy? What about a recipe for physical health? Or mental and emotional well-being? What are the ingredients in the recipe for financial freedom?

Our expertise is in the area of finances—of money mastery and the creation of wealth. We're master chefs when it comes to financial freedom, and we'd like to share with you our cookbook with our favorite recipes for financial success. It's time for you to achieve the abundance and success you've always hoped for.

I NEED TO MAKE SOME SERIOUS MONEY *NOW*

There are hundreds of slow-cooking, Crock-Pot-type recipes for cooking up a financial feast. But let's face it, today, most of us have a need for speed when it comes to earning extra money. This book will focus on microwave recipes that can generate a fast flow of cash in ninety days or less. We'll show you how to set up your financial kitchen, assemble the ingredients, acquire the proper tools, and learn how to organize yourself to cook the fullest, richest life in the fastest time possible.

It doesn't matter why you need to make some serious money. Maybe something unexpected happened—like an accident, a job loss, a financial reversal, or a sudden illness. Maybe you've been a master procrastinator all your life and you're finally up against a looming deadline—like paying for a college education or retirement. Perhaps you don't have an immediate emergency but you've come to realize that a way to escape the paycheck-to-paycheck prison is to generate some extra cash or cash flow on the side. Or you might just be sitting on an opportunity and don't know what to do with it. Whatever the reason, this book will show you how to create the cash you need and the life you've always desired.

Neither of us was born with a silver spoon in our mouth. We've learned to earn our fortunes through hard work and many, many mistakes. We can teach you the shortcuts that we've learned along the way. We'll share with you the recipes that really work and tell you how to avoid the recipes that we've discovered aren't worth your time and effort.

You might be wondering if using the metaphor of a recipe is appropriate to the concept of success and wealth. When people think of success, they usually think of a formula, a method, or a blueprint. They rarely think of a recipe.

For example, in his classic book *Think and Grow Rich*, Napoleon Hill talks about the thirteen principles of success: desire, faith, autosuggestion, imagination, specialized knowledge, decision, organized planning, persistence, the power of the mastermind, the mystery of sex transmutation, the brain, the subconscious mind, and the sixth sense. In essence, Hill teaches that if you "add" these principles to your life—desire + faith + persistence, and so on—you'll become rich just by thinking about it.

Financial expert Suze Orman shares her insights in *The 9 Steps to Financial Freedom*—such as being honest with yourself and recognizing true wealth. Follow these steps and, according to Suze, you'll be financially free.

Such basic formulas list the steps or principles to achieve wealth, but in no particular order or intensity. On the other hand, a recipe is much more precise. It lists which key ingredients need to be mixed in which specific proportions in exactly the correct sequence for a specific period of time.

We believe that using the metaphor of a recipe is a better and more effective way to think about money and the creation of wealth. But there are pitfalls. Some people may look at the "bakeries" of wealth around them and wonder, "How did they bake those cakes? What recipe did they use? What ingredients?" and then try to figure it out on their own through trial and error. Following someone else's recipe would be much faster and easier.

These amateur chefs try to re-create the recipes of the top wealth chefs but can't seem to get their own cash cake to rise. We think it's because they've been adding ingredients that spoil the recipe—such as a negative attitude or a poisonous relationship. Or they've been leaving out key ingredients—such as persistence or faith in a Higher Power.

For example, suppose you were trying to bake a chocolate cake from scratch. You'd need a few key ingredients: flour, sugar, eggs, chocolate. Suppose you left out one of the key ingredients—like flour. Your cake wouldn't be very tasty, would it? What if you followed the *exact* recipe, with every ingredient mixed in the proper proportion and sequence. But just before you poured the batter into the cake pan, you added an extra ingredient that wasn't in the recipe—say, a cup of vinegar, or six crushed cloves of garlic, or a pound of sausage. How would your chocolate cake turn out?

We'd like to teach you several specific recipes for creating enlightened wealth. We'll share with you which key ingredients are necessary and how to combine them to achieve unlimited prosperity.

Are you ready to cook your way to wealth?

Recipes for Riches

CHUNKS AND STREAMS

When it comes to wealth creation, there are two basic ways to think about money: chunks and streams.

In our first book, *The One Minute Millionaire,* we laid out the strategies for earning chunks of money in short periods of time, such as a million dollars in ninety days. We specifically chose to create such a large amount of money in such a short time frame because we wanted to stretch your mind to the possibility of becoming an enlightened millionaire.

There is no doubt that a million dollars is going to go through your fingers before retirement. Our objective is to raise the possibility of earning double or triple that amount while simultaneously shortening the time to do it.

Earning an extra million in twenty years is a very realistic goal. After reading *The One Minute Millionaire,* many entrepreneurs have been able to do it in five years or less. Some did it in less than a year. Thus, fast chunks.

In this book, we have tackled an entirely different financial problem—the need for fast streams. We realize that the goal of most people is not to become a net millionaire with a million in assets (chunks). The more pressing goal is to bring money in the door immediately—streams of monthly income to support a struggling family *now.*

Like most, you've probably procrastinated too long. You've awakened to the fact that retirement is racing toward you and the thought of living on Social Security is not that appetizing. You need to bring money in the door in the next ninety days. Maybe your home is in foreclosure. Maybe you've just lost your job. You don't have time to take a night school class to train for a new career. You barely have enough time to read this book.

You need an extra stream of income *fast!*

TWO TYPES OF MONEY STREAMS: LINEAR AND RESIDUAL

When people think of making a stream of money, their first thought is to get a job and earn a salary. But this might not be the best long-term solution. If you just got laid off from a job, you don't want to go begging for another job, do you? You've had enough of that kind of "security." Nope. You need cash flow that you can count on.

Before we go much further, let's explain the difference between linear income and residual income. Linear income is when you work for money. Residual income is when money works for you.

Linear income usually comes in the form of a salary—working for someone else. You rent yourself out to some employer, usually on an hourly basis. One unit of your time yields one unit of money—X number of dollars per hour. We call this type of money linear income because you only get paid once for every hour you work. If you want some more linear income, you need to put in another hour of work. If you stop working, the stream of money also stops.

Residual income usually comes in the form of profits—earned when your money is invested wisely. Instead of renting yourself out to some employer, the goal is for you to rent out your money to do the work for you.

The power of residual income is that you get paid multiple times for every hour you work. For example, both of us are authors. We work very hard to write our books (many units of time), but once these books are completed, they continue to be sold over and over again to new readers. We've been paid thousands of times for hours that we invested twenty years ago. And we'll continue to be paid for these same hours for as long as these books continue to be sold.

Do you want to be paid only once for your time—or would you like to be paid hundreds, even thousands of times for every hour you work?

Ultimately, this is the difference between financial servitude and financial freedom. Many couples work two or three linear-income jobs and still can't make ends meet. It's because they're only getting paid once for their time. In this book, we'll share with you multiple ways for getting paid multiple times for every hour you work. Eventually, you'll be able to retire and let these multiple streams continue to flow into your life without you having to go out and earn more.

RECIPE FOR AN EARLY RETIREMENT

Essentially, this is a recipe book for early retirement. For example, suppose you were tired of driving to work every day and wanted to stay home—to take care of your kids, to nurse an aging parent, or just to take a needed break. Suppose you needed to bring in an income of at least $50,000 a year to support yourself. How could you do it?

The traditional (and longest) approach to retirement is to sock money away in your IRA or 401(k) for several decades until you have enough to buy yourself your own gold watch and retire on your savings. This is simply too long to wait in this volatile world.

Are there faster ways to cash?

Absolutely.

The fastest (and least likely) way would be for you to inherit a large chunk of cash—let's say a million dollars. You invest this money in a safe certificate of deposit at your local bank earning 5 percent interest. This generates a predicable stream of interest—approximately $4,000 per month—for the rest of your life. In other words, if you had a million invested, it would throw off residual income every year that you could spend for retirement. So without lifting a finger, you could stay home on this modest income and devote your full time to things and people that are more important to you.

The recipe that we have just explained is precise. The ingredients are:

A relationship with someone who will name you in his or her will
Inherit $1,000,000 in cash
Invest it in a safe bank account
Make sure it pays 5 percent interest yearly

Unfortunately, very few of us have a chunk of money like that—or even the prospects of inheriting it. By the same token, very few of us want to work at the proverbial career for forty years. That's the long and the short of it.

Are there other nontraditional ways to early retirement? Yes, there are.

What if you wanted to retire in less than forty years? Is that possible? Absolutely. Could you retire in forty months? Or forty weeks? Maybe in as few as ninety days from start to finish?

Yes.

Is this realistic?

Of course not! Yet we hope to stretch your mind to a new way of thinking and, ultimately, a new way of seeing how retirement wealth can flow quickly toward to you, not away from you. Thus, fast streams.

What if your life depended upon you solving your money problems in the next ninety days? More important, what if the life of a child—even your child—depended upon it? Could you do it? The only thing that might stop you from saying yes is that you have no idea how you'd accomplish it.

This book is about teaching you several key nontraditional recipes for creating perpetual streams of monthly cash. What if we told you that you could comfortably retire this year by investing as little as an hour a day of your time—right from your kitchen table? If that interests you, then read on, because we'll teach you the recipes in the chapters to follow.

THE RIGHT-SIDE STORY

The story on the right-side pages of this book introduces the principles of fast cash in the form of a fictional tale. Some people learn better though the use of a right-brain story. We'll weave the financial recipes through the lives of five women and one young man, with various financial challenges. You'll probably relate to one of their stories so the process can become more real to you. Perhaps you'll be like Francie, who is facing financial ruin. Can she follow the recipe back from the brink to achieve a stable, secure financial future? Perhaps you'll be like Kanisha, who has an immediate need to make some money to support her new baby girl.

The principles work the same for anyone and everyone—male, female, young, or old.

THE LEFT-SIDE PAGES

The left-side pages will teach the principles and recipes in a straightforward, left-brain way. If that's the way your brain works, you'll be able to quickly learn and apply our techniques and strategies. By reading both sides, you can educate both sides of your brain so that you get the message and gain the courage to implement the recipe that fits your personality and circumstances of your life. Whether your need for income is immediate or somewhere off in the future, the recipe you'll use has the same essential ingredients.

In the next chapter we'll share with you what we believe to be the key ingredients of immediate financial success.

NOTE TO READER

In the later sections of this book, we'll be teaching you several specific recipes for generating cash in a flash. To help you implement these recipes, we encourage you to be a frequent visitor to our accompanying website, www.cashinaflashthebook.com. On our website, we have expanded the moneymaking recipes into detailed ninety day plans. Why don't you go there right now and check it out? :) MVH and RGA

MICHELLE'S STORY
FAST CASH IN
SLOW TIMES

THE THREE KEY INGREDIENTS:
WOW NOW, INNER WINNER, DREAM TEAM

If you look through any ordinary cookbook, you'll discover that there are a few basic, essential ingredients that are found in almost every recipe. Most dessert recipes contain sugar. Many breakfast recipes contain eggs. The majority of recipes contain flour or salt or butter.

No matter which recipe you select, there will be three or four key ingredients. They form the foundation of every recipe. If you try to leave out any of these key ingredients, your creation will likely fall flat, and in the end you will fail.

When it comes to financial success, what are the key ingredients? They

"You followed the recipe but it's missing the secret ingredient: Mom."

Prologue

While the rest of the country was preoccupied with personal electronic gadgets and the transition from oversized SUVs to luxury hybrids, the quaint Colorado town managed to hold on to its small-town charm. It was a life without the pressure of keeping up with the Joneses. Here, an automobile was transportation, not a status symbol. Houses were full of life and love. Calendars marked weekly PTA meetings and soccer games, and four times a year a town fair would celebrate the change of seasons. Yes, life in Idyllwild, Colorado, was simple and people liked it that way, but everything was about to change. The lives of five women, including Michelle Erickson's, would never be the same.

It had been eighteen months since Michelle Erickson won custody of her children, Nicky and Hannah, from her overbearing father-in-law, Anthony Erickson. Her husband of ten years, Gideon Erickson, had died in a violent car crash on a cold January evening as he drove home from work in Deer Creek, Colorado. His parents, Anthony and Natalie, had never liked Michelle, but that didn't bother her much, because the feelings were mutual. "They are stuffy and condescending," she often snarled to Gideon. He didn't disagree; Gideon disliked the fact that his parents were rich braggarts. Michelle had loved this about her husband. She once whispered to Gideon as they drove past the guard gate of the Erickson estate that visiting his parents was like having a tooth pulled, over and over again. He laughed.

Michelle would often whisper things out of the children's

are simple yet profound. We'll touch on the three key ingredients briefly in this chapter and revisit them in the chapters that follow.

THE FIRST KEY INGREDIENT

Although it seems obvious, *the first key ingredient in* every *recipe is a clear vision of what you are trying to create.* We don't know about you, but we both find it easier to follow a cooking recipe when we can see a picture of what the ultimate dish will look like after it comes out of the oven. We can more easily imagine it—taste it, smell it, experience it—as we try to recreate it. Do you have an image of the lifestyle you are attempting to create?

Any book on success will tell you the importance of imagining your ultimate objective. Although this is important, we'd like to share with you our "secret sauce" when it comes to visioning.

It's a process that we call Wow Now.

Have you ever been wowed by something you experienced in your past? Scan back and remember something that blew you away. Maybe it was a special moment in an important/meaningful relationship. Maybe it was the experience of receiving a unique reward or extraordinary acknowledgment. Maybe it was the birth of a child. Maybe it was a well-earned accomplishment—a diploma, a degree, or a certification. What was it about that experience that knocked your socks off?

As you remember that special experience, we encourage you to remember it more vividly. Remember it as if it was happening again, right now. Remember what it felt like—what it feels like. Remember what sounds were (are) going on all around you. Remember what you smelled, what you tasted, what you saw. See, smell, and taste it. Step into that special memory and experience it in all five senses. Now. Become so absorbed in the memory that you begin to notice details that escaped you the first time. Make the colors more vivid. Remember part of it more precisely. Make it *more* real than you remembered it.

Why do this?

This is excellent practice for a visioning process we call "virtualization."

earshot. This was her way of keeping the adult friendship with Gideon alive and spunky, while preserving the children's perception of their egotistical grandparents. No matter what Michelle thought of the Ericksons, they were still Gideon's parents. As long as she had Gideon, she didn't care what the Ericksons said about her parenting skills. She knew the love she shared with Gideon was a once-in-a-lifetime kind of love. It was a love that made her feel like she was forever standing in the afternoon warmth of the setting sun.

For ten years, her life, as she saw it, was perfect. Then it happened. The day she would never forget. It was a cold, lonely day in January. Michelle walked in with an armful of groceries when she saw the flashing red light of the answering machine. She wasn't sure how many times she would listen to the message in the weeks that followed. With each listen, she hoped the ending would somehow miraculously change. It never did. Gideon was singing the kids' favorite song, "Puff the Magic Dragon," during the message when Michelle first heard the horrific sounds of crushing metal. Gideon had been involved in a four-car pileup caused by a drunk driver. Hoping to ease her pain, the highway patrolman told Michelle that Gideon had died instantly. It didn't work. Gideon was dead, and she was devastated and now alone. Nothing could change the emptiness in her heart.

Upon hearing the news of his only son's death, Anthony Erickson released a team of high-paid intellectual muscle on Gideon's financial affairs. They quickly discovered that Michelle and Gideon had let the life insurance policy lapse and that Gideon's business venture, a new product invention firm known as Gideon's Gadgets, was bankrupt. Their savings account was minimal, and now with Gideon gone, Michelle was broke. Michelle couldn't afford to raise the two children on her own. She would have to sell the house, but even then, she wouldn't be able to afford the costs of raising two

It's more intense than visualization, which just uses visual inputs. To virtualize it, you imagine it in all five senses—as if you were virtually experiencing it. This drives the memory deeper into your psyche. It imprints your brain and body with what it feels like to be living your ideal lifestyle. It makes it more real.

Scan forward in your mind to five years in the future. Skip over your current money worries and income challenges. Fast-forward through your credit card pressures and short-term cash crunches. Imagine living your ultimate lifestyle of financial freedom—of freedom in every sense. Freedom to live the life of your dreams. Never mind how you might have accomplished such a lifestyle. Just imagine that you've found an honest and ethical way to achieve your dreams.

Imagine what kind of house you live in. Walk up to the front door, open it, and walk inside. Imagine what you might see as you enter. A chandelier? A grand staircase? An open view to the ocean?

It's your dream, so imagine it exactly the way you want. Smell something cooking in the kitchen. Your favorite recipe! As you walk down the hall toward the kitchen, feel the flooring beneath your feet. Is it wood? Or carpet? Or marble? Follow your nose toward where the chef has created a masterpiece for your taste buds. You enter the kitchen and the chef offers you a taste on a silver utensil. It's even better than you thought! You smell deeply. How delicious!

You absorb yourself in the sensations of your surroundings. You've created a space where the best of your love of life can grow and flourish. You hear music. The sound of laughter. The warmth of a crackling fire. The view out to the back lawn. Down to the stream or river or ocean or lake or forest or golf course. Step into the image as if you were experiencing it *now* in all five senses.

Wander the rooms of the home in your dream lifestyle. Notice how every room is a special place for the special people in your life. What kind of relationships do you want to nurture and enhance? Whom do you picture enjoying each room? Your home is the center of your world. From this center, your influence spreads to bless those around you.

See it. Feel it. Smell it. Taste it. Hear it. Make it virtually real. As if it

children on a minimum wage job. Seizing the opportunity for control, Anthony Erickson immediately filed for custody of Nicky and Hannah and won a questionable decision when Michelle was found to be an unfit mother, unable to care for her children.

She wasn't sure how it happened, partly because she didn't understand how someone could be so cruel, but Anthony Erickson was used to getting what he wanted. Somehow, Michelle found the strength to fight back when she remembered, almost instinctively, something Gideon said about being an inventor and living an entrepreneurial life: "When you risk big, you win big." After carefully checking with her intuition, Michelle drove to her father-in-law's house and asked, "How much is it going to take? How much do I have to make before you consider me a good mother? A thousand? Ten thousand? A million dollars?"

"A million." He laughed. "Don't be ridiculous. You made thirty-five thousand dollars last year, and that was before taxes."

Michelle dug in and fired back. "Care to make a wager?"

"Excuse me?"

"If I make a million dollars in twelve months, will you agree to give me back my children?"

A condescending smile crept across Erickson's face.

"Very well, but you'll have to earn it."

"Fine," Michelle shot back.

"And it cannot be gifted to you."

"Fine."

"And . . . the time limit is ninety days."

"Ninety days? That's not fair."

"Life isn't fair, Michelle. That's the offer. Take it or leave it."

"Fine. Ninety days. Have your lawyer draw up the papers."

Based on her limited education and the ability to hold nothing more than a salesclerk position in the past, Anthony Erickson

had already happened. Now, heighten your virtualization and ask yourself the following questions.

Whom did I build this for?
Why did I build it?
Where did I build it?
What did I build?
When did I build it?

Don't concern yourself with how you did it. For now, just imagine having already achieved it.

Without question, it's fun to imagine the ingredients of an ideal lifestyle. But that's not the only reason we do it. There's a deeper reason.

There is an unwanted ingredient that most people add to the recipe of their life that ruins almost every meal. That dangerous ingredient is fear. Fear is a destroyer. Fear entices you to vividly imagine the worst possible outcome.

How real are your fears? Have you ever hesitated moving toward your goals? Have you ever been burned by the fear of rejection? Has the fear of failure ever stopped you? Just the thought of failure can cause even a courageous person to hesitate. These fears are real! Your palms sweat. The bile in your stomach starts to burn. Your brain goes blank. Your heart begins to pound like a bass drum. The voices in your head begin to shout, "You can't do it. You've never done anything like this before. Who do you think you are?"

You feel it. You hear it. You smell it. You taste it. You see it. Most of us experience our fears in all five senses! That's why fear is so real. Fear is intense. Fear is absorbing. Fear virtually seizes every cell in your body. Are your dreams *more* real than that? Most of your dreams are just fleeting fantasies—nice images of possibly positive outcomes. But do they wow you?

This is the secret. For you to achieve your dreams . . .

Your dreams must be more real than your fears!

chomped down on the bait like a hungry shark. What he hadn't counted on that day was Michelle's sudden discovery, albeit crisis-driven, of a sense of self-worth. These were her children. This was serious. To Michelle, this was war.

With the help of her newfound mentor, Samantha Munroe, a self-made, enlightened millionaire, and a ragtag dream team of new-bie entrepreneurs, Michelle was able to make a little over a million dollars in ninety days. Through a combination of hard work, real estate deals at the last minute, product inventions, and Web-based businesses, Michelle's life was changed forever. She got her children back and discovered that a person can do just about anything as long as she truly knows—not just believes but *knows* on the most basic, soul-filled level—that her mission is connected to her heart. What seemed like a roadblock at first, this million-dollar challenge from Anthony Erickson, enabled Michelle to discover her true, authentic self. She was powerful. She was unstoppable. She was finally becoming the woman she used to dream about as a little girl. "Life couldn't be sweeter," she thought to herself in the months that followed her victory. She beat up the bully and she was proud of that. (Read the complete story in *The One Minute Millionaire*.)

The hardest thing for Michelle now was learning how to face the truth about who she had become during that ninety-day, million-dollar challenge. It was a series of hypothetical questions that would haunt her each time she found herself truly happy in a given moment. If it weren't for Gideon's death and the Ericksons' cruel intentions, would she have come to this place of empowerment on her own? Why did she have to lose Gideon, and ultimately her old self along the way, to come to this level of self-awareness? Why couldn't this discovery of inner peace be manifested on her own volition, without the loss of her beloved? Was Gideon an angel sent into her life so she

If your dreams don't wow you, then they aren't real enough to combat the fears that will eventually arise to stop you. Your dreams *must* be more real than your fears. Your dreams must be connected to your soul. They must *excite* you. Simply thinking about them must cause you to stay awake at night.

When a fear comes in contact with such a dream, the fear itself must be wowed into submission.

Therefore, when we say Wow Now, we mean for you to go out into the future and create a vision that wows you. The first step in this wow process is to virtualize your ideal dream lifestyle. Make it as real as possible—in all five senses.

In Part One, we'll teach you more powerful techniques to more quickly turn your now into wow.

THE SECOND KEY INGREDIENT

The second key ingredient in any success recipe—from better health to greater wealth—is to make friends with your Inner Winner. There is an inner world inside all of us that few people have learned how to manage. Are you aware of what is going on in there?

As we speak to audiences around the world, we ask a few simple questions.

"How many of you have a critical voice—a nagging, negative part of you that often brings you down?" The vast majority of every audience raises their hands. Then, we ask, "How many of you have a true voice—a part of you that whispers to you, encourages you, supports you, leads you in the right direction?" Once again, most everyone raises their hands.

Everyone has at least two inner voices. All of us have a nagging, negative, or critical voice that tries to talk us out of almost everything that we do to better our lives. Have you ever berated yourself for thinking about doing something to improve your life and then gotten down on yourself for not doing it? We call this the Inner Whiner.

How prevalent is this critical self? Experts say that *everyone* has one—although this critical voice is louder in some of us than in others. If you

could become the person she was today? It was this sobering debate of spiritual enlightenment that was a daily struggle for Michelle.

Over time, her thoughts of happiness began to overpower her thoughts of guilt. She learned to be grateful for who she was, her role as an enlightened millionaire, and the mother she was becoming. She was a living testament that wealth was an energetic vibration, not a possession to hoard. Money comes and goes in life, but spiritual enlightenment and self-awareness last forever. Which is why, when Michelle woke up in the middle of the night and felt the call to move away from Deer Creek, Colorado, she didn't think twice. She sold her house, making a tidy profit, of course, and began the transition to a new life.

The Ericksons tried to put up a fight when Michelle told them she was moving away with the kids, but the fight was short-lived because Michelle could now afford the same powerful lawyers as the Ericksons. Anthony Erickson lost his ability to bully Michelle. Ironically, it was his bullying that had caused her to overcome the poverty mind-set she had carried with her ever since her mother died of cancer when Michelle was fifteen. However much she disliked him personally, she found a way to be grateful for Anthony Erickson because he pushed her to become more of the woman she now was.

Knowing the importance of family, Michelle agreed to periodic holiday and birthday visits. Gideon would've liked this, she thought before calling Anthony with the news. She enjoyed the conversation that day, which caught the bitter Erickson off-guard. Michelle was learning that her happiness had nothing to do with the circumstances or appearances of her life. Happiness was up to her, and she was now learning to be happy from the inside out. Michelle was finally learning to like herself.

Even though she was happy with her decision to move away, Michelle had trouble silencing the pestering doubts associated with

were to listen in on the conversations that people have with themselves incessantly throughout the day, you'd wonder how anyone got anything done.

Where does this critical voice come from? There are dozens of psychological theories. Did it come with you at birth? Is this part of your personality? Is it your ego? Is it a mechanism you learn in childhood to protect yourself? Is it your anti-self? Frankly, who knows? No matter where it originates, one thing is certain: this critical voice definitely affects your life—primarily for the negative. It slows you down, sometimes even stops you.

What about that other voice—your true voice? Have you ever had a hunch where you just knew something was going to happen? Have you ever heard a faint whisper encouraging you to do something that would be good for you? Have you ever found yourself being nudged toward something positive or away from something negative? Most likely this was your Inner Winner.

Sometimes we don't hear our Inner Winner because the Inner Whiner is so loud. You'll be amazed at what you hear when you become more attentive to your true voice. Your true voice *is* your friend. That still, small voice you hear wants you to win, to succeed, to triumph.

Could it be that most of us are held back in our pursuit of success by an inner critic that talks us out of it? Could it be that the most successful among us have learned how to silence their critical voice, while listening more to their true voice?

The really interesting question to ask yourself is: where are these voices? Generally speaking, the critical voice is heard in your mind. It's a "mind" voice. The Inner Winner, your true voice, is heard in your heart. It's a voice you feel in your heart.

Throughout this book, we'll teach you techniques to remove the unwanted ingredients from the field of your mind—such as the bitter messages from the critical voice. And in Part Two we'll show you how to add the second essential ingredient to your recipe for success—learning to notice the sweet assuring heart whispers from your true voice, your Inner Winner.

facing the unknown. As these thoughts came into her awareness, Michelle tried to remember the spiritual principle she'd learned during her ninety-day ordeal with the Ericksons: once you determine the *why*, the *how* will soon follow. It was one of the laws of the universe, and who was she to think otherwise? But, where would she go? What would she do? As the uncertain thoughts raced through her mind, she decided that she would wait for a clear message before she made her next decision concerning the move out of town.

The message came to her while visioning one night in her living room. These visioning sessions, otherwise known as *conscious dreaming*, was a practice Samantha had taught her. It was a practice of sitting still with her thoughts. She loved looking into the unknown of tomorrow by opening herself up to the grand possibilities of who she was and what she was doing, moment by moment.

It had been three weeks since she'd first made the decision to move. The house had been sold, the closing was imminent, and Michelle faced the formidable task of packing up their lives. She laughed at how much stuff she and Gideon had accumulated over the years. But now she was yearning for a more simple life. It was hard for her to throw anything away that evoked a connection to Gideon, but she knew *possessions* were just *things*. To Michelle, love was a dance between two souls and wasn't defined by achievements or the possessions of *things*. The love she'd shared with Gideon was pure, and trinkets had nothing to do with that love.

The children were fast asleep in their beds when the message came to her. The summer rain had begun to lightly drum on the rooftop. This was one of the things Michelle loved about living in Colorado, the unpredictable weather. For her, the sound of rain somehow came with a soothing, romantic view of life. It calmed her soul.

THE THIRD KEY INGREDIENT

In America today, there are more that twenty-four million separate businesses. Less than 2 percent of those businesses take in more than a million dollars a year in gross revenue. The vast majority of entrepreneurial enterprises are solopreneurs—sixteen million businesses that are operated by a single proprietor. Most of these solopreneurs are men. But women are coming on strong.

Here is a shocking statistic: as many as 95 percent of the businesses that launch today will be out of business within five years. There are a lot of reasons for the high failure rate, but in our experience, one of the key reasons is that most entrepreneurs don't know how to team up.

The odds of going it alone—of solopreneuring your way to financial freedom—are not promising. To say it bluntly, the solo way can be said this way: so low! The success rate is so low and the failure rate is so high, it's foolish to go solo.

We see bright spots on the horizon of entrepreneurship. In the past decade, the fastest-growing segment of the business world has been made up of women entrepreneurs. This is the century for women entrepreneurs. Women find it more natural to team their way up to success.

One of our mentors, Dr. Stephen Covey, teaches that there are three stages of maturity on the continuum of success:

Dependence II⬛➡ Independence II⬛➡ Interdependence

In our opinion, many women find themselves at either end of the spectrum. They're familiar with being depended upon by their young children and often find themselves dependent on an outside source of income—a job, a spouse, public assistance. But most women have successfully achieved the third stage of interdependence. Why? Women are more people-friendly. They know how to support and be supported by a wide array of female friends.

Men are usually stuck in the middle—to a fault. They're too independent. They want to do it by themselves. It's the American tradition: they

Sitting on the living room floor, she closed her eyes and let her thoughts drift toward her new life . . . in a new town . . . away from the watchful eyes of the Ericksons. It would be a fresh start for everyone, she thought. The message came almost in an instant, like a lightning bolt of inspiration! She would open a small bookstore in Idyllwild, Colorado. She knew opening an independent bookstore was a counter-intuitive notion given the presence of superstores and the downturn in the economy, but she trusted the message. She knew if she opened a bookstore, it would have to be unique. It was in that moment her idea took shape. She wanted to open her eyes and rush to the computer to write down the inspiration, for fear of losing it, but she reminded herself that nothing is ever lost in the mind of God. If an idea is connected to a person's soul-filled purpose, any fear of lack will dissolve away into nothingness. This was her understanding of faith: trust the small stuff, because in the end it's all small stuff.

Letting go of her own perceptions of what she thought might be possible in life, Michelle began to concentrate on the idea further. Deep, soul-filling breaths calmed her soul. After fifteen minutes inside this visioning stillness, Michelle began writing what she would later refer to as her *vision manifesto*—which, to her, was nothing more than a to-do list for dreamers. She was a single mother of two, thirty-five years old, and about to start her life.

want to pull themselves up by the bootstraps. Their theme song is Frank Sinatra's "My Way." That's the male way.

Women are much more team-oriented. This is good, because it is essential. You need a team. In *The One Minute Millionaire* we called it a Dream Team. The forming of a tight group of like-minded people is the third key ingredient to your success.

Our literary agent is Jillian Manus. This book would not exist without her. She's incredible. When we asked her about the most essential ingredient to her amazing success, she replied without hesitation, "My Broad Squad." This is the name she uses to describe her women's group, made up of highly successful women who go to extreme lengths to support each other. In *Think and Grow Rich,* Napoleon Hill talks about the power of the mastermind. Whether you call your group a Mastermind, a Dream Team, a Chick Clique, a Guy Tribe, a Dude Crew, a Bro Patrol, or a Broad Squad isn't important. What is important is to decide to form such a group. The forming of a support team is as essential an ingredient to your entrepreneurial activities as flour is to a rich chocolate cake.

We've done special research with women to capture the essence of how women entrepreneurs bond to make results happen. We've also drawn heavily on women's microcredit groups worldwide. After thirty years of experience, Muhammad Yunus's microcredit movement has discovered that the ideal number of women per group is never less than five and never more than six. When we get to later chapters, we'll share with you how to find, form, and perpetuate your team—your own Broad Squad, Guy Tribe, or Dream Team.

Once your team is functioning, we'll teach you strategies for earning rapid streams of income. Then, as an enlightened entrepreneur, we encourage you to "send the elevator back down." Transfer your new skills to other groups of men and women who are searching for a way up.

So let's review the three key ingredients:

- **Wow Now.** Make your dreams more real than your fears. Experience your ideal future now. No matter what you're experiencing now,

1

The Wealth Menu
What Are You Ordering?

Drifting in and out of focus, the images were confusing at first. Colors blurred into each other like a Salvador Dalí painting, melting in the hot Colorado sun. The video camera jerked back and forth before landing on Michelle, tailgating the rusty pickup truck in front of her, as it dodged in and out of the morning rush hour traffic. She checked her watch, hoping the time had somehow stalled on her behalf, but it hadn't. She was late.

Moving to pass the pickup truck and get away from the choking black smoke belching from its tailpipe, Michelle looked over her shoulder to make sure the road was clear. As her eyes came back to the road ahead, she saw the crimson brake lights of the pickup truck coming directly at her. The driver of the pickup heard Michelle's screeching tires but didn't care as he casually made the illegal left-hand turn onto Oxnard Street. Michelle jammed on the brakes with both feet, but it was no use—she was about to smash into the pickup.

Michelle took her foot off the brake pedal, yanked the steering wheel to the right, and hit the accelerator, narrowly missing the edge of the truck's dented, spray-painted bumper. They were safe, but the momentary sigh of relief was cut short as she slammed into a large pothole in the middle of the street. Loose change from the ashtray jumped into the air like popcorn in a hot pan as the camera jerked back and forth again.

your goal is to find the wow in it. We want to wow your soul and make your pocketbook grow.

- **Inner Winner.** Learn how to befriend your Inner Winner and silence your Inner Whiner.

- **Dream Team.** Create as quickly as possible a unique support team—your own unique Broad Squad or Guy Tribe—that will guide you toward your dreams, in the shortest and easiest way possible.

Before we begin our moneymaking adventure into the Wow Now, Inner Winner, and Dream Team, let's explain the bird on the cover of this book—the hummingbird.

What comes to your mind when you think of a hummingbird? Speed. Agility. Flexibility. Boundless energy. The hummingbird is the perfect example of making the nearly impossible appear quite effortless. Have you ever known someone like that? Does this describe you? By the time you're finished reading this book, we hope you'll begin to identify and access your "inner hummingbird."

The hummingbird is a multitasker—feeding and buzzing off to the next responsibility with lightning speed. It hovers and darts from project to project, focusing intently on the nectar that's needed, and then speeding off to insert itself into the next project with intensity. It can fly up, down, sideways, and backward with amazing flexibility. But one of the most powerful and little-known aspects of the hummingbird is the speed at which it learns and can be trained. And if anything is needed in today's rapidly evolving world it is the ability to acquire and assimilate new ideas. Our modern world requires speed. Information is multiplying exponentially,

"Mom, I'm rolling back here," Nicky, her nine-year-old, blurted out, attempting to steady the video camera. Hannah, Michelle's excitable seven-year-old, buckled into the seat next to her brother, reacted as if this were some kind of an amusement park ride. Michelle managed to smile at her daughter in the rearview mirror. Ever since the move to Idyllwild two years ago, Hannah's personality had finally begun to blossom. She was no longer a shy little girl who had trouble making friends in school. She was fearless for a seven-year-old, Michelle thought as she focused on the road ahead.

During the months following Gideon's death, Michelle had spent many sleepless nights, worried how her children would react to the violent and sudden death of their father. Would they blame her for his death somehow? Perhaps suffer a crippling dysfunction at school, struggling to fit in with the new kids in Idyllwild? At first Michelle thought Hannah's sudden transformation had something to do with the distance from the Ericksons, now some two hundred miles away, but it was her big brother, Nicky, who made the difference in Hannah's life. The two had become friends and rarely fought since their father died. Their friendship had a sweetness that couldn't be taught by a parent. It was instinct, Michelle thought. She was proud of who they were. With the exception of Nicky's new-found love of filmmaking, Nicky and Hannah were inseparable.

Armed with a digital video camera Michelle had bought him for his ninth birthday, Nicky was at work on his latest short film, *Another Endless Summer Without a Dog*. Nicky loved the title. It was his way of lobbying with his mother for a golden retriever puppy. Michelle, on the other hand, was lobbying in return for Nicky to learn how to keep his room clean. Nicky had become somewhat of an artist, calling the room his "creative expression." Michelle called it a pigsty, which left the puppy negotiations at a standstill. She

and we have a need to assimilate new information and convert it into usable daily food.

In this book, we'll be sharing dozens of new ways of thinking and acting in today's ever-changing world. Five hundred years ago, the world sped up dramatically as Gutenberg created the printing press. In the past twenty years, the digital age is causing the next massive revolution. A lot of people will feel dislocated and disoriented as we go from one iteration to the next. The world is speeding up. It will take all of your hummingbird instincts to keep up with it.

In addition, the world of money is becoming increasingly volatile. Almost every traditional moneymaking method has recently suffered substantial shocks. Is there such a thing as a secure job anymore? What about the stock market? The real estate market? The bond market? The arena for small business? Where is a safe haven for your money? Although today's turbulent economy might cause you to wonder whether financial freedom is still possible, we assure you that the three essential ingredients in the recipe for financial freedom will never change. Yes, you can still become financially successful! There are many ways to create cash although some of them may be unfamiliar to you. Throughout this book, we'll share with you our best financial recipes for times like these.

Now that you're beginning to understand these three essential ingredients, let's explore some specific recipes to rapid financial freedom.

knew she'd give in to the demands soon enough, perhaps for Christmas morning, she thought, but for now, she was intent on teaching Nicky the valuable lesson "chores before stores." Michelle thought if you wanted something bad enough, you had to be willing to work for it. The pride of ownership follows the pride of earnership. It was a good ideal and she stuck to it. It was important to Michelle that her children learned about money.

Nicky now framed his camera on Hannah, who was busy brushing her Barbie's hair. Sensing the camera, Hannah slowly looked up and scowled at Nicky before turning away. Nicky's first piece of work had been a three-minute exposé on Hannah's life, aptly titled *My Baby Sister, Hannah Banana*. As a result, Hannah was on strike. It wasn't so much the nickname Hannah Banana that bothered her as much as the notion that she was still considered the baby of the family. Hannah was seven years old and about to start the second grade. "Babies wear diapers," she'd yelled after seeing the film screened in the family room that Sunday night.

Nicky pushed in for a close-up on Hannah. Clearing his throat, he asked in his best anchorman voice, "So, Hannah Erickson, what do you think about golden retriever puppies? Shouldn't every kid have a dog?"

"Mom," Hannah quickly protested.

"Come on, don't be a baby."

"Mom!"

Turning onto the frontage road outside Idyllwild Elementary School, Michelle spun around.

"That's enough, Nicky. Put the camera away."

"Mom!"

"We're almost there."

"But I'm working." Nicky took his new hobby seriously and had

3

THE FORMULA FOR
SUCCESS: S = M + H + T

In the field of wealth, success, and personal achievement, there are dozens of excellent books that teach hundreds of valuable principles, strategies, and techniques. It could take you decades to read them all. We know, because between us, we've spent close to a hundred years reading, studying, and teaching on the subject of success.

The purpose of this book is not to teach you every success strategy. We're assuming that you don't have time or money for a master's degree in personal growth and financial success. This book is for someone who wants or needs to make rapid progress with limited time and resources. You don't need slow Crock-Pot recipes. You need the microwave success system for generating fast, almost immediate results.

Let's assume that you're a procrastinator. You have less than ninety days from this moment to turn your life around. This is your last chance. These are slow times and you need some fast cash! We believe that by focusing on only three key fundamentals, you'll make the most progress in the shortest period of time.

In this chapter, we give you a taste of the three most important ingredients in any success recipe. As we said in chapter 2, these ingredients are Wow Now, Inner Winner, and Dream Team. To recap, Wow Now refers to an awareness of how your mind works and a simple system of mental skills to focus it like a laser beam to attract what it is that you truly want. Inner Winner describes the power to access your powerful inner guidance system that leads you quickly from where you are toward where you want to be. Dream Team is an incredible way of attracting, organizing, and operating your mastermind team.

begun watching the nightly news so he could research how the professionals did it. He was nine years old going on twenty-five.

"And you know the rules, mister. Your sister's off-limits."

"It's not like I posted it on YouTube or nothing."

"Stop it!" Hannah shouted.

"Nicky. Hand it over."

"But Mom—"

"Don't *but Mom* me, hand it over." Nicky's eyes narrowed in frustration, but he quickly relented when he caught the single look from his mother in the rearview mirror.

"Okay, fine. My chip is full anyway." Slapping the viewfinder shut, Nicky muttered something about freedom of the press before handing over the camera. They rode in silence until Hannah giggled and said, "That sounds funny."

"What does, honey?" Michelle asked.

" 'Don't *but Mom* me.' "

Michelle ran it over in her head a few times before she started to laugh. Nicky tried to hold out, but when it was isolated, "don't but Mom me" did sound funny. He joined in the laughter, and just like that, the pouting was over.

Michelle loved the relationship she had with her children. No matter what the Ericksons thought of her skills as a mother, they couldn't deny she was raising two great kids. Nicky's laugh reminded her of Gideon, and there wasn't a day that passed where she didn't think of her husband. She missed him dearly, but was forever thankful for the beautiful reminders sitting in her backseat, now laughing hysterically with each other.

As the car pulled up to the drop-off curb in front of Idyllwild Elementary School, the doors flung open in unison as the school bell rang.

"Okay, guys, Justine will pick you up at three-thirty. I have book

To simplify even further, the concept of Wow Now deals with your *mind*. The concept of the Inner Winner deals with your *heart*. And the concept of the Dream Team shows you how to harness the *minds* and *hearts* of the chosen few people on your mastermind team.

Albert Einstein once said, "Make everything as simple as possible, but not simpler." It is our hypothesis that success in any area of life—especially financial—all boils down to the foundation formula of all success: $S = M + H + T$.

Success = a focused mind + a determined heart + a focused, determined team

Surely it can't be that simple!

Think of someone you admire. What makes this person special? Why has this individual been able to accomplish so much in comparison to most other people? Is it because he or she is smarter? More knowledgeable? Has the person read more books, been to more seminars? In our experience, what makes people successful is being able to focus their minds and harness their hearts. In addition, they've been persuasive enough to focus and harness the minds and hearts of a few other people to help them accomplish their goals.

Following this basic recipe, they are able to acquire all of the other ingredients necessary for success—money, skills, knowledge, connections, and so on.

No doubt you've heard of the 80/20 principle: 20 percent of what you do gives you 80 percent of your results, and 80 percent of what you do gives you only 20 percent of your results. The three critical key ingredients—heart, mind, and team—are the 20 percent. If you get them right, you're 80 percent of the way to your goal. Most students of financial success do just the opposite. They spend 80 percent of their time learning the strategies and techniques of making money and zero time on the mind, heart, and team. No wonder wealth eludes them.

Since the 20 percent of heart, mind, and team generates the most

club tonight, so don't give her any trouble," Michelle said. "And no dilly-dallying, Nicky. I don't want you to keep her waiting."

"Mom, nobody says *dilly-dallying* anymore," said Nicky, who in the past five weeks had discovered what "being cool" really meant, at least to a nine-year-old.

"You just be on time."

"Will you please think about the puppy today?"

"Honey, I think about the puppy every day, and until you learn how to keep your room clean, the answer is still no."

"You're so mean," he said, hanging his head, which was a bid for sympathy. Michelle wasn't buying it.

"I know, I'm horrible. Now give me a kiss." He rolled his eyes as he leaned forward and gave her a kiss good-bye. Hannah quickly did the same, then dashed out the door, catching up with her brother as he entered through the main doors of the school.

When the kids were safely inside, Michelle eyes drifted upward to the leaves falling from the giant maple tree hanging overhead. Fall had arrived, and it was the first day of school. The skies were dark with an approaching storm. The air was crisp, and Michelle couldn't believe that another school year was about to begin.

Down the street at Lei Kim's Diner, Mayor Brady Wilson sat in the front booth reading the newspaper. He was forty-three, but his wavy blond hair kept him looking like a man in his early thirties. He was on this day, much like every day, impeccably dressed in a black pin-striped suit with a crisp red paisley tie. He was a big fish in a small pond, but he preferred it that way. "Small-town living with a big-city mind for progress" was the platform he'd used to win his second

results we'll focus our attention on those three ingredients. But in the final chapters of the book we'll address the other 80 percent of what you can do, and teach you a few powerful moneymaking strategies organized into a few fundamental moneymaking recipes.

MAGNETIZE YOUR MIND
AND ENGAGE YOUR HEART

People are notoriously impatient. They want results and they want them *now*! Therefore, they rarely take time to lay a strong foundation. That means they're always building on sand. The three key ingredients of mind, heart, and team are the foundation of fast cash. We will show you how to *magnetize* your mind and *engage* your heart to get what you want in the fastest way possible.

Minds and hearts. This is the essence of success. Getting these two centers of your power to align in yourself and others is essential to whatever endeavor or project you are attempting to accomplish.

Have you ever tried and failed to accomplish something? Have you ever set a New Year's resolution that is still undone? More than likely it was either your mind and/or your heart that didn't buy into it. If your mind can see it but your heart can't feel it and get excited about, it ain't gonna happen. If you've always wanted something but you can't imagine yourself doing it, likewise, no can do.

Any book on success talks about the importance of goal setting. Yet success is much more than goal setting. Between you and your ultimate goal are dozens of distractions that can slow you down and divert you. The successful person translates his or her goals into doable daily projects with deadlines, benchmarks, resources, and accountabilities, then applies single-minded, wholehearted thinking to drive those projects to completion.

For example, you might set the goal to create an extra $5,000 a month income in the next ninety days. As long as this remains a goal or a dream, it will probably remain undone. The project coordinator (that's you) needs to assemble all the necessary ingredients—money, people, knowledge, skill, and so on—to make the project a success. But without the prime

election as the mayor of Idyllwild. He was well informed, educated, and a student of the game. Mayor Wilson pushed the importance of current affairs, not just for the politicians of the world but also for every citizen of the community. You'd think he owned the *Wall Street Journal* the way he recommended reading it daily. "How can you vote on the issues if you don't know what's going on in the world?" he often lectured to anyone who would listen.

Lei Kim, a Korean-born woman in her late sixties, wiped her hands on the floral print apron tied around her plump waist as she retrieved Mayor Wilson's order from the pickup counter: scrambled eggs, hash brown potatoes, one crisp piece of bacon, a sausage patty, two slices of fresh avocado, and double-toasted wheat toast. Lei Kim never minded the special order—after all, he was the mayor, and he was sitting in her diner, something he did five days a week. The diner had a faithful following, not because the food was so good, which it was, but because Lei Kim made everyone feel as if each meal was prepared by the loving hands of the customers' own mothers. She was sweet, caring, and knew her way around the kitchen.

Balancing the plates like a pro, Lei Kim hipped her way through the double doors next to the lunch counter. As she passed the back booth, she saw her only son, Johnny Kim, texting on his phone in the back booth.

"Put the phone away and get back to work," she said with a disapproving glare.

"You see a customer who needs waitin' on, and I'll snap to, Mom. I promise," Johnny said, continuing to type away on the keyboard of his phone. While he was certainly the poster boy for a lazy, self-entitled generation, Johnny did have a valid point. With the exception of three tables and two counter jockeys—a term Johnny had coined for old customers who dined alone—the diner was all but empty.

The decline in meals served had begun ten months ago when a

ingredients of mind, heart, and team, the project remains uncompleted. The cash cake you're trying to bake will most likely fall flat.

Many of our students assume that the fastest way to financial freedom is to learn nitty-gritty moneymaking techniques. They want to get right to the meat of how to make money. In essence, they say, "I'm financially upside down. Teach me how to generate some serious cash flow *fast!*"

There certainly are hundreds of moneymaking strategies. In teaching people how to achieve financial freedom, we find that a small percentage actually take our specialized knowledge and go out and create wealth. The vast majority get sidetracked by fears of rejection and failure, in the distraction of procrastination, in the confusion of not knowing what to do first, in the quicksand of low self esteem, in the doubt and discouragement and overwhelm. **They know what to do but they don't know how to get themselves to do it.** The heart/mind stuff is the meat of the matter. You get *that* right, and you can accomplish anything you put your mind to. *Fast!*

In *The Seven Habits of Highly Effective People,* Stephen Covey quotes President Abraham Lincoln, who reportedly said, "If I had eight hours to cut down a tree, I'd spend six hours sharpening my ax." Although we know that you're champing at the bit to get out there and start chopping, we are going to show you the sharpest shortcut to wealth. It might seem like a detour, but it's the fastest way.

There is a scene in the 1984 movie *Karate Kid* that has become almost a clichéd example of what it takes to succeed. You may have heard this metaphor before, but have you applied it to yourself recently? (If you haven't seen the movie, rent it. If you have, it is worth watching again with your Dream Team on a free night you might share together and then discuss the insights that you glean.)

If you remember, the film's main mentor is a handyman/karate expert, Mr. Miyagi. He has been recruited by a bullied boy, Daniel, to teach him some quick karate techniques so he can defend himself. His eager student wants to immediately start learning karate moves and is very frustrated when his mentor instead assigns him days of menial chores.

He gives him several cars to wash and wax. "Wax on," Miyagi says, and demonstrates with a clockwise movement with his right hand. "Wax off,"

Starbucks moved into town. It was a sign that the get-up-and-go lifestyle usually reserved for big-city America had finally arrived in here Idyllwild. But it wasn't just Idyllwild, and Lei Kim knew it. People everywhere were becoming more and more impatient with daily life, and it was this fast-food mentality that somehow had caused a shift in traditional values. And now, sadly, small-town America was being replaced by strip malls and corporate chain stores.

Lei Kim stopped dead in her tracks. If you listened hard enough, you would probably have heard her sneakers skid to a halt. She did an about-face and with silent authority she took a step back toward Johnny.

"Get up, grab the dustpan and the broom, and sweep up around here. I'm not paying you to text your friends."

Lei Kim didn't need to tell him twice. While Johnny did have a smart mouth, Lei Kim ruled. Johnny grabbed the dustpan-and-broom combination from the utility closet and began to carelessly sweep his way through the diner. Making sure his mother was busy delivering the mayor's breakfast, Johnny pulled out his iPod Nano and snuck the earbuds into his ears. Like most kids his age, Johnny was a walking LCD light if you counted all the electronics he carried at one given time.

"Okay, here we go, Mr. Mayor," Lei Kim announced over his *Wall Street Journal*.

Folding his paper, Mayor Wilson thanked Lei Kim, and smiled as Michelle entered through the front door in a rush. He'd liked her from the minute he first saw her standing in line at city hall nearly two years ago. Michelle had been applying for her business license, and Mayor Wilson had been on the campaign trail for reelection. For the past six months, Brady Wilson had been a man on a mission. He was attempting to court Michelle, but she didn't think it was appropriate yet to introduce a new man in her children's lives, so they

he says with a clockwise movement of his left hand. "Breathe in. Breathe out. Very important."

The next day, he delegates Daniel another task—to polish his deck with sandpaper. "Right circle. Left circle," Miyagi says, and demonstrates.

The next day, he assigns Daniel to paint the fence using up/down brush strokes. "Up. Down. Up. Down. Don't forget to breathe."

On the fourth, day Daniel arrives to see a note on the door: "Paint the house. No up/down. Side to side. 1/2 right hand. 1/2 left hand." When the pupil finally rebels over all of this meaningless make-work, Miyagi reveals, in a powerful scene of martial arts movements, how the muscle memory Daniel has built from the seemingly meaningless repetitive movements are necessary building blocks of coordination for specific defensive moves in karate.

Just like Mr. Miyagi, we're going to ask you to wax on, wax off. If you wonder why we're asking you to do these homework assignments, just trust that there is method to our madness.

So here is your first wax on/wax off assignment. Notice what time it is right now. Then, for sixty uninterrupted seconds, ponder this question: *What does it mean to be single-minded?*

Next, for sixty uninterrupted seconds, ponder this question: *What does it mean to be wholeheartedly committed to an objective?*

For sixty uninterrupted seconds, scan back over your life and find three examples where you succeeded—often despite great odds.

1. _____
2. _____
3. _____

remained just good friends. Her spirit was light and he needed that in his life. It had been three years since he'd lost his wife to a long battle with cancer. He was ready to start again, but Michelle wanted to take things slowly. He understood this, but liked her nonetheless.

Lei Kim greeted Michelle with a warm hug.

"Are you hungry, dear?" she asked.

Michelle was running late and didn't have time for breakfast. "Just a coffee to go." While Michelle greeted the mayor with a quick smile, Lei Kim began to lecture, something she often did, on the importance of a healthy meal.

"Breakfast means breaking the fast. Now you can't do that with coffee and a doughnut, now can you?" Lei Kim didn't wait for an answer, as her attention was drawn to Johnny trying to sweep a piece of paper into the dustpan. After his third stroke, he braced the broom against his neck and tried to sweep the trash into the dustpan.

"Maybe just bend down and pick it up next time."

"Stupid broom gave me no leverage. What am I gonna do?"

Mumbling to herself out of frustration with her son, Lei Kim crossed back in to the kitchen with a purpose.

Michelle turned to Mayor Wilson and delivered an apologetic smile.

"Sorry I can't stay—first day of school has put my morning behind. I have to get the store ready to open up. Are we still on for Thursday lunch?"

"Actually, I have a better idea. What time do the kids go to sleep?" he said, leaning in with a smile. "I could come over, make dinner, and we could . . . watch a movie or something?"

"Brady . . ." Her words trailed off. "I think it's probably best we keep with lunches for now. I'm just not ready for anything serious right now. Is that okay?"

Before he could answer, Lei Kim returned with a brown paper bag for Michelle.

For sixty uninterrupted seconds, scan back over your life and find three instances where you set a goal but failed—where you did not achieve your objective.

1. _____

2. _____

3. _____

Bring the insights you gleaned into Part One, where we'll learn more about the first key ingredient to rapid success: Wow Now.

"What's this?" Michelle asked.

"Fresh fruit and oatmeal. You can eat in the car."

"But I didn't order—

"No, you didn't. Your body did, and you can thank me when you get to be my age," Lei Kim said with a smile. Even though she was probably thirty pounds overweight and a recent convert to veganism for medical reasons, the woman was an expert on food. Nobody could doubt that.

Michelle thanked Lei Kim and said good-bye to the mayor. His eyes followed her out the door. Michelle looked back and delivered the smile he loved so much. Mayor Wilson smiled back and returned to his breakfast, but Lei Kim was still standing over the table.

"She's one of the good ones, you know," Lei Kim offered.

"Yes, I know." He was about to take a bite of toast when she leaned forward like an overprotective mother

"Have you ever visited New Orleans, Mr. Mayor?" she asked.

"I believe I have."

"Did you try the gumbo?"

"It's a little early for me to start thinking about gumbo. I'm still trying to eat my breakfast."

Lei Kim stopped his hand just as the toast was about to reach his mouth. She looked into his eyes. "It's never too early to talk about gumbo, and the secret to a good gumbo is to not rush it. If you rush the roux, you'll ruin the gumbo." Then she walked off. The mayor caught the eyes of the old man sitting at the counter.

"I guess she told you," he chuckled to the mayor, sipping his coffee.

The mayor offered a "thanks for playing" smile, then bit into his morning toast, which was now cold. Tossing it onto the plate, he returned to his *Wall Street Journal*.

PART ONE

The First Key Ingredient: Wow Now

2

The Last-Minute Millionaire

The Birthing of Desire

With rustic awnings hanging over the old wooden sidewalk, Idyll-wild's Main Street was a throwback to Colorado's silver-mining days. The Heartlight Bookstore occupied part of a two-story brick building that ran the length of the short city block between Cedar and Van Ness Boulevard. There were three distinct spaces in the bookstore. The one to the left was called "Book of Dreams" and was specifically designed for children. The name of the room came from a workshop Michelle had held last summer that taught children to dream out loud. This merely meant she taught them how to express their creative impulse. Through the process of journaling, she was able to teach children the expression principles of "Don't think it, ink it" and "Speak it, then see it."

Equipped with Apple computers, toys, and zebra-patterned bean-bag chairs scattered about the floor, the Book of Dreams was meant to foster creativity and learning through the practice of free writing. The only thing missing from the experience for the children were the latest titles in video games. It wasn't as if Michelle was taking a stance against video games in general; she was simply *for* creativity. She had a habit of never being against anything. Rather, she was always for some-thing, and she wanted kids to come to the store to expand their ability for conceptual thought, not to learn how to shoot a gun through com-puter simulation or learn things by memorization. The decision to

4

VOICES, VISIONS, AND VIBRATIONS: FAST MONEY BEGINS FROM THE INSIDE OUT

All wealth begins from the inside out. The two places where you combine the ingredients to inner wealth are your mind and your heart.

But just what is a mind? We're obviously not talking about the physical three-pound mass of brain neurons atop your shoulders. Your mind is where and how you think about success and money.

And what is a heart? We're obviously not talking about the muscle pumping in your chest. Your heart is where and how you feel about success and money.

How you think and feel (in your mind and heart) has an enormous impact on how you convert inner wealth into outer cash. Both of us have been able to accomplish amazing goals precisely because of the way we think and feel. We want to share with you how we combine our secret inner ingredients to create outer wealth. In Part One, we'll focus exclusively on your mind—how to think your way to prosperity.

The first major ingredient to wealth, Wow Now, is a way of focusing your mind so that you remain calm and yet confident even in times of stress and pressure like these. It's a way of communicating to yourself a clear vision of exactly what you want. It's a way of vibrating at a higher frequency so that you attract all of the resources necessary to accomplish your objectives. It's easy to be distracted by negative headlines, plunging stock markets, and declining economic indicators. It's easy to be diverted by shrinking 401(k) balances and layoff announcements.

Wow Now is a special state of mind where doubt, worry, and fear are not allowed to exist. So how do you build such a state of being?

exclude video games from the store was applauded by parents and teachers alike, which only added to the community appeal of the Heartlight Bookstore. At any one time during the weekends, the room was filled with ten to fifteen kids, buzzing with creativity.

While other shops along Main Street discouraged schoolkids from hanging out after school, Michelle welcomed them because the Heartlight Bookstore was "more than just a bookstore," as she was quoted in the local paper's community profile section. In two short years, Michelle had managed to turn the store into something of a community center where people came to mingle and engage in fellowship. The Heartlight Bookstore was indeed more than a bookstore; it was an interactive book-buying experience.

The room off to the right was known as the "E-Book Room." Filled with more Apple computers and high-speed Internet connections, the room offered customers a place to purchase and print out what had become known as the "ten-minute e-book." Ten-minute e-books were the latest phenomenon to hit the publishing world, and one that had become Michelle's hottest-selling item in the store. The e-books offered customers a condensed version of most every literary title available. Publishers thought this "drive-through" approach to the written word ultimately would lure customers back to purchase the entire book. The idea worked. Michelle was selling more books as a result of the e-book system than ever before. The idea was first conceived as a promotional tool by the publishers, but turned out to be another source of revenue for everyone involved.

In the middle of the main room sat a giant coffee table in front of two comfy slipcovered couches. If it weren't for the retail activity going on inside the store, it would appear as if you were sitting in someone's living room. This had been Michelle's intention when she first conceived the idea for a bookstore—she wanted people to feel at home. If she was going to compete against the online and

In order to have a single-minded focus, we need to understand what a mind actually is. When you think of your mind, what do you think of? Your mind is a playing field of thought. Your mind is how you think and process the information coming in from your inner and outer worlds.

Close your eyes after you read these instructions and time yourself for an entire minute—a full sixty seconds—in complete silence. Become aware of your breathing. Breathe in. Breathe out. Go ahead and start your minute right now.

You may have noticed several sensory inputs that connect you to the outer world. Did you hear any sounds that may have been beneath your awareness before you began to heighten your consciousness? Did you notice any smells or tastes? Did you feel anything physical where your body made contact?

Do it again. This time try to notice even more sensory input. Don't forget to breathe.

This is the beginning of awareness—to recognize what you're experiencing.

What else was going on in there? What other inputs were you noticing? In addition to these physical sensory inputs—sight, sound, smell,

brick-and-mortar giants like Amazon and Barnes & Noble, she knew she had to offer something more than a good price. She needed to sell the entire book-buying experience. Which is why when she saw a print-on-demand machine in Europe, which could print and bind any book while you wait, Michelle did research to find out more about the process. Foyles, the European company that perfected the print-on-demand business model, offered all types of books. They had softbound, hardbound, oversized trade, ancient, out-of-print, and specialty textbooks instantly available in print or to be put on your memory stick, iPod, Kindle, or any PDA, for that matter. The one thing they didn't have, however, was the desire to bring the service to America. When Michelle discovered this, she immediately saw the opportunity. She wanted to do for books what Tom Black had done for ATM machines in the United States. Tom Black was an entrepreneur she'd read about in *Fortune* magazine who started the ATM terminal machine business in America and subsequently made millions. Every entrepreneur has at least one billion-dollar idea, and the print-on-demand idea for America was Michelle's.

She also installed a self-service popcorn machine, and each table carried a candy jar, just like her Grandma Mohagen had always had. There was something inviting and soulfully warm about the smell of freshly popped corn and Michelle knew it. Every time a new batch was popped, sales would jump, and as a result, people in town were talking about the different bookstore on Main Street. Word of mouth was more than good—in fact, business was great—but Michelle knew fads would come and go, so she kept thinking of ways to keep things fresh. To bolster weekend foot traffic, Michelle began "Acoustic Night at the Heartlight." Every Saturday evening, a local artist would perform as customers shopped. The concept was a perfect combination of artistic expression, community fellowship, and retail promotion.

taste, and touch—there were inputs from your inner world. There was an additional layer of thinking going on. You are having thoughts constantly.

WHAT IS A THOUGHT?

How would you describe your thoughts? What exactly are they? You have three primary types of thoughts:

Self-dialogue—things you say to yourself
Images—pictures you conjure up with your imagination
Feelings—impressions that often result from what you imagine or say
    to yourself

For simplicity, we'll refer to these three forms of thinking throughout this book as *voices, visions,* and *vibrations.* These are the main ingredients of your thinking.

VOICES, VISIONS, AND VIBRATIONS

Successful people combine these three mental elements into amazing results. People who fail use the same three elements to no avail. How good is your thinking?

The outer walls were lined with old wooden bookshelves, which held the literary works of fiction. The rest of the bookcases were like the spokes of a wheel, angling outward from the center couch area. Michelle was particularly proud of her financial book section, but the section with the highest purchase volume was romances. On the other end of the spectrum were the nonfiction titles, which barely made the sales needle move. *It must be the weather,* Michelle thought, and the more she thought about it, the more it made sense. Curling up in front of a fire with a self-help book didn't sound as inviting as curling up with a romance novel by Nora Roberts as the snow fell outside.

The Heartlight's book-of-the-month club met the first Tuesday of every month. Francie Huffington was the first to arrive, but this wasn't unusual for the rich Texas-born socialite, who had trouble filling her days since her husband's death three years ago. Her husband, Christopher R. Huffington, had been a third-generation oilman from Texas who took up the habit of smoking at the age of thirteen. The habit Christopher referred to as "the only thing he could count on" killed him two months shy of his fifty-seventh birthday. The death was hard on Francie, but she never let on. She was fifty-nine, beautiful, outspoken, and egocentric. The combination made it hard for most people in town to like her, but that was the thing about Francie—she didn't care about other people or what they thought of her.

Sharply dressed with perfectly styled, platinum-blond hair, Francie entered under the protection of a large black umbrella, dripping with rain. Peeling off the purple Calvin Klein raincoat she'd special-ordered from Barneys New York, Francie announced a weather update to Michelle, who at the moment was across the room, preparing to close up shop.

"Storm's gonna be a gully washer for sure," she said, hanging up her raincoat. Even though she and Christopher had moved to

Let's test out your thinking right now.

Do you ever talk to yourself? Sure, everyone does. Say something to yourself right now in the field of your mind. Notice the exact sentence and remember it word for word.

Notice where you spoke to yourself in your mind. Take your finger and actually touch the spot where you "heard" this internal voice. Notice how far inside your mind the voice is being heard. Notice if you can pinpoint precisely where this voice is. How loud was the voice? Imagine a volume dial in your mind that gives you the ability to turn the volume of your self-dialogue much louder. Say something to yourself in a louder voice. Even louder. Louder still. Now, shout it to yourself internally at the top of your mind. Now lower the volume to a whisper. Speak to yourself in an even quieter tone.

The volume dial above represents the volume at which you speak to yourself. Each person has a unique volume setting. As you think about your internal dialogue, what volume is it set at? Just point to the spot on the dial. Ask friends or family members about their volume setting. Find out how their internal dialogue compares to yours. Here are the questions to ask them: "Do you talk to yourself from time to time?" If they say yes, then ask: "On a scale of 1 to 10, with 1 being soft and 10 being loud, how loud is your self-dialogue?"

Now that you've determined the volume level of your internal dialogue, notice the quality of the voice. Then, notice if you have the ability to

Idyllwild some ten years ago, just before he got sick, Francie's Texas accent was still evident.

"Is it starting to come down?" Michelle asked, removing the cash drawer from the register.

"Oh yes. She's puddlin' up over there on Maple Drive, gonna make it hard for folks to get home," Francie said, looking around at the empty store. "Just you and me tonight?"

Before Michelle could answer, Lei Kim entered through the back door, as she often did. Carrying a tray of her latest culinary invention, she shook off the rain and closed the door behind her. While she made her reputation as the best short-order grill chef around, Lei Kim's food inventions had become something of a legend. Her latest was fueled by her customers' on-the-go lifestyle and her own diet restrictions. Lei Kim was constantly searching for something that would not only provide the necessary nutrients one would get from a full meal but would taste good as well. The latest culinary concoction was a vegan chocolate chip raw food bar, which was sweetened with a slight touch of molasses, which made the bar irresistible despite the lack of butter and sugar in the ingredients.

Michelle looked at the grandfather clock near the front counter. The oversized hands indicated that it was 6:45 P.M.

"Let me put this in the safe and we'll get started," Michelle said as she moved around the front counter to enter the hallway. She noticed the somber look on Lei Kim's face. She was preoccupied with something and it showed.

"You okay?" she asked quietly.

"Oh yes, thank you," Lei Kim replied, offering a half smile. She was perhaps one of the sweetest people in all of Idyllwild, Michelle thought, forever polite and always with a smile, but Michelle had come to learn how to read Lei Kim and she knew when something was wrong.

change the quality of your internal voice. For example, remember the sentence you spoke to yourself a few moments ago. Say the same sentence as if spoken by a little child . . . by a person in their eighties . . . by a member of the opposite sex. Sing the message to yourself. Say it as if you were angry. Say it lovingly. Say it playfully.

So, you have the ability to modify the volume, the tone, and the quality of your internal dialogue.

Here's your wax on/wax off assignment for today.

Notice your internal dialogue—become more aware of what you say to yourself. More specifically, notice *how* you say it to yourself. Where is it? How loud is it? How would you describe the nature of the voice?

Become more aware of your inner world. Most people pay very little conscious attention to it. They're talking to themselves constantly with little or no awareness of it. For one entire day, just monitor what's going on up there.

Notice what words you use to address yourself. Do you use the pronoun *I* or *you* or *we*? For example, do you say to yourself, "*You* really must get going or *you'll* miss *your* appointment"? Or do you say to yourself, "*I* really must get going or *I'll* miss *my* appointment"? Or do you say to yourself, "*We* really must get going or *we'll* miss *our* appointment"? Is your internal dialogue in the *I* form, the *you* form, or the *we* form?

Wax on and off on these kinds of questions for the entire day, and meet us tomorrow at the beginning of the next chapter.

"Married life?"

"My son," she said, almost embarrassed.

"Trouble at school?"

"That would mean he'd have to be registered in school." When Michelle's eyes widened, Lei Kim continued. "He just informed me that he won't be going back to Boulder."

"I thought he was on a scholarship."

"He did not attend class last semester, so they pulled the scholarship."

"I'm sorry."

"It's okay."

"No it's not," Francie shot as she dug in her purse for a piece of chewing gum.

"Francie. . . ."

"Worst thing you could do right now is to help him out. Young people today need to understand that actions have consequences. Just my two cents, mind you, but Lei Kim . . . you have to stand firm with the young man. It's about the only way he'll learn."

"She's right," Michelle said.

"I don't know what I did wrong," Lei Kim said, frustrated.

"Honey, it's not your fault," Francie said. "Free will has to account for something. He made his bed, now he has to lie in it. You just take my advice."

"I'm worried about him," Lei Kim replied.

"He's young. He's got many mistakes to make, and this isn't the last of them. Trust me, he'll be fine." Francie smiled.

"I hope you're right," Lei Kim said, unable to hide her concern.

As Francie led Lei Kim over to the couches, Michelle put the cash drawer in the office safe.

Next to arrive was Lisa Garcia. Entering through the front doors,

5

NEGATIVE VOICES: SILENCING YOUR INNER WHINER

Welcome back. So, what did you learn?

Do you have an *I* voice, a *you* voice, or a *we* voice?

You might be wondering to yourself, "*I* wonder why they're asking *me* these kinds of questions."

Did you catch that?

If you said those words to yourself, then your voice is an *I/me/my/mine* voice. Your high school English teacher would have called this voice first-person singular.

On the other hand, you may have wondered to yourself, "Why are these guys asking *you* these kinds of questions?" If so, your second-person singular/plural voice would use *you/your/yours*.

It's possible that you use the first-person plural, as in *we/us/our/ours*.

First-person singular	*I-me-my-mine*
Second-person singular/plural	*you-your-yours*
First-person plural	*we-us-our-ours*

Is there an ideal way to talk to yourself?

That's a good question . . . which we won't answer at this time. This was just an exercise to help you become more aware of your chattering mind. First, just notice how you are communicating with yourself. Later on, we'll show you how to become more single-minded. Continue to monitor your dialogue from time to time throughout the day.

dressed in her usual Marmot jacket, blue jeans, and worn-out Asolo hiking books, Lisa fit the part of a woman who loved to go camping. But that was the funny thing about Lisa—she had never been camping a day in her life. She couldn't stand mosquitoes, and she'd never been one for roughing it. Lisa just liked the way the warm clothes made her feel comfortable and safe.

Shaking the rain from her jacket, she fought with her umbrella, trying to close it as she entered. It was a losing battle because the umbrella refused to cooperate. She tried to force it shut, but nothing worked. Just when she was about to throw a fit, something she was good at, Lisa froze.

"I smell chocolate," she said as her eyes searched the room like a satellite dish looking for a signal. Lisa had a thing about sweets, but chocolate was her weakness. She was never without it. Some people had a gum fascination, but Lisa was a chocoholic.

Lisa had met Michelle two years ago at the semiannual parent-teacher barbecue for Idyllwild Elementary. Held each year, the party gave parents a chance to network with other parents as well as teachers in hopes of making the most of their children's educational experience.

Lisa had grown up in Idyllwild, and she spent a year in California with a girlfriend before finally starting college two years after high school. Once in college, Lisa became something of a loose cannon. Late-night parties and missed classes was her major for her first year. During her second year, at the age of twenty-two, Lisa became pregnant. The problem for Lisa was she didn't know who the father was. After all, she was dating three different guys during the summer before her sophomore year, so when a visit to the doctor confirmed she was indeed pregnant, Lisa packed up and moved in with her parents on the south side of Idyllwild. Nine months later she

Did you hear any *other* voices as you were tuning in to the conversations going on in your mind?

We have asked audiences worldwide this question: "How many of you have a critical voice?" Almost every hand goes up. Let us ask you, the reader, this same question: "Do you have a critical voice?" Have you ever noticed a nagging, judgmental voice that speaks to you—berates you or brings you down?

Is it the same voice as the self-dialogue you noticed during your assignment yesterday? Ask yourself that question right now. Don't say it out loud, think it. Ask yourself: "Is the self-dialogue voice the same voice as the critical voice?"

Hmmmmmm . . . interesting question, isn't it? Could there be two different voices in your mind? The first one is just your normal, internal thinking voice. The voice you use every day to think through problems and solutions—the part of you that ponders, wonders, questions, and otherwise just thinks.

Often, there is a more negative voice—a critical voice. This voice is your inner critic, your Inner Whiner. It talks you out of things that are good for you: "Who do you think you are? You can't do that. It's too scary. Do it tomorrow." And when you don't do them, it criticizes you for *not* doing them: "What's the matter with you? You should have done it yesterday when you had the opportunity. What an idiot!" It gets you coming and going!

Or it talks you into something that isn't good for you: "Come on. You can do it. Just this once. It won't hurt. No one will know." And when you do it, it beats you up for having done it: "That was stupid. What got into you? You're such a screw-up. You're worthless."

THE INNER WHINER

Do you have a critical voice? Take a moment to notice it. Remember a time when you got down on yourself for something you either did or didn't do. Notice where this voice "talks" to you. Become more aware of it. Specifically, where is it? Actually point to the spot where your inner critic

gave birth to a healthy baby boy she named Russell. Russell was the same age as Nicky, which seemed to strengthen the friendship between the two single mothers.

When Lisa lost her job at McGregor's Department Store after payroll cutbacks, Michelle had hired her to help run the day-to-day responsibilities of the Heartlight. After only six months of work, Michelle gave Lisa a raise that eclipsed her salary at McGregor's. Michelle's entrepreneurial philosophy was simple—"pay more to get more." If you wanted an employee to perform at their highest level, reward them. The philosophy worked. Lisa gave the job 110 percent and Michelle, in return, treated her not like an employee but as a business partner. The problem with Lisa, however, was that she was always short on two things: time and money. She made living paycheck-to-paycheck an art form.

Michelle and Lisa shared the most reliable babysitter in town, Justine Dawson, a college student majoring in child development, which in the end was like having a schoolteacher as your babysitter.

"I know it's here. I can smell it," Lisa said, slowly taking off her jacket.

"Special batch, just for you," Lei Kim answered, rising from the couch.

"Are you going to make me share like last time?" Lisa joked.

"There's plenty for everyone. And I tried something new this time. These are 100 percent vegan goodies," Lei Kim said, peeling back the aluminum foil covering the chocolate treats.

"You know, Cameron Diaz is a vegetarian," Lisa said, scooping out a chocolate chip bar.

"Who's that?" Lei Kim asked.

"Who's that?" Lisa said with a mouthful. "Lei Kim, come on. Don't you watch the movies?" The blank look on Lei Kim's face quickly answered the question. "Here, look," Lisa said, grabbing a

resides. When we ask audiences to point to the place where they hear the critical voice, the vast majority of people point to their head.

Who is this critical voice—this Inner Whiner? Whose voice is it? Is that voice you? Why would you talk to yourself that way? What positive outcome is your critical voice trying to achieve?

As you did before, imagine that there was a volume control dial in your mind where you could raise or lower the volume of your critical voice.

Play with that dial for a minute. Turn the volume of your critical voice louder. Notice how you feel when the volume of that voice plays louder in your mind. People report that they feel angrier, more pressured, less in control, more confused. It can even become painful.

Now do just the opposite. Lower the volume of your critical voice. Make the sound so faint that you have difficulty hearing it. Now, how does that feel? Most people report that a sense of peace comes over them when the noise from their critical voice is turned off. They're happier, less overwhelmed, less confused.

Throughout the day, notice how many times your critical voice interjects itself into your thoughts. When you become aware of your critical voice, ponder this question: "Is this critical voice my friend or my enemy? Does it want me to win or lose? Does it want me to succeed or fail?"

In our opinion . . .

The critical voice is *not* your friend.

The most important lesson is to become aware that there is an enemy

copy of *People* magazine from the magazine racks. She quickly flipped to a page about celebrity vegetarians. Lisa was an avid reader of the celebrity rags and knew the who's who of Hollywood like a preacher knew the Bible.

"She's pretty," Lei Kim replied, digging out a second helping of the dessert.

"Vegetarianism is really popular in Hollywood. I'm even thinking about doing it," Lisa said as she took another huge bite of the vegan bar.

"Thinking about what?" Michelle asked, exiting the office.

"Lisa's turning vegetarian because it's popular in Hollywood," Francie said with a tone of skepticism.

"Don't make fun, Francie. I'm really considering it."

"No more turkey at Thanksgiving?" Michelle asked with a smile.

"They have that Tofurkey thing, don't they, Lei Kim?"

"Yes. But I will admit, Tofurkey is not as good as the real thing," Lei Kim answered.

"If you cook it, I'm sure I'd find a way to eat it," Lisa said, popping the last bite of her second bar into her mouth. Blessed with an overactive metabolism, Lisa was never shy when it came time for sweets, especially anything with chocolate. Lei Kim loved this about her, but was envious Lisa could eat whatever she wanted, whenever she wanted it. Lei Kim, on the other hand, had always said she could gain ten pounds just by smelling dessert.

Looking around the store, Michelle checked her watch and decided to close five minutes early. It was, after all, Tuesday, and the approaching storm, which promised to pack a punch, seemed to have driven most people home early. The weather was hard to predict along the Rockies. Storms could arrive in an instant, or never materialize at all. This storm, however, seemed to have vengeance on its mind.

in there that doesn't want you to win. As soon as you recognize the effects of this enemy, you can quickly gain control by turning down the volume.

What does this talk about voices in our head have to do with your success? Suppose you've been mixing all the right success ingredients in the right proportions, but all of a sudden you feel a wave of anxiety come over you. You begin to doubt whether or not you can do it. You're wondering to yourself, "What makes you think you can do this? Who do you think you are? What if you fail? Don't do it." You find yourself feeling depressed, heavy, upset. Your motivation to move forward is gone. Your enthusiasm wanes. You wonder where it went.

Suddenly, you realize what happened. You become aware of your inner world. It was this nagging inner voice in your head that caused you to doubt yourself. You pause. Dial down the volume on that critical voice and calm your mind. Notice the connection between your feelings of discouragement and the presence of a nagging critical voice.

According to experts, *everyone* has a critical voice.

Dr. Robert W. Firestone further explains in his book *Conquer Your Critical Inner Voice:*

> *The critical inner voice exists to varying degrees in every person. It undermines our ability to interpret events realistically, triggers negative moods, and sabotages our pursuit of satisfaction and meaning in life. The voice essentially keeps us locked into our defense systems, while our healthier side (the real self) strives for freedom from the constraints of these defenses. These destructive internalized thoughts lead to a sense of alienation—a feeling of being removed from ourselves and distant from those we love. When we believe the negative interpretations of the voice and fail to challenge them—that is, when we "listen" to the voice—we tend to act in ways that have negative consequences for us.*

Some people have a loud, insistent voice that makes their life miserable. For others, the voice is barely beneath their awareness.

"I'll get the front door," Francie announced as she straightened her perfectly ironed blouse and moved to the front of the store. Just as she reached out to lock the antique stained-glass doors, they were pushed open by a young black woman. Disheveled and unkempt, with baggy clothes, the young black woman was about to step out of the falling rain before Francie stopped her.

"I'm sorry, but we're closed for the evening," Francie said, blocking the door with her arm.

"It ain't seven o'clock."

"It isn't seven o'clock," Francie said, correcting the young woman's grammar, "and that doesn't matter. We are closed."

"Your sign right there says seven o'clock." She pointed to the hours of operation posted in the front window.

"Like I said, we are closed for the evening. You'll have to come back tomorrow."

"Please, I need to look for a book," the young woman said, not backing down from Francie. She was maybe seventeen or eighteen years old. Her hair was cut short, but tangled and badly in need of a shampoo and a brush. Dripping wet, her honest face wore the hardship of life on the street. Her eyes were sad.

"I'm sorry," Francie replied after a quick beat of consideration

"I said please," the girl fired back, putting her hand on the door to push it open.

"Young lady, remove your hands from this door."

"Francie, it's okay. She can come in," Michelle said, approaching from behind.

Francie kept her arm up, blocking the young woman from entering, while she whispered back to Michelle, "Look at her, she's obviously homeless."

"It's okay. Let her in," Michelle whispered back.

"Michelle, the girl stinks," Francie said as she leaned in closer.

When the critical voice speaks in your mind (if you notice it), what volume level does it use (from 1 to 10)? If your life is not plagued with such a critical voice, feel blessed. If you were to eavesdrop into the minds of many of the people you see today, it would shock you.

Your critical voice might be wondering why we're spending so much time asking these seemingly strange questions about voices. Okay, let's give you some rationale. Suppose an ordinary reader of this book is anxious to get started and flips ahead to the chapters on moneymaking strategies. She's looking for a kick-butt method for earning some serious cash in no time flat. She's broke and on her way to bust. She doesn't have time for all of this psychological mumbo-jumbo.

She devours the moneymaking chapters, and now all she has to do is to take action. We've seen it over and over again. Her critical voice starts to kick in . . . activating a host of negative emotions, including fear, doubt, and worry. It's almost as if there's an opponent in there that is trying to talk her out of moving forward. This opponent doesn't want her to win! So she hesitates, second-guesses herself, procrastinates. And nothing gets done!

She knows *what* to do. She just doesn't know *how to get herself to do it*!

Not everyone is like this. A few gifted people just seem to get things done. They aren't distracted by fears or doubts. The vast majority of the rest of us are plagued by self-doubt, worry, and fear. We spend an enormous amount of time getting ready to take action and worrying about the fear of rejection and failure—and get very little done. It's time to become single-mindedly focused on getting through the fears and getting more results!

To be single-mindedly focused means refusing to be distracted by *anything*. First, don't be distracted by the critical voices in your own head. Second, don't be distracted by the critical voices that are screaming in the minds of many of the people around you. They profess to be concerned for your safety, but often they're just repeating aloud the words spoken by their own internal critical voice.

Often your critical voice floods you with a myriad of reasons why your project won't work. *Yeah, that sounds like a great idea, but you aren't prepared for that kind of growth. Better wait till next month, when you'll have more time.*

Yeah, but . . .

Michelle gave Francie a compassionate smile, then welcomed the young woman into the store. "You can come in, but I need you to make it quick. We have a meeting starting in five minutes."

"No problem," the young woman said as she stepped out of the rain. As she passed by, she shot Francie a nasty glare. Francie's eyes narrowed, not willing to be bullied by the younger woman.

"What kind of book are you looking for?" Michelle asked, leading the woman into the store.

"Parenting. I mean, ya know, stuff about babies," she replied quietly, suddenly embarrassed that Lei Kim and Lisa were now watching her as well. Before Michelle could get a word in, the young woman offered up that her sister was about to have a baby. Michelle smiled and tried to make small talk with the woman, who mumbled more than spoke, but she grew quiet when Michelle showed her the section on parenting.

"I'll be right over here if you need anything," Michelle said, but the woman picked up a new release and began thumbing through the pages.

Michelle smiled and walked away. Watching the events closely, Francie delivered a condescending huff and crossed back to her purse for a quick shot of antibacterial gel. Francie was a clean freak. She was, after all, a Virgo. Just as she snapped the cap onto the antibacterial gel bottle, a giant thunderclap announced the hailstorm arriving outside.

Ice pellets the size of marbles began to bounce off the cars parked along Main Street. The women gathered around the front of the store to watch as the street quickly became white as snow. The howling wind whistled through the cracks of the old building like in a spooky Vincent Price film. The storm, however violent it appeared, made Michelle smile because the white streets made her think of Gideon and their honeymoon in the Great Smoky Mountains of

But is one of the favorite words of your critical voice. Often, whatever reason follows the word *but* is just an excuse to stop your progress. There is a free, downloadable illustrated book that shares a humorous message. It's called *The Devil Only Knows One Word* by James Skinner, Mark Victor Hansen, and Roice Kruger.

Here is the entire text of the book:

THE DEVIL ONLY KNOWS ONE WORD . . . BUT!

But, I'm not old enough.

But, I'm just a kid.

But, I'm not popular.

But, I didn't graduate from college.

But, I don't have any experience.

But, I don't have enough money.

But, I'm too busy.

But, I'm not pretty enough.

But, I'm not handsome enough.

But, there's too much competition.

But, somebody is already doing it.

But, my boss doesn't agree with me.

But, the economy is so bad.

But, it's so hard.

But, I'm too old.

But, it's too late.

Stop listening! Before it's too late . . .

Download a fully illustrated copy of this excellent book by visiting our website at www.cashinaflashthebook.com/gift.

Someone once said, "If you really want something, you'll find a way. If you really don't, you'll find an excuse." Your critical voice is the master of excuses. Anything to divert you.

So let us ask you again: how did that critical voice get in there? Is it

Tennessee. It was hard to believe so many years had passed since that amazing week.

The two had planned on hiking to the hot springs, kayaking the river, and many nights with good food and better wine, but none of that ever happened. Michelle and Gideon spent the entire week in the cabin, buried in a sea of down pillows and blankets, as the biggest storm on record hammered the area. Looking back on it, as she often did when the streets were dusted white, Michelle could feel the love they'd shared as if it were yesterday. Fond memories she would never soon forget.

She wasn't sure how it happened, but Michelle's past had become a source of celebration and not pain. She'd learned in losing Gideon that there were no good or bad situations in life, just varying degrees of what is. The pain and pleasure of life were there to make each moment, each day, a little bit sweeter. There were tears for times gone by, but for the most part, Michelle felt blessed to have shared a once-in-a-lifetime love. It was this kind of love she'd hold out for, but there was no rush, she told herself whenever she felt lonely. She wondered at times if she would find that with the mayor. Was he the one for her? All she knew right now was that she was enjoying the storm outside, which was beginning to show off its sharp, jagged teeth.

Francie, on the other hand, was visibly shaken each time the lightning hit, dimming the lights of the store with every strike.

"Makes you feel like a kid again, doesn't it?" Lei Kim asked with a smile.

"Not really " Francie said.

"I love it," Michelle said, putting her arm around Lei Kim.

Lisa cleared the coffee table to get ready for the meeting. Lei Kim eased into one of the antique rockers by the front door. Her smile seemed to widen as the wind whistled through the antique front doors of the shop.

just part of being human? Is that voice you? Why would you say those kinds of destructive things to yourself? It is your ego? Your anti-self? Your parents' voices? Frankly, there are many professional opinions.

Here is our unprofessional opinion. For whatever reason, your critical voice is not your friend. It doesn't want you to win. It primarily wants you to lose. It will try to talk you out of your growth and happiness. And then, having succeeded in stopping you, it will berate you for not having the courage to act.

For some people, just hearing this voice creates a flood of negative feelings and emotions, such as fear, anxiety, worry, apprehension, dread, panic, low self-esteem, worthlessness, not-good-enoughness, unworthiness, undeservedness, guilt, blame, self-reproach, and shame.

CRITICAL SELF-TALK	NEGATIVE EMOTIONS
"What will happen if the market turns? You could lose everything."	Fear, anxiety, worry, apprehension, dread, panic
"You don't know enough to pull this off. Whom are you trying to kid?"	Low self-esteem, feeling worthless, feeling not good enough, feeling unworthy, feeling undeserving
"You're always only thinking of yourself. You're so selfish."	Guilt, blame, self-reproach, shame

Suppose you knew a person who professed to be your friend. She seemed to give you good advice from time to time, but upon reflecting, you began to notice that this so-called friend took every opportunity to subtly bring you down and make you feel fear, low self-esteem, and guilt. How long would you hang around a person like that? You'd likely drop that relationship the moment you became aware of it.

Suppose you were getting ready to run a marathon, but your friend kept nagging at you: "I doubt you'll be able to finish. You haven't trained enough to make it. Only masochists go through this kind of pain to run a silly race. You could hurt yourself. You waited till too late to get started, better wait till next year." How long would you hang around that so-called friend? Not very long.

With all the action going on, they forgot about the young woman still inside the store. Oblivious to the storm raging outside, the young woman flipped through the pages of a book like a student looking for the answers to a pop quiz. Suddenly, the wind became deafening as the hail began to pelt the windows, which rattled beyond their limits. The chorus of violence finally exploded as a tree limb, about eight inches in diameter, crashed through the store's front window.

Broken glass flew inside the store and the wind rushed in uninvited. Lei Kim's chair tipped over backward. Lisa quickly hit the deck, scrambling under the coffee table like a rabbit down its hole. Francie fell back behind the front counter, more startled than hurt. Behind a stack of new arrivals, Michelle peered out in fascination. The violent storm, once outside, was now inside her store, wreaking havoc. Hail mixed with rain began to pelt the new carpet. Paperbacks were getting soaked, loose papers flew into the air like confetti, and cardboard displays toppled over without argument.

Over the howling wind, Michelle yelled over to Lei Kim, but there was no answer. Lei Kim was motionless, facedown under a large portion of the tree limb. Worst-case scenarios shot through Michelle's mind in an instant. Was Lei Kim dead? Had the tree limb crushed her?

Shielding her eyes from the pelting hail and rain, Michelle crawled her way over to Lei Kim's side.

"Is she okay?" Francie yelled over to Michelle.

"I don't know. She's shaking."

As Michelle leaned closer, she realized Lei Kim was shaking because she was laughing.

"I think I peed my pants," she said, wiping the rain from her eyes.

"You scared me!" Michelle said.

That's what we're encouraging you to do with your critical voice. Don't spend another minute listening to it.

How do you do that?

Well, if you're like most of us, you've become rather accustomed to listening to your critical voice, under the false assumption that since it was in your own mind, it must be part of you and is trying to help you and give you sound advice. Your critical voice is *not* the real you. It is *not* your friend. It is *not* your conscience.

THE INNER WINNER

There is ANOTHER voice that we'll train you to listen to called your True Voice that IS your true self, IS your friend, IS your conscience. Learning to listen to your Inner Winner is a almost a spiritual process—a sensitivity to the hidden path you are following. You begin to be led toward your destiny in miraculous ways. In later chapters, we'll share with you specifically how to do it.

In our experience, a short detour on how to manage your mind and your internal world can set you free to move forward more rapidly toward what it is that you really want.

Here is your wax on/wax off assignment for today:

For one entire day this week, become more aware of your internal dialogues. Try to distinguish between your normal thinking voice and your critical voice in your mind.

"Scared you? How do you think I felt?" Lei Kim returned as they began to laugh together. Just then Michelle remembered the young woman. She glanced over to the parenting section, but she was gone.

"Where'd she go?" she yelled out over the wind.

"Where'd who go?" Lisa shouted from under the table.

"Lisa? Where are you?" Michelle asked.

"Under the table," Lisa said, crawling out. "Hey, I wasn't taking any chances when I saw that tree coming at me. Stop, drop, and roll, right?"

"That's for a fire," Francie said, correcting her.

"Where's the girl?" Michelle asked again.

"She was right there a second ago," Lisa replied.

"Hopefully the stinky thing got the message and left."

"Francie, be nice," Michelle said, rising.

"You see, that's your problem, Michelle. You're too nice. What that girl needs is a good swift kick in the pants," Francie offered.

"Poor thing. I hope she's okay," Lei Kim added.

"Oh, enough about the girl. What are we gonna do about the window?" Francie added.

Looking down the hall, Michelle saw the young woman lying on the floor just inside the open bathroom door.

"Call 911!" Michelle said, running down the hallway.

"For a window?"

"Oh my God," Lei Kim said, getting to her feet as she saw the young woman.

"Is she breathing?" Lisa shouted as she slid to her knees next to Michelle, who was bent over the young woman.

"I think she fainted. Here, help me turn her over," Michelle said.

"All circuits are busy," Lei Kim yelled from the phone.

"Keep trying!"

"What's wrong with her?" Francie asked from a distance.

Notice your normal thinking voice—how you banter with yourself. Then notice if you have a critical voice.

Here is how you'll tell the difference. Sometimes the easiest way is to notice how you feel. Do you feel encouraged, empowered, and uplifted? Or do you feel discouraged, disabled, and beaten down?

Often, when the critical voice is talking, it makes you feel "down." Trace these feeling back to the actual words in your mind and it will be obvious why you were feeling down. Anyone would feel down if there was an inner voice saying things like, "You're broke and stupid and out of work. You'll never get your act together."

The first part of your assignment is to become more aware of how some of your feelings can be directly linked to the words you say to yourself.

The next part of your assignment is to notice *what* you say to yourself when the critical voice is talking. Notice if your critical voice speaks to you in the *I* or the *you* form. Does it say "I'm so stupid! I can't do it" or "You're so stupid! You can't do it"?

Then change the way the voice speaks to you. If it's a *you* voice, change it into an *I* voice. Does this make you feel more down? Or less down? Notice if there is a difference.

If you've been able to notice what the voice is saying, let's tinker with *how* the voice talks to you.

First, try to adjust the volume of your critical voice. What if there was a volume dial to make the sound louder and softer? Try it out. Turn the volume louder. Yes, that sounds strange . . . but adjust the volume so your critical voice speaks even louder in your mind, and notice how this makes you feel. Then turn the volume lower and notice if that feels any different. More likely you'll feel much better when the voice isn't screaming at you. As soon as you notice it, turn the volume down on this critical voice. Better yet, just turn off the sound entirely. Refuse to allow it to affect you.

Since you're becoming aware that you're in control of the knobs and dials of your brain, try these experiments.

Change the tone of your critical voice to match the voice of Minnie Mouse or Mickey Mouse—high-pitched and squeaky. Notice how that makes you feel.

"Straighten her legs out," Michelle ordered.

When Lisa moved around to grab the young woman's legs, she made the discovery. "Oh no!"

"What's wrong?" Michelle asked, gently brushing the young woman's hair from her dirt-smudged face.

"I think this girl's pregnant," Lisa replied.

"What?"

Before Lisa could repeat what she'd said, a bolt of lightning struck a power pole outside, lighting up Main Street like the Fourth of July. Sparks showered down from the power lines hanging overhead, plunging the women into complete darkness. Francie screamed.

"What are we going to do? I don't know how to deliver a baby," Lisa said, panicking.

"Still no answer!" Lei Kim screamed, beginning to panic as well.

"Calm down! Lisa, get the flashlight from the supply closet. Lei Kim, you keep trying 911," Michelle said in the darkness. Before Michelle finished, Lisa was scrambling to her feet and digging into a utility closet for the flashlight.

"I got it," she said, snapping it on. The single beam of light cut through the darkness like a scalpel.

Michelle called back to Lei Kim, "Any luck with 911?"

Lei Kim appeared from out of the darkness. "No. I think the lines may be down."

"Oh dear God," Lisa said quietly to herself, looking down on the unconscious girl.

The grim situation sank in for all of them.

"Fine, we're on our own," Michelle said in realization. "Lisa, grab the blankets out of the closet. Francie, get my keys out of the office. You'll need to pull the Range Rover around back."

"I'm not driving anywhere."

Then try making the voice seem far away, as if it's outside your front door and can't get in.

Make the voice as seductive as your favorite movie star.

Try moving the voice around to different locations in your mind.

ROBERT ALLEN: At a Wealth Retreat I was teaching in San Diego a few years ago, I noticed a woman in the audience who had a scowl on her face. She didn't seem to be enjoying the moneymaking techniques I was teaching. It was as if she couldn't concentrate. I saw her at lunch and had a hunch. I asked her if she had a critical voice. She looked at me with a puzzled expression. She hadn't really thought of this before.

She focused inward and replied, "Hmmmmm . . . yes, I do. I never noticed it."

"Whose voice is it? Is it your voice?" I asked.

She thought, then said, "No, it's my dad's voice."

"What does he say to you?"

She pondered again for a few moments. "He's saying loudly, 'You're no good. You're stupid. You'll never amount to anything.'"

"Really?" I said. "How does that make you feel?"

"Not very good."

"Let's try something," I said. "Change his voice into the voice of Mickey Mouse—all high-pitched and squeaky."

She tried it, and immediately started to chuckle.

I said, "Whenever you notice that critical voice, just change it immediately into Mickey Mouse's. Or turn the volume down on it entirely."

Then I asked, "Do you have a true voice? A voice that encourages you, that wants you to win?"

This took her longer to ponder. "Yes," she replied. "It's much softer. Much more subtle. But it's there."

"How does this voice make you feel?"

"Hmmmmmm," she said, searching for the right words. "Peaceful. Yes, peaceful."

"Then you stay with her and I'll drive," Lisa said, springing to her feet.

"I will not."

"Francie, we have to get this girl to the hospital," Michelle told her.

"No. Please. I can't go to the hospital," the young woman said, sitting up and grabbing Michelle's arm.

"Sweetie, you're about to have a baby on Berber carpet—I don't think that's the best way to start a life, do you? If I can get you to a doctor, I'm gonna get you to a doctor."

"Aaaaahhhhhhhhh!" The young woman fought back the contractions and pulled Michelle closer. "I don't have insurance. I don't have any money. Please, you can't take me to the hospital.' She was screaming now.

"This baby's coming out right now," Lei Kim announced. "We don't have time."

Lisa shrieked with panic, "What are we going to do?"

"Let's carry her into the office. Francie, grab her legs!" Michelle ordered.

"I said I'm not touching that girl."

"Dammit, Francie, get over here," Lisa barked.

"I'll do it," Lei Kim said, moving past Francie.

"I don't know who that girl is, and I don't really care to, either. You heard what she said. She's broke. She's got no insurance, and God forbid something happens to her—y'all be held responsible. If you want to help her, you go right ahead. I'm going home."

Before anyone could react to Francie's cold declaration and abrupt exit, the young woman screamed from another painful contraction. The wind howled through the hallway. There would be no time for doctors. There would be no time for any more discussions. The baby was coming.

We parted ways, and when the seminar resumed, I noticed her out of the corner of my eye. She would have a scowl on her face as I was teaching and then she'd stop. I could see her concentrating, and then she'd break out in a huge smile. She'd take a deep breath, and I could see a sense of peace glowing on her face.

More than six months later I was teaching a seminar in Anaheim. She met me in the hall at the break. She was so excited she could hardly contain herself. This one technique had released her to make enormous progress. She had learned why she had been procrastinating and putting off her dreams.

You may not have an obvious critical voice.

In his book *Voice Therapy: A Psychotherapeutic Approach to Self-Destructive Behavior*, Dr. Robert W. Firestone describes a "demonic inner voice" that represents the "dark side" of every one of us. He states:

> *In general, the average person is largely unaware of his self-attacks and of the fact that much of his behavior is influenced and even controlled by the voice. Indeed, "listening" to the voice predisposes an individual toward self-limiting behavior and negative consequences. In other words, people make their behavior correspond to their self-attacks.*

Your wax on/wax off assignment is to simply notice if you have such a critical voice. If so, how do the volume, timbre, and location seem to affect how you feel about yourself? Can you adjust these to make yourself feel better? Can you turn your critical voice off completely? It may take several days, even weeks, to train yourself to do those things, but being aware of your critical voice and learning how to control it are the first steps toward feeling more empowered, enriched, and excited more often.

The first step toward creating a powerful Wow Now is to control the voices in your head. See you tomorrow.

3

The Agreement of the Soul

It's Up to You

Located on the south side of town, Idyllwild Memorial Hospital looked more like an upscale retreat center than a corporately owned hospital. Utilizing the abundance of trees and plant life native to the Idyllwild area, the architects had designed a building that was inviting. It was a stark contrast to the usual stale construction of most hospitals and fit into the community perfectly.

The morning air was crisp and the streets were still damp from last night's storm. Leaving behind a wave of destruction, the five-hour storm had dropped power lines, littered sidewalks with fallen leaves, and snapped tree limbs. Residents and city employees had risen early and were hard at work on the cleanup. The downed power lines had canceled school and shut down city hall for the day.

Talking on the phone with her son, Johnny, Lei Kim paced the hallway outside Kanisha Peterson's hospital room. That was the name of the young woman who had given birth to a healthy baby girl just twelve hours earlier on the floor of the Heartlight Bookstore. Lei Kim had been up all night and the diner was about to open, so while Johnny wanted to talk about borrowing money, something he often did, Lei Kim first reminded him to turn on both burners of the stove. It was an older stove and needed adequate warmup time. Her cell phone battery was dying, so Lei Kim talked fast.

6

POSITIVE VOICES: EMPOWERING QUESTIONS AND HIGH-ENERGY WORDS

Are you beginning to notice that you have more control over your thoughts and feelings?

Once you've learned to manage your critical voice, it's time to learn how to use your normal voice to speak to yourself in ways that empower, embolden, and encourage you.

ONLY ASK YOURSELF EMPOWERING, UPLIFTING, EMBOLDENING QUESTIONS

Learn to monitor the questions you ask yourself. The mind works best when it is asked questions. Your mind works like Google. If you ask it a question, it searches through the vast database of all the experiences you have ever had, all the lessons you have ever learned, all the books you have ever read, all the television programs you have ever watched, all the schooling you have ever received, all the conversations you have ever taken part in. It sorts through all of this data, processing your question, and soon answers begin to pop up in the field of your mind.

Your brain/mind is the most powerful computer on the face of the earth. The three-pound machine inside your head right now is amazing. Most people misuse the amazing resource of their mind by asking questions that disempower and discourage.

Who do they think they are?!
What's the matter with me?

"And I said you're welcome to move in with your father and me, but I don't have the money to support you. You drop out of school, you get a full-time job—that's the deal," Lei Kim said as she smiled to Michelle, who was rocking the newborn baby inside the room. "You should have thought of all this before you quit school." *Beep*— the battery was reminding her that it was about to die. "My battery is low. Don't forget—make sure you turn on the burners of the stove. The left burner won't ignite, so you have to—" *Beep*. The battery was now dead.

Lei Kim looked at the phone and shook it a few times, just to make sure it was dead. It was. She stopped a nurse passing by.

"Excuse me. Is there a phone I can use?"

"Yes ma'am. You can use the phone inside the room, but they charge an arm and a leg," the nurse said. "There are pay phones by the elevators."

"Thank you," Lei Kim replied.

The baby had ten fingers and ten toes, and although she was only twelve hours old, she seemed to smile up at Michelle from the soft blanket wrapped around her. Michelle bounced her lightly up and down. Looking down at the newborn baby reminded Michelle of the feeling she'd had when she held her children for the first time. It made her think about Gideon.

Slowly Kanisha opened her eyes and smiled for a brief second at the sight of her newborn baby. Then, suddenly, she panicked.

"Is she okay?" she asked, sitting up.

"She's fine. See?" Michelle said, turning the baby so Kanisha could see her.

"Can I hold her?" Kanisha asked, her voice trembling. Michelle

When will my life stop being so hard?

Where is the justice in this world?

How long will I have to put up with fools like these?

Why do some people seem to get all the breaks?

When you "Google" these kinds of questions in your mind, the answers it provides often get you stuck in a downward spiral of negative emotions. You don't want to go there.

Scholar, philosopher, and researcher Dr. Jean Houston asks a more empowering question: "What is the purpose of your mind? It is to do whatever you tell it to do." Since you have access to the most powerful computer on the face of the earth, learn to ask it questions that empower your life and bring you the results you're seeking. Don't tell it what you don't want; tell it only what you *do* want.

Who can I call to help me resolve this issue I'm dealing with?

What's the fastest way to overcome this hurdle?

When is the best time to get started on this project?

Where can I find the answers that will get me fast results?

How can I turn this into success?

Why am I so blessed?

When you train your mind to ask only empowering questions, you begin to tap into the powerful answers that have always been there.

Buckminster Fuller said, "Your mind ultimately answers every question you ask it." So if you say, "How do I go bankrupt?" your mind figures it out. (We both tried that. It's not a good question.) Now, if you ask, "How could I retire rich in ninety days?" your subconscious mind will spring forth with the answer. Obviously, when it gives you a thought flash or a hunch, you must immediately *take action on it to get the results that you desire.*

This subtle shift in your thinking can immediately cause you to see a completely different world that is surrounding you right now. Instead of a

gently laid the baby in Kanisha's arms. Kanisha had tears in her eyes as she looked at the baby, then up at Michelle.

"Thank you."

"You're welcome."

"Did you talk to the doctor? Everything where it should be?"

"She's perfect."

Relieved, Kanisha finally smiled widely. "Yes. She is perfect."

"Have you thought of a name for her yet?" Michelle asked, pouring a glass of water for Kanisha from the plastic water pitcher sitting on the nightstand.

"Her name is Faith."

"That's beautiful, Kanisha."

"She's beautiful. A little wrinkled, but look at that cute face."

"Don't worry, the wrinkles won't stay . . . they just come back when you get to be my age," Michelle said with a laugh.

Kanisha's smile slowly faded as Faith seemed to look right into her mother's eyes. Kanisha was struck by the innocence and helplessness of the newborn baby squirming in her arms. It was a sobering moment for the young mother, and it didn't go unnoticed by Michelle. Before either of them could comment on what was going on, a nurse entered and announced it was time for the baby to return to the nursery.

Kanisha lay back in her bed and watched as the nurse carried Faith out, but she was crying even before her head hit the pillow. Michelle recognized what was happening—Kanisha was crippled with thoughts of fear.

"It's going to be okay," Michelle said, patting Kanisha's arm.

"No it's not."

"Kanisha, you can't talk like that."

"I told you not to bring me here," she said sternly, keeping her voice down.

world of problems and disasters, you begin to see a world of wonders and opportunities. More important, you begin to see the wisdom in problems and the opportunities in disasters.

The last century was full of turmoil, war, disease, murder, death, and depression. Instead of wringing their hands in despair, a few courageous souls saw the opportunity to make the world a better place: Mother Teresa, Nelson Mandela, Lech Walesa, the Dalai Lama, Muhammad Yunus, Mahatma Gandhi, Dr. Martin Luther King Jr.

Despite everything, it was an amazing century. The average life span in North America went from forty-eight years to seventy-eight years. Diseases were eradicated. Communism was discredited. The Internet now connects the world in a nanosecond.

This century will be even better. On a macro scale, as positive people search for positive solutions, the world is getting better and better. On the micro scale of your life, it will get better and better as you learn to search for positive solutions by constantly asking yourself positive, empowering, enriching, enlightening, and emboldening questions. The universe expands at the level of the requests and questions that you ask.

Many people speak positive affirmations to themselves: "You're awesome. You're amazing. You can do it. You have the power in you." We believe it is even more empowering to ask your mind empowering questions. Like a thoroughbred, your mind hungers to run. It's champing at the bit to solve problems and seek solutions. Just a flick of the whip and it's off and running. Flick your mind with an empowering question and let it race to cross the finish line with your answer. Your mind delights in making things better. Like a dog, it is eager to play fetch. Throw it an empowering question and let it speed off to retrieve the answer for you.

Whom can I serve excellently in order to tenfold my value to the world?

What do I need to know to find my fastest path to cash in ninety days or less?

When is the right time to take action? Answer: *now*.

Where is the best opportunity for me to pursue?

"I figured it was better than the carpet of my bookstore."

"I can't pay for all of this," she said, indicating the room, her hospital gown—basically everything around her. "And where are my clothes?"

"Kanisha, you have to trust that everything is going to be okay."

"Lady, I'm from Torrance . . . everything isn't going to be okay. I know better."

"Why do you say that?"

"Because unless you got a wand under that shirt of yours, you're no fairy godmother. Why are you here, by the way?"

"What?" Michelle asked.

"What do you want from me?" Kanisha said.

"What are you so afraid of?" Michelle finally asked.

"I got a baby . . ." Kanisha's emotions suddenly welled up and choked her quiet. She fought back the tears before gathering herself to continue. "I got a baby who's gonna look to me for guidance and I haven't even graduated from high school, okay?"

"Maybe it's time you did."

"Do I look like I got time to go back to school?"

"What about getting your GED? My father always said that a diploma is just a piece of paper. What you do with it—what you do next, he'd say—that's what is important."

"We back to the fairy godmother again? What world do you live in? I need to get a job, that's what I need to do next. So, what, you gonna wave your magic wand and make my life all better? I've been poor my whole life . . . nothin' you can say or do is gonna change that."

"Just because you've been poor, that doesn't mean you have to stay that way," Michelle said, smiling back at her.

"Why are you smiling at me? Don't you get it? I don't have anywhere to go," Kanisha fired off.

"I'm smiling because you remind me of myself. A much younger

How can I make my fortune this year, this month, this week, today,
and in an hour?

Why was I so blessed to be born in this great country?

ONLY SPEAK IN HIGH-VIBRATION WORDS

The words that flow out of your mouth come from the source of your
thinking. How can you learn to speak more positive, high-energy words?

Yvonne Oswald, Ph.D., has written a book entitled *Every Word Has
Power*. She explains that every word you speak has energy. Some words
have higher energy than others. Take the two words *good* and *bad*. Which
word do you think vibrates at a higher energy? Say the following words to
yourself and notice what kind of reaction (energy) they create in you.

Happy	Sad
Strong	Weak
Optimistic	Pessimistic
Easy	Difficult
Beautiful	Ugly

In Dr. Oswald's workshops she has the participants play a game to
teach how pervasive is the use of low-energy words.

> *Each individual gets twenty coins on the first day. Participants are told that
> if they use a low-energy word, they will forfeit a coin to the person who
> catches them. The catcher says, "Switch!" and the person who's been caught
> must replace the low-energy word with a high-energy word or phrase.*

For example, one person describes ~~a problem~~ . . . *switch* . . . <u>a chal-
lenge</u> they're dealing with. "I work at a job ~~that I hate~~ . . . *switch* . . . <u>that
I don't love.</u> My boss is ~~a real jerk~~ . . . *switch* . . . not a nice person. But
I need to make money because ~~I have so much credit card debt~~ . . .
switch . . . <u>I had too much fun using our credit cards.</u> Now it's time to ~~pay
the piper~~ . . . *switch* . . . <u>learn how to be more financially savvy.</u> But ~~I'm~~

version, but . . ." Michelle got momentarily lost in the realization of how life seems to race by without permission.

"But what?" Kanisha asked.

Michelle snapped out of the thought and continued, "I want you to come live with me until you get back on your feet. You can work at the bookstore—if you stay long enough, you can qualify for health care—and during that time, I'm going to teach you about making money, big chunks of money. And we'll find a way to get that piece of paper too."

The look on Kanisha's face was more skepticism than excitement.

"How?"

"First I'm going to help you change your mind."

"About what?"

"About what you think is possible. A good friend of mine—her name was Samantha, you'd love her—Samantha said money is energy, which is why they call it currency. Isn't that cool?" Michelle didn't wait for an answer. "You say you've been poor all your life. Well, it's time we change that current into one of abundance, filled with possibilities."

"Would you mind if I joined in?" Lei Kim said, standing from the doorway. "The way my family's going, I will need to make more money."

"Sure. Why not? We could start a group," Michelle replied.

"A group? What are you talking about?" Kanisha asked, sitting up.

"A group of women who want to learn about money. Not only learn about money, but how to make it . . . lots of it," Michelle said, liking the idea the more she talked about it.

Just then a nurse walked in. "Well, that sounds great, ladies, but you can't have your little group in here. Not right now, at least. Visiting hours are over. Time for you to go."

~~stuck in this dead end job~~ . . . *switch* . . . <u>I'm in a place where I don't have the freedom I'd like to have.</u>"

The fun in the game is that it teaches the participants to become very sensitive to the words they speak.

Notice what kinds of words are coming out of your mouth and the mouths of those who you converse with today. To prepare yourself, watch the nightly news on television. As you hear a word that's not high-energy, say *switch* in your mind. Count up how many times you say *switch* in only five minutes.

It will ~~shock you~~ . . . *switch* . . . <u>amaze you.</u>

Now, spend an entire day listening to the *quality* of the words that you and others use in your daily conversations. Make a conscious effort to switch your language to higher-energy words and thoughts. You'll soon become sensitive to the feelings you have as you listen more closely. You'll also understand why some people are just more fun to be around. They make you feel good. Others make you ~~feel bad~~ . . . *switch* . . . <u>feel not so good.</u> Imagine how much more positive you'll sound and feel to yourself and others after only a week of retraining your vocabulary in this way.

Here are some examples of some negative statements that you're probably making or hearing every day and how to turn them around:

ENERGY-DRAINING STATEMENTS	ENERGY-EXPANDING ANSWERS
I haven't got any money.	I'm temporarily low on cash and en route to being rich.
I'm out of work.	I'm discovering my perfect right livelihood.
The economy is bad.	There is a lull in economic expansion and I've decided not to participate.
Everyone is getting fired or laid off.	I'm working on making myself indispensable.
I don't have enough skills.	I'm learning at least one new money-making skill a month.

"Can't they stay a little longer?" Kanisha asked.

"They've been here all night, and honey, I'm a real nice lady, just ask anyone, but rules are rules," she said. She was the kind of nurse you didn't argue with. "You'll just have to come back later."

"But when can I get out of here?" Kanisha asked.

"Honey, if all goes well, you could be released tomorrow."

"If all goes well? What does that mean?" Kanisha said, sounding panicked. "Is there something wrong with my baby?"

"Your baby's fine. Sure is a cute little thing. I saw Mary with her down in the nursery when I came on my shift," the nurse said as she pulled the lid off the water pitcher to refill it.

"Who's Mary?" Kanisha asked.

"You just relax—your baby's fine. Right now you need some rest. And you two—out you go," the nurse said, ushering Lei Kim and Michelle out the door.

"I'll call you later!" Michelle said just as the nurse shut the door in her face.

"Kind of a bossy nurse, don't you think?" Lei Kim asked as they walked toward the elevators.

"She's doing her job."

"This sounds exciting, this group about money. Do you think Lisa and Francie might want to join us?" Lei Kim asked as she pushed the down button.

"We'll have to see," Michelle replied as they stepped onto the elevator.

Back at the store, Michelle couldn't stop thinking about Kanisha. While Lisa had written last night off as a freak occurrence, Michelle knew that the combination of Kanisha's arrival, the fact that she was

If you've ever written anything such as a journal or a blog, go back and read what you've written with this new lens. Notice how many times you could have used higher-energy words.

REFUSE TO THINK NEGATIVE THOUGHTS

Oops. Did you notice that? Read the above heading again. *Switch.*

ONLY THINK POSITIVE THOUGHTS

It's obvious which of the above two headings makes you feel more empowered.

So, from now on we encourage you to exercise your "positive" brain muscles ~~by refusing to see the negative~~ . . . *switch* . . . <u>by focusing on the positive</u> in everything that happens to you—even if it appears at first not to be so positive.

Here's a great quote from our friend Bob Proctor, host of the popular DVD *The Secret:*

> *Let's get rid of the idea that there's anything negative. Let's just see everything as good. It doesn't matter what we're thinking about, let's see the good in it. I believe if we can train ourselves to do that, we're going to catapult ourselves ahead. Quantum leaps will become common. We want to see the good in everything. When the negative thought comes up, say, "Wait a minute. What's good about this?" And just start to look for the good. Whenever anything happens that appears negative, let's just say, "What's good about that?" I don't think anything is gained by looking for what's wrong with something. I think a lot is gained by looking for what's right in it. You're not going to correct something by focusing on the negative. You're going to correct it by focusing on the positive. Don't get critical about things. Look at the people who are critical, who are looking at what's wrong. They're generally not very happy people. They're in a bad vibration. They're attracting to themselves more of what's wrong. Any dumbbell can find out what's wrong. It's fairly obvious. We want to train ourselves to find out what's right. There's something good about*

pregnant, the violent weather, and the members of the book club all arriving at the same time were the makings of a tipping point for change, where each woman, if she was willing, could begin to reach for an agreement with her soul. The idea of a financial Mastermind Group would be the perfect arena for this agreement to take place, Michelle thought, but it wouldn't come without a challenge.

Knowing there was a thirty-day waiting period before health coverage could begin, Michelle had Lisa fax in Kanisha's health insurance forms, listing her as a new employee of the Heartlight Bookstore. Lisa thought the move was odd at first, since they didn't need the extra help, but understood why Michelle was doing it.

Standing by the fax machine as the papers fed into the machine, one after another, Michelle pitched Lisa on the idea of the financial Mastermind Group.

"Who'd be in the group?" she asked.

"Kanisha, of course. You. Me. Lei Kim. Maybe even Francie."

"Probably not a good idea for me," Lisa said.

"Why not?"

"Ah, let's see. How shall I put this? Maybe because you're my boss?"

"So?"

"So what happens when I don't agree with what you're saying? You of all people should know I'm not the type to just keep quiet."

"I wouldn't expect you to," Michelle replied.

"Like I said, probably not a good idea."

"You have to trust me. I'm not there as your boss."

"Okay, then, who's leading the group?"

"I am, but—"

"Michelle, I like you. I like what you're trying to do for this girl. I think it's great, but I want to keep my job. I need this job!"

everything. Now, granted, you sometimes have difficulty finding it. Sometimes you never find it. But I know one thing, if you don't look for it you're never going to find it. Seek and ye shall find is very good advice.

Notice the empowering questions in what Bob says. He asks, "Wait a minute. What's good about this? What's good about that?"

One of our close friends, Dr. Ken Blanchard, author of the colossal best seller *The One Minute Manager,* recently had the opportunity to practice "finding the good." On October 14, 2007, he was informed that his Escondido home of thirty years had been burned to the ground in the California wildfires.

A few days later, he appeared on *Larry King Live* to talk about it. When Larry asked him about his devastating loss, his answer was simple and profound: Some things are important and some things are just stuff. You can always replace stuff. It was hard to lose his stuff, but since everyone in his family was safe, he was grateful.

Later, Ken Blanchard released a four-page summary of his reflections on losing his home. (Go to www.cashinaflashthebook.com for a full copy.) In it he referred to an exercise in a book by John Ortberg, *At the End of the Game, It All Goes Back in the Box.* The exercise goes like this:

> *It's 4:00 P.M. in the afternoon and you have decided to head home. There are two pads of Post-its on your desk. One says "Important—Forever" and the other says "Stuff—Temporary." As you leave your office, put a Post-it on anything you see—your computer, your desk, your secretary, the soda machine, the receptionist, your car, your house, your spouse, your kids— anything you see. Which Post-it do you put on what or whom? What is important and what is stuff?*

Then he described what it was like to see his once-beautiful home burned to the ground.

> *That afternoon Margie, Debbie, Tom (Margie's brother, who is President of our company), and I all headed to the site of our former home. When we*

"Why?"

"Why do I need this job? Kind of a stupid question, don't you think?"

"No, really. I'm curious. Why do you need this job?"

"Because I gotta pay the bills just like everyone else."

"And if you worry about just paying the bills, that's what you'll get . . . just enough to pay the bills."

"I'm worried about getting fired," Lisa said.

"Okay, then—if you don't come, you're fired," Michelle quickly replied.

"Excuse me?"

"If you aren't willing to learn how to get unstuck, it's probably not a good idea for us to work together anymore."

"You're joking." Lisa stood in shock.

"Try me," Michelle said as she walked back to her office.

"Wait a second. You can't say that and just walk away," Lisa called, moving after her.

"Don't you get it? I want to teach you about money so you don't need this or any job ever again."

Lisa remained silent. Michelle waited for a beat, then continued down the short hallway to her office.

"Fine. I'll come to your stupid meeting," Lisa said just as Michelle was about to close her office door.

"Great Now figure out a way to get Francie to come too and you can keep your job," Michelle said as she shut the door to her office. She smiled to herself. Challenging Lisa was a risk, but Lisa was predictable with her fear. Her life ran on it and Michelle knew she didn't want to babysit Lisa any longer. If she didn't like the group, she could leave.

Looking at her watch, she grabbed her keys and left her office.

"She's not answering her phone," Lisa told her, hanging up the receiver behind the front counter.

arrived, Carlos and Sharon, Scott, Mad and the three boys, and friends Tim Vannervien and Pat Zigarmi were already there raking through the rubble to see if anything was salvageable. It wasn't. As Margie and I walked down the driveway, our beautiful view was there but the house was ashes. Earlier in the day I had received a call from a dear friend, Tom Crum, author, Aikido expert and wonderful spiritual being. He said in his meditation room is an old Japanese quote, "Now that my barn has burned to the ground, I can see the moon." That really took on a whole new meaning during that moment.

"Important—Forever" or "Stuff—Temporary." Once you understand the difference between these two concepts, the world makes a lot more sense. Even when things don't appear positive, it's useful to be grateful for everything that happens. Most of what happens is just "stuff."

ROBERT ALLEN: I had a terrible car accident six years ago. I was a few moments from death. When I awoke from a medically induced coma, I was so grateful to be alive. The loss of my beautiful Lexus 430 SC convertible was insignificant. It was just stuff. Every minute of my newfound life was *wow* to me. I kept saying under my breath, "Thank you, God. Thank you. Thank you. Thank you." Hundreds of times day. I still do, six years later. Life itself is such a miracle.

So what does this positive thinking have to do with making fast money? Whatever moneymaking method you choose to use will involve other people—their ideas, their connections, their resources. Why would they want to do business with you? Do you exude confidence? Or does the room brighten when you walk out? How you think creates hope. Hope is contagious. Speed happens on the wings of hope.

Ask yourself only empowering questions.

Speak only high-energy words.

Think only positive thoughts.

"Then if I were you, I'd figure out a way to find her," Michelle said, crossing to the front doors.

"I don't get it. Why can't you just call and invite her?"

"And then what happens when she finds out Kanisha's going to be part of the group? You heard her the other night."

"Right," Lisa said, seeing the difficulty in the situation. "You think tricking her is going to work?"

"You just get her here. I'll handle the rest," Michelle said, about to exit.

"Wait a second—you're leaving?"

"Is that okay?"

"Yeah. I mean, no. Michelle, what is going on here? All of a sudden, everything seems out of whack. You tell me I'm going to lose my job if I don't join the group, and also that I've got to trick Francie into joining a group I know nothing about. What is all of this?" Lisa said in protest.

"You've been working here a year, right?"

"Yeah. So?"

"So, I'm trying to help you." Michelle stepped closer. "Look around. Look at all these books in here. Yet I haven't seen you crack one of them. Not one book that might improve your life."

"I didn't know my life needed improving," Lisa said, now getting defensive.

"Two weeks ago you sat right there on that counter after we had Thai food and said you were bored," Michelle reminded her.

"I said I was bored because it was slow in here," Lisa replied.

"So boredom is a result of your surroundings?"

"What? No, I didn't say that." Lisa was getting confused.

"Boredom is just something people do when they don't want to be creative. So here's your chance to get un-bored and keep your job at the same time," Michelle said with a smile as she turned and

If you do, you'll find yourself saying "Wow" faster and more often. *Wow* is a word that you will learn to say, under your breath, a hundred times a day. Notice all the ways in which your life is blessed: wow! Count how grateful you are to live where you are with what you have—as compared to the almost seven billion other people on the planet who will never enjoy a fraction of the freedom you enjoy: wow! Notice those around you who are achieving or who have already achieved their dreams: wow!

Notice the invisible miracles as they happen: WOW! Notice how amazing you are and how each moment in life is a gift. Look past the fear and know that you are divinely guided. This is your time to shine! WOW!

~~Refuse to notice the bad~~ . . . *switch* . . . Only notice the good. Change your perceptions and look forward to your ultimate wow. Look for what good might come of any apparent ~~failure~~ . . . *switch* . . . delayed success. What could you learn now? How could this lesson serve you in the future? What is the good hidden in it? Notice the good as quickly as you can. The faster you notice the good, ~~the less pain you'll experience~~ . . . *switch* . . . the more pain-free you'll be. As soon as you discover the good, say under your breath, "Wow!"

~~In this way, NOTHING *or no thing* of a long-term nature can hurt you. No "realistic" fear can harm you if you~~ . . . *switch* . . . Always look for the immediate benefit camouflaged inside every experience of life.

There is a wow in every now. Find it.

Positive thinking gets positive results that pay positively.
—MARK VICTOR HANSEN

walked toward the front door. "I have to go. Somehow I have to convince Hannah to move into Nicky's room to make room for Kanisha and Faith."

"You're having this stranger move into your house?" Lisa asked in amazement.

"That's the idea."

"Michelle, I'll play along—I'll get Francie down here somehow, but . . . I don't get it. Why are you doing all this for someone you barely know?"

"Because I can," Michelle said as she left the shop.

Here are your wax on/wax off assignments.

Pick one of these assignments each day for the next four days.

1. Notice the kind of questions you're asking yourself. Convert them into empowering questions. Remember, the size of your question determines the size of your result. Ask "How can I earn a penny?" or "How can I earn a million?" and your mind will find the answer.

2. Notice the energy of the words that are coming out of your mouth. Count the number of times you silently say the word *switch* today.

3. Put a mental yellow Post-it note on everything you see today. Is it Important—Forever or Stuff—Temporary?

4. Each time you notice something that you're grateful for, say silently to yourself, "Wow." Don't stop until you've said *wow* at least a hundred times today.

See you tomorrow.

4

Finding a Balance
Letting Go of Yesterday

Michelle took the kids for dinner at Gary's Outdoor Grill. Located near Idyllwild High School, Gary's was known for its incredible hamburgers and french fries. While she knew this was her chance to do something special for Kanisha, the way Samantha had helped her, Michelle wouldn't go through with it unless both Hannah and Nicky agreed. Through all the struggles of the past few years, Michelle had managed to develop a strong friendship with her children. Some said it was impossible to do this, to be friends with your kids, but Michelle thought the best way to get her children to act like adults was to treat them like adults.

Michelle was not surprised that Hannah loved the idea of having a little sister to watch after, but Nicky, forever the eccentric artist, objected to sharing his bedroom with his sister. His room, he said, was his "creative workshop," and he needed his "space." Michelle couldn't help noticing how much Nicky was like his father already.

After some debate, as well as a second chocolate shake with extra whipped cream, Nicky finally agreed to have Hannah move into his bedroom . . . but not without negotiating two conditions. First, he would be allowed to make a movie of the entire experience. He confessed he wished he'd caught on film the storm tearing through the

7

CHANGE YOUR PAST AND ENVISION YOUR FUTURE: STEPPING-STONES FOR SUCCESS

The last few chapters have been about "voice work." How you manage your voices has a direct effect on your feelings. If you feel down, it's likely you have been talking to yourself using "down" words. If you want to feel up, learn to ask yourself empowering, uplifting questions. Speak to yourself and others using high-energy words. Learn to say the word *wow*.

Why spend so much time on this? We'll soon be teaching you financial recipes that require strong, focused action. There will be ~~no~~ only time for ~~hesitation~~ decisiveness, ~~worry~~ confidence, ~~or procrastination~~ and action. Voice work helps sharpen the blade of your mind so you can cut to the chase and create some cash.

CHANGE YOUR PAST:
TURN YOUR OWS INTO WOWS

Some memories from our past are intense. We can still experience them today. We can taste, smell, feel, hear, and see them.

Some memories are far in the distance. We only observe them. We don't feel them anymore. They don't have the same intense impact they once did. We see them from perspective. We can take a god's-eye view and learn from them.

Scan back over your past. Some of your memories were painful (dark). Some were exciting (light). Some lifted you. Some dragged you down. Some were heavy. Some were light. Uppers and downers.

bookstore, but the aftermath of the blown-out window was "brilliant footage," he told his mom. "Brilliant" was the new catchphrase he'd picked up from watching the BBC, his favorite channel after the Discovery Channel. As long as it wasn't a music video channel, Michelle was happy. The second condition was simple: before the year was out, Michelle would agree to finally get a golden retriever. Michelle smiled because she knew Nicky was going to be a fine businessman one day. His negotiating skills were keen.

Kanisha and Faith settled into Hannah's room the day they got out of the hospital. Michelle was impressed with Kanisha's ability to adapt to her new surroundings. The kids liked her from the very start. Hannah said it was like one big sleepover. Although Kanisha wasn't getting much sleep with the night feedings and diaper changes, she was eager to help around the house. Through all of this, Michelle couldn't help wondering about Kanisha's past and how she'd ended up here.

On day three of the new living arrangement, while Nicky and Hannah got ready for school and Faith was sleeping, Kanisha helped Michelle clear the breakfast table. Michelle noticed that Kanisha had a sweet habit of humming while she worked. The habit reminded Michelle of her own mother. After the last plate had gone into the dishwasher, Michelle turned to Kanisha.

"Have you thought about what you want to do?"

Putting away the orange juice, Kanisha answered, "We have an appointment with Dr. Carlson at ten-thirty, and . . ."

Kanisha's words quickly trailed off as she turned and realized by the look on her face that Michelle was asking a bigger question. Michelle was asking a life question, and these were the types of questions Kanisha had spent a long time running from. Michelle watched as the young woman's body language quickly changed, almost daring Michelle to challenge her. Michelle could see that

Here is your assignment. Scan back over your memory and find three positive memories and three ~~negative~~ not so positive memories. Three light arrows and three dark arrows. Just write a word or two in the arrows above to remind you of each memory.

Look at your three positive memories. Remember them in "experience" mode. Make the memory even more intense. Crank up the feelings by remembering more details that you might have forgotten. Make it *more real* than you remember it. Intensify it. Enjoy it even more.

Look at your three ~~negative~~ not so positive memories. Why would you evaluate them in such a way? As we learned in previous chapters, your critical voice might be getting down on you for having done such a ~~dumb~~ not smart thing. Take the signal out of the memory, by turning that voice down.

Remember to ask yourself empowering questions. "What's the matter with me?" is ~~the wrong~~ not the right kind of question. "What could I learn that would transform those ~~painful~~ challenging events into valuable lessons?" This is a more empowering question.

Don't get sucked into a painful memory. See it from perspective. Watch yourself up there on the television screen going through a challenging experience. Notice how you handle the situation. Notice what you can learn from it. Don't feel it.

Kanisha was scared inside, and talking about that fear was something that frightened her even more.

Fear had arrived in Kanisha's life right after her father was killed two months shy of Kanisha's ninth birthday. The victim of a gang-related shooting, her father was dead at twenty-six years old. Her mother, Shantal Peterson, had become pregnant with Kanisha when she was just seventeen years old. Now Shantal began to use drugs as a way to mask the pain of losing her husband, who'd been her high school sweetheart. Unskilled and a high school dropout, Shantal began to sell marijuana for a living. Kanisha tried to think her life was normal, but the late-night parties and the string of different men in the house the morning after the parties made her finally face the truth. It was this truth she wanted to run away from, but it was choking her.

They lived in a tough section of Torrance, California, and while Torrance wasn't South Central L.A., it was still a battleground for gang life and drugs. At fifteen years old, Kanisha was arrested for selling pot at school. Other than taking a sip of wine with some friends one Saturday night in the summer, Kanisha had never touched drugs or alcohol. When she found her mother's stash one day after school, Kanisha devised a plan. If she could make enough money selling the drugs, she could find a way to get out of Torrance. A few of her friends wanted to go to college after graduation, but all Kanisha wanted was to get away from her life. She wanted to start over somewhere new. But the idea backfired when she sold the marijuana to an undercover officer.

The arrest sparked a string of events that would change Kanisha's life forever. A search of the house brought about her mother's third strike. Shantal Peterson was sent to prison for ten years, and

If you do this faithfully, you might begin to notice that the less positive memories are turning from down to up—from dark to light. You might begin to wonder why you labeled them as less positive in the first place. How could something that caused you to grow so much and gain so much wisdom be labeled anything other than a fully positive, vibrantly up experience?

Some people say you can't change your past. Oh, yes you can! You can remember your past successes even more vividly, more powerfully, more experientially. You can remember your so-called failures more successfully, with more wisdom and learning. By doing this, your past becomes a more powerful resource for you.

As a friend of ours, Clive Swersky, says, "You have to take your ows and turn them into wows."

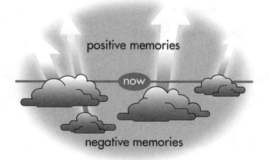

LOOKING TO THE FUTURE: THREE WAYS TO MAKE YOUR DREAMS A REALITY

How do you think about your future? Is your future predominantly positive? Negative? Or neutral? Do you have hope for the future? Can you imagine a brighter day? By brightening the memories of your past, you can brighten your future. Your dreams are future memories. They are events in the future that haven't occurred yet. Can your dreams of the future have an effect on your daily activities in the now? Absolutely!

Just as memories of the past can affect your present, future memories

Kanisha was sentenced to two months in a juvenile facility. Then she was transferred to a group home.

The summer before her senior year, Kanisha finally found a way to escape her dismal life. She would take the city bus to the neighboring town of Redondo Beach. For her, being there was like living someone else's life. Even though she stuck out like a sore thumb in the predominately white city, Kanisha found her escape. For a few hours every day, she felt like she was someone else.

Things started to look up when she got a job working as a cashier in the gift shop at the Redondo Beach Yacht Club. The job paid minimum wage, but the association with the success and money displayed by the yacht owners was all Kanisha wanted. She didn't know how to make lots of money, but knew she loved being around it. Kanisha's good looks quickly opened doors, but her attitude often closed them just as fast.

Even though it was against policy for employees to fraternize with yacht club members, Kanisha met a boy two years her senior. Jake Underhill was born a millionaire and his family had more than a few yachts around the harbors of Southern California.

One day, when Kanisha was working alone in the gift shop, Jake came on to her. She turned him down, trying to explain the club rules for employees, but Jake said he was an Underhill. That meant he was used to getting what he wanted. It had been this way his entire life. For his seventeenth birthday, his father, a luxury yacht designer out of Newport Beach, gave his only son, Jake, his own yacht. At just over fifty feet, it was small compared with his father's, but the yacht was Jake's haven for parties.

Lined with polished teak and outfitted with a flat-screen television, the inside of the yacht was nicer than any home Kanisha had ever lived in. Being there made her feel like she was finally someone, and Jake treated her nicely. Summer love had taken her over. At

of planned events can make your life today more exciting. By transforming your past memories, you can change your past. For most people, however, the past contains painful experiences that create fear for the present and dread for the future. Look at the illustration below. Here is someone who has a few positive memories that they're disconnected from and many intensely negative memories that they're fully connected to. These fears ruin their past, infect their now, and destroy their future.

This is a fearful life: past, present, and future. The goal is to change the past by intensifying the positive memories and disconnecting from the not-so-positive memories. You don't want the signal from intensely painful memories to bleed into now and infect the future, do you? When you think of your past, you want to remember it as a series of predominatly positive experiences. Yes, there were some bumps, but you learned from them and moved on. There will also be some bumps in the future, but you can handle them. This gives you peace in the now (Life was and is good) and hope for the future (Life will be good), as in the illustration on the next page.

In daily life, most people get disappointed very easily. They are hoping for good things to happen and expecting positive outcomes, and if instead they experience a temporary setback, they get quickly disappointed. Then they dwell on this disappointment by conjuring up sad pictures—images of themselves missing out on their dreams, failing to meet their obligations, making their friends and family unhappy.

nineteen, Jake was already six-two. This was ideal for Kanisha because she already stood five foot eight. Jake had perfect teeth and his tan redefined the term "California golden boy." During their second week together, the relationship became physical, and then the unthinkable happened: Kanisha became pregnant.

When she told Jake the news, he told her not to worry, that everything would be okay. But it wasn't. Jake soon started acting differently. He became busy with his father's business in Newport Beach and stopped returning her phone calls altogether. She was devastated.

When she took the bus to pick up her paycheck, she saw Jake in the yacht club, laughing and carrying on with his golfing buddies, preparing to end their day of drinking on his boat. Jake caught her eye and dismissed Kanisha without a second glance. She knew it was over and she was alone again. Humiliated, Kanisha turned to walk away, but her anger took over. She wanted answers from this rich kid. When she confronted Jake, he denied ever spending time with her. The commotion brought the yacht club's security, but it immediately escalated into something of a Jerry Springer episode when Kanisha punched Jake in the face. She was mad, kicking and screaming. Jake was furious at being assaulted by a club employee. He demanded she be fired on the spot.

Inside the manager's office, Kanisha was informed she would be fired for the incident. When she tried to explain what had happened, the manager said he didn't want to hear it. She could tell it to the police, because Jake was pressing assault charges. Knowing this would send her back to juvenile hall, Kanisha bolted out the back door of the club and ran across the street to catch the bus home.

Sitting on the bus, dazed at how in just a few weeks' time she could go from bliss to this, Kanisha didn't get off at her stop in front of the group home because there was a police car parked outside. She

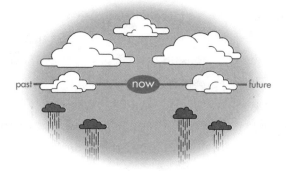

past — now — future

To compound this, they have angry conversations with themselves: "How stupid!" They magnify it by asking themselves disempowering questions: "What's the matter with me?" These thoughts send immediate signals to their body in the form of negative vibrations. Almost instantly they begin to feel the effects of these thoughts in the form of discouragement, disillusionment, and despair. This affects their now immediately and negatively impacts their future. The thought of succeeding is dampened with doubt. Their motivation is lessened. They just don't feel like trying. They procrastinate—put it off until tomorrow, when they'll feel better.

Well, if this has ever been your pattern, it's time to fix it. You don't have time for this kind of "stinking thinking," as Zig Ziglar has often said. Like we learned in the last chapter, you can't afford the luxury of a negative thought. You only have time for a positive environment. When a setback happens, it's more empowering to be positively expecting it. Instead of being disappointed, you're anticipating the positive lessons and the wisdom you'll gain as a result of the setback. Setbacks are just stepping-stones to make you stronger.

You actually welcome a change in plans. Plan B is like a surprise present you get to unwrap. Your imaging process is positive. You're looking for the good: "There's got to be a pony in there somewhere." Since you're looking for it, you find it. You're asking yourself more empowering questions: "Why would God love me enough to give me this growth experience? What

rode the bus until its last stop near East L.A. Cashing her final paycheck, Kanisha bought a bus ticket and left town with the clothes on her back.

With little money and no family to speak of, Kanisha was leaving California for good. She had no destination. She had no home. She lived on the streets and traveled by bus when she could afford it. She'd already had a lifetime of hard-knock lessons and she was only eighteen years old.

Michelle asked the question again: "Have you thought about what you're going to do?"

"Why do you ask?" Kanisha replied, folding her arms across her chest and staring back at Michelle with a challenging glare.

"Because it's an important question to consider."

Kanisha didn't reply. Michelle continued, "If you don't choose your life, life will choose for you. And you'll end up with a bunch of things you don't want."

"Is that what you think I'm doing?" Kanisha fired off.

"I didn't say that. I was asking the question to—"

"Do you want us to leave? Is that it?"

"Now hold on a second."

"Because we can be gone this afternoon, no problem. I don't need—"

"Stop it," Michelle barked at the young woman.

"I wasn't doing anything," Nicky complained, entering from the hallway with his video camera rolling.

"Nicky, put the camera down and go brush your teeth."

"I would, Mom, but Hannah's been in the bathroom forever," he answered, moving into the kitchen for a better shot.

could I learn from this to share with people who might be having this same experience?"

Skeptics call this Pollyanna thinking. They are sometimes right. At times, there is no good that comes from an experience other than the opportunity to exercise your positive-thinking muscles and strengthen the habit of constantly trying to find the good in everything.

This form of thinking infuses your experience with a sense of optimism. Life is basically good. People are predominantly good. This is one of the reasons why watching a lot of television is such a waste of precious time. How many episodes of *Law & Order* can you watch until you begin to form the attitude that life is basically bad and that people are predominantly evil? Watch the news and ask yourself, "Does the newscast generally portray the best of humanity or the worst?" Focus on activities that foster the best in yourself and others and you'll begin to attract the best like a magnet.

> *There is always sufficiency. Start with the consciousness that there*
> *is always enough, and you'll find enough. If you start with the*
> *consciousness that there is not enough, then you'll find not-enoughness.*
> —MARK VICTOR HANSEN

So let's create positive, powerful, impactful future memories. Here are three techniques.

VIRTUALIZE IT

The first technique we've already discussed in chapter 2. We call it virtualization. Imagine your most ideal lifestyle in all five senses! Step into your future dream and imagine what it feels like to experience this lifestyle. Feel it. Smell it. Taste it. Hear it. See it. Make your dreams more real than your fears.

Don't Wait! Experience Your Dream Now

If your fears are overwhelming and intense, then they'll blot out your dreams like an eclipse of the sun. Make sure your dreams are brighter than

"Well, girls tend to do that."

"Well, I tend to not like it," Nicky quickly replied. "You said I could make a movie."

"Not right now! Put the camera away and get ready for school."

"But you said—"

"I know what I said, baby. Please. Not this morning."

"You guys fightin'?" he asked.

"Go."

Nicky slapped the viewfinder shut and disappeared back into the hallway. Michelle turned her attention back to Kanisha, who was staring out the window.

"I know what you're going through."

"No you don't," Kanisha said, her voice cracking as she fought back the tears.

"You're right. I don't. But I know you're scared. It's not the end of the world. It's only the beginning."

"The beginning of what?" Kanisha asked.

"That's up to you. And I know you're unable to see this right now, but you're going to look back on this whole situation, this time of your life, and you're going to smile."

"For what?"

"Because your life has finally started. Your future is happening right now, and God has a plan for you."

"Then God sure has a funny way of showing it." Kanisha felt embarrassed because the truth was, she hadn't thought of her future. "I *am* scared," she said softly.

"I know . . . and that's okay."

"Why?"

"Because that fear is telling you that you're about to make changes in your life. Use it. Feed on it."

"I thought fear was a bad thing."

your fears. Step into your future dreams in all five senses. Imagine how good life could be if you stepped into your future dreams more often. How good could life be if you tamed your inner critical voices and learned to follow your true voice? How good could life be if whenever you experienced a bump in the road, you immediately looked for the positive in it and instantly learned from it? This kind of thinking would transform every bump into a stepping-stone for success.

This virtual place is a space of awareness, a place of total receiving.

How can you access your future dreams, brilliance, wisdom, love, joy, happiness, and infinite ability and capabilities? There's only one way—virtualization.

Virtualization is a form of meditation where you go to a state of having something before you have it. It starts as an idea, concept, hunch, notion, hope, or dream. You cogitate, ruminate, meditate, and ponder it again and again in your heart. You feel it, touch it, taste it, and celebrate it.

Everything Starts as an Idea

Ideas start as fiction, become theory, and are then melded into fact.

Moneymaking ideas are deep-seated. You start to inwardly smile and joyously desire the next step or idea or dream that you want to come true.

Inside our minds we can orchestrate anything we want to be, do, or have. As we virtualize it, we five-sense it into reality. Your five inner senses need to embrace it completely, as though it was a true living reality, before it comes to be an actual truth.

For example, virtualize a situation where you write out and carry with you a $1 million check paid to yourself for excellent products, royalties, or services rendered.

You need to feel and touch it—that is, wear your ideal watch in your mind before you buy it, smell the new-car smell, hear the compliments before you achieve them. Taste the meals of celebration that you will enjoy. Hear the congratulations of those closest and most important to you, giving meaning and purpose to your accomplishments. Believe in its existence before whatever it is hardens into fact.

"Only if you allow it to consume you. Trust in what you're doing," Michelle said with a smile.

"What am I doing?"

"Asking bigger questions from your life. Bigger and better questions will eventually bring bigger and better answers," Michelle said, allowing the words to sink in.

"I don't understand," Kanisha confessed.

"You want to ask yourself how you can make enough money now so that you can survive—and ultimately thrive—without giving up your freedom as you get older."

"Oh," Kanisha said, still a bit confused.

"I'm going to take the kids to school and then I'm going to work. I should be home around five-thirty. We can talk more about this kind of stuff tonight."

"Michelle?"

"Yes?"

"Thank you."

"Don't thank me yet. We have lots of work to do."

While she loved owning the bookstore and working real estate deals from time to time, Michelle had enjoyed the mentoring session with Kanisha more than she'd anticipated. As she drove to work, her mind raced with all sorts of moneymaking possibilities. Would she focus on real estate? Product inventions? Brokering? Her mind then drifted to Francie. She wondered where she'd fit into the mix. After all, she was already rich. What help did she need? She lived in a large house on the east side of town and drove a Jaguar. Maybe Michelle could convince her to co-chair the group. She loved the fact that Francie was older—it would bring a different level of life experience

Your inner being is an exciting place to move, live, and be. It has the predictive values of all of your future experiences.

Your desire goes into your subconscious as an idea and gets transformed into a result. One idea goes in and the entire universe responds.

Your state of mind creates your state of result. Your state of heart creates your state of future. Your state of future is boundless.

Experience just how boundless it is by downloading the free e-book *Say Hello to Riches* at www.cashinaflashthebook.com/gift.

What positive images of your future are you creating in your mind, multiple times, every day?

Feeling Is the Virtualization

It is important to stress again that your heart and mind need to be in alignment for what you virtualize to come to fruition.

The only way for you to have the end result you desire is if you are brimming with self-worth, so your creative mind is thrilled that you are going to have more wealth.

So the question becomes, do you have a high enough self-worth to create a high future value?

It is time for you to destroy the old model of trying to meet outrageous standards and believing you are not good enough. Who set those standards, anyway?

Get comfortable and try this virtualization now: As you read these words, experience voices, visions, and vibrations in all five senses. Don't just read these words, FEEL these words.

I am happy.
I am joyful.
I am blessed.
I am a blessing to myself, all others, and the planet.

and insight to the group. What good would it do to have all the members the same age, the same race, with all the same sensibilities? Diversity would be their strength. It would keep them honest.

In her office later that day, the idea finally came to her. She would first focus on the mental energy it takes to become a millionaire. Sure, she could teach them the ABC's of making money, but the mental energy—that's where people falter. That's where the juice was, Michelle thought. They had to think like millionaires first. "Yes, that's it," Michelle said to herself. "That's the focus." She was certain this was the reason they'd all come together. And she knew the best way to do something was not to start at the beginning, where questions and fear usually reside, but at the end, where she held the vision that these women were already living extraordinarily rich lives.

Exiting the office, Michelle found Lisa behind the counter, reading a magazine.

"I'm going to Starbucks. You want anything?" she asked, crossing to the door.

"No thanks. I'm trying to quit," Lisa said, flipping the page of the magazine as if she was annoyed at the declaration.

"You? Quitting coffee?"

"I know. Absurd, isn't it?" Lisa snapped.

"How you holding up?" Michelle smiled at Lisa's playfulness.

"I'll let you know after I get through the morning."

"Day one?"

"Yeah, and I'm already not happy about it. First they take away coffee. Then it's red meat. Carbs. Hell, even blow-drying is going to kill you now. What's next, chocolate?" She shook her head. "If they say I'm gonna die from eating chocolate, then you better bury me in the largest Nestlé's 100 Grand bar wrapper ever, because I will not give up chocolate."

I am healthy physically, mentally, and spiritually.

I know that I have an inner and outer self.

I can easily see my outer self by looking in a mirror.

I can see my inner self by breathing deeply and going quietly within.

I love working on my inner self.

I know the road to my self-improvement and development is always under construction. I am on an exciting, never-ending journey that delights me.

I feel good inside and it shows up outside. My face ultimately reflects and radiates the truths that I have held deep within my inner being.

I am elated and thankful to do my personal inner work.

I love decorating my inner mind—my "home entertainment center"—with images that are good, true, lovely, noble, and of high report.

I live in the assumptions of my wishes fulfilled.

I have fixity of thought and feeling. I know that my words and vibrations shall not return to me void and shall accomplish the missions where I send them. I dream it and it comes to pass.

My imagination is my looking glass.

It is our goal to instill in you a strong sense of self so that no matter what you may encounter in your future, especially your financial future, you can handle it with ease.

In summary, the first visioning technique for creating powerful future memories is virtualization. The second technique is to megasize your dream.

MEGASIZE IT

Ponder this powerful quote from Arnold J. Toynbee:

It is a paradoxical but profoundly true and important principle of life that the most likely way to reach a goal is to be aiming not at that goal itself but at some more ambitious goal beyond it.

Michelle smiled and turned back toward the door.

"Oh, by the way, I guess I get to keep my job," Lisa said, not looking up from her reading "Got an idea to get Francie to come down to the shop."

"Really?" Michelle said. "How?"

Before Lisa could respond, the front door opened and Francie walked in. Michelle glanced at Lisa with a look of amazement and then said to Francie, "We were just talking about you."

"Slow news day?" Francie said, joining them at the front counter. Michelle noticed Francie wasn't making eye contact with them She wasn't sure, but it looked like Francie had been crying.

"Francie? You okay?" Michelle asked.

"Oh yes. My allergies got a good hold on me this morning. Just out doing my morning shopping. I need a few books today," she said, tearing a page from her leather Filofax planner. Even though Francie was quick with a smile, Michelle couldn't help sensing there was something wrong with her.

"Francie, when are you going to trash that old-school date book you've been luggin' around and get yourself an iPhone?"

"If you haven't noticed, dear, I *am* old-school. I like to write it. When I write it, I see it. When I see it, I remember it," she said, handing the list to Lisa.

"Real estate?" Lisa asked. looking up from the paper.

"Yes. I'm thinking about some investments and wanted to see if you had anything on foreclosures. Buying them, I mean."

"Well, this is perfect," Michelle said, looking first at Lisa and then at Francie. "We're starting a new discussion group about money and investing. Every Tuesday night at seven, here at the shop."

"A discussion group?" Francie asked.

"It's more than a discussion group . . . it's a financial Mastermind Group for women who want to make money," Michelle said.

Create a vision that is over the top. Don't aim for a realistic goal; aim "at some more ambitious goal beyond it." Make your dream bigger than life. Don't just supersize it, megasize it!

Warning: Objects in Mirror Are Larger Than They Appear

Since we live in a world where the predominant messaging is negative, we need to overcompensate for this negativity. The little sign on the side mirror of your car reads: *Warning: objects in mirror are larger than they appear.* Most media reports paint the world in a negative light. Warning: objects in the news appear worse than they really are.

You need to paint your world not just in a positive light but in a brilliantly positive light—almost too bright. Learn to make things *much* better than they appear to be in *all* the mirrors of your life—your rear-view mirror, your near-view mirror, and your peer-view mirror. Past, present, and future.

For example, our first book, *The One Minute Millionaire,* was a huge success. But right from the first brainstorm, we envisioned our book ultimately being made into a feature-length movie. The probability of any book being made into a movie is highly unlikely. One in a million.

We megasized our movie vision by writing an imaginary future article for the *Hollywood Reporter,* one of the major media outlets for the movie industry. Before a word of our book had been written, and before a sentence of the screenplay had been put on paper, we went into the future in

"Francie's got money. Why would she wanna sit around and talk about it with a bunch of women who don't?" Lisa joked. But just as the last word left her mouth, she realized from the look on Michelle's face what she'd done. "I mean, I can't answer for you, of course, and I'm sure it's going to be fun."

"Thank you, but no," Francie replied with a smile. "Life is a bit busy at the moment. Maybe another time."

The phone rang. Moving to answer it, Michelle shot daggers at Lisa. Saved by the bell, Lisa took Francie over to the real estate section.

"Good morning, Heartlight," Michelle said.

"Any baby deliveries today?" the mayor asked jokingly.

"Nothing yet, but we might have a death later," Michelle shot back, still watching Lisa.

"What?" he asked, confused.

"Nothing. I'm kidding. What are you doing calling me at eleven-thirty? I thought you had back-to-back meetings today."

"I did, until my budget meeting got pushed to the afternoon. The controller's kid got sick or something, so now my morning's wide open. Thought I'd swing by and take you to an early lunch."

As he spoke, Michelle noticed Francie's Filofax sitting on the counter. An official-looking letter stuck out from the pages. Looking closer, Michelle could partially see a word in bold, just below a bank's letterhead. Making sure Francie was still preoccupied with Lisa, Michelle eased the letter out just enough to see that it was a foreclosure notice on Francie's house.

"Michelle?" the Mayor finally asked.

"What? Yes. I'm here. Sorry . . . lunch might be difficult today." They chatted a bit longer, then agreed to meet for breakfast another day.

our imagination and wrote the following fictional report on what we envisioned:

THE HOLLYWOOD REPORTER

The One Minute Millionaire Makes Movie History
#1 Movie in America Completely Sold Out Thirty Days BEFORE It Opens

If you want the hottest ticket in America, you're too late. You'll have to wait for at least another four weeks. The One Minute Millionaire *is already sold out for each showing of its five-day opening week, with over ten million tickets presold to movie-goers nationwide.*

For the first time in movie history, there will be no lines forming in front of movie theaters to purchase tickets for the release of a new movie. The tickets have all been sold. This is good news to studio executives, who usually spend the last few days before the launch of a major movie in frenetic strategy meetings or in nervous group hand-wringing sessions. Not so with this movie. Just like the title suggests, the money is already in the bank gathering interest. It is a guaranteed winner no matter what promotional magic competing studios try to pull out of their hat.

What made all of this possible was a completely new marketing model for promoting a blockbuster movie. Advance tickets to the new movie have been in presale for almost a year and the success of this innovative campaign has exceeded all . . . (see **Millionaire** *on page 76*)

What sets this imaginary newspaper article apart is its wildly improbable outcome. In crafting this story, we purposely aimed far beyond what anyone could realistically expect.

We went for the wow.

We've shopped our movie idea to most Hollywood studios through dozens of dead-end meetings, yet we never lost touch with our ultimate goal: *The One Minute Millionaire* as a hugely successful movie in theaters around the world reaching ten million people on the very first opening day. After eight years, our constant enthusiasm has finally paid off. We've landed a major movie deal with an award-winning production house. The

As Francie and Lisa brought a pile of books over to the counter, Michelle smiled at Francie. "What are you doing later? Maybe you and I could have lunch. I don't think we've ever gone out to lunch, have we?"

"Neither have we," Lisa said to Michelle.

"What do you say, Francie? Would you like to have lunch with me today?" Michelle asked, ignoring Lisa.

"Thank you, but no. I . . . have lots of reading to do," Francie replied, giving Michelle a polite smile.

"That'll be $42.53," Lisa announced. "That's with the 20 percent book club discount, of course. Pays to be part of the family, doesn't it?" Francie handed over her American Express, and Lisa ran the card. The credit card machine beeped with a decline message.

"Hmmm," Lisa said, leaning down over the machine.

"Is there a problem?" Francie asked.

"Says your card was declined. Probably just something wrong with our phone lines. Been hinky ever since the storm. Here, let me run it again."

"No," Francie said quickly, "I'll pay with cash." Francie retrieved her American Express card and dug out the exact change from her purse.

"Wow, right to the penny." Lisa smiled as she counted the money. Francie collected her books and headed toward the door.

"Francie, wait. Your receipt," Lisa called out after her.

"That's okay. I don't plan on returning them." And just like that, she was gone.

"That was weird," Lisa said, looking out the window as Francie pulled away in her Jaguar.

"Maybe she's having a bad day," Michelle offered, not wanting to reveal what she'd discovered.

"By the way, what did you say to get her to come in?"

screenplay for *The One Minute Millionaire* is finally complete, and as you read these words, the money is being raised to manifest our dream. It's happening! Wow!

For the promotion for this book, we see ourselves on the cover of *Time* magazine for having helped get America out of the most crippling "repression" since the Depression of 1929.

Our hero, Sir Winston Churchill, said, "Success is the ability to go from failure to failure without losing your enthusiasm." To maintain enthusiasm in the face of failure, you need to create a vision big enough to be enthusiastic about—to be worth the risk of failure. By challenging you to aim for a more ambitious goal, our intention is to make the goal of financial freedom appear less difficult.

HABITUALIZE IT

The first step to create a wow future vision is to virtualize it. The next step is to megasize it. The final step is to habitualize it. Step into your vision several times a day and imagine how good it could be. As you go to bed tonight, wander through your dream home and your dream lifestyle. What kind of art is on the walls? What kind of enlightened activities resonate around your life? Keep this clearly in your mind, especially as you encounter negative people or circumstances.

MAKE A HABIT OF SUCCESS THINKING

Repetition is the mother of learning. If you really want your dream, drive it deep into your mind and heart. Every day, step into your dream and make it more real than your fears—over and over and

"What?" Lisa asked, a bit confused.

"You said you had an idea to get her to come to the store."

"I did, but I never talked to her—she just came in. That was just a coincidence."

"Yeah, maybe. But what was your idea?"

"I thought if we said we found her Calvin Klein scarf here at the store, she'd come in to get it. We could tell her that if she didn't come get it, we'd give it to Goodwill or something. Ya know, scare her into action."

"Did she leave a scarf?"

"No, but that doesn't matter. If Francie hears *anything* Calvin Klein is about to go to the Goodwill, I'm bettin' five bucks she comes a-runnin'."

"Well, try it out. See if you can get her to come in tonight around seven."

As she walked to Starbucks, Michelle was preoccupied with the thoughts running through her head. Should she just go over to Francie's house and see how she could help? Or was it better to wait until Francie came to the shop? There were no answers.

over and over and over and over and over and over and over and over and over and over and over and over and over and over and over and over and over and over and over and over again.

If you do not see great riches in your imagination, you will never see them in your bank balance.

—NAPOLEON HILL

Every day, as you move through this negative world and the "realists" that surround you, you will be tempted to abandon enthusiasm for your ultimate dream lifestyle. Expect it. Expect resistance. People don't like such positive thinking. It makes them uncomfortable. It's not realistic, they say. It's even ridiculous.

Whenever you experience the skeptics' stare, just remember that they are seeing your dreams through walls of their own fear. Since their fears are more real than their dreams, all they can see is fear. And that's all they ever get—fear!

Do you want *their* fears or *your* dreams?

Stop. Ask yourself that last question one more time until you really get it.

Do you want their fears or do you really, really, really want your dreams?

Smile as skeptics tell you what might go wrong. Agree that they might have a point, but keep bringing your wow into the now and nothing can stop you.

Whatever you focus on, you manifest. If you focus on your fear, fear will expand in your life. Fear will grow. Fear will find a place in your home. Don't let fear into your home. The home of your body is a sacred temple. Don't let fear into the temple of your body. Focus on your fortune and your fortune will expand. Focus on your blessings and your blessings will expand. Focus only on what you want. If you focus on what you don't want, what you don't want will sprout up all around you. So the key is to focus intensely on what you want. Be convinced that you're going to get it.

5

Whatever It Takes

Finding a Way to Begin

When Lei Kim walked into the store that evening, Lisa was excited to see her, but soon she realized that Lei Kim wasn't carrying her usual tray of fresh-baked goodies. Dejected, Lisa returned to the copy of *Us Weekly* spread out on the front counter.

Just then the front doors opened and Francie stepped in, dressed to the nines in a black Dolce & Gabbana suit with a Marc Jacobs purse. The woman had great taste and knew her fashion.

"Francie, you keep showing up at the store like this, we're going to have to give you a time card," Lisa joked.

"Come sit down and have a cup of tea," Lei Kim urged.

"Ladies, I can't stay. I'm just here to pick up my scarf."

Lisa and Lei Kim exchanged a look, and Francie immediately became suspicious. "All right, what are you two up to?"

When Michelle came out of her office and joined Lisa and Lei Kim, Francie sighed. "I didn't leave my scarf, did I? What's going on?"

Michelle spoke up. "You want to come back to my office?"

"No. I want you to tell me why Lisa lied to me."

"Because if I told you why I wanted you to come down, I didn't think you'd come. I tried to talk with you today, but you blew outta here like there was a fire."

Have a burning desire to get it and it will begin to be attracted to you like a magnet.

Virtualize. Megasize. Habitualize.

And you will realize your fortune. It awaits you in your thought escrow, requiring the requisite stimulus—your feeling that you deserve to have it. You merely need to vibrate at that level of accepting your desired outcomes and ultimately and inevitably it will be yours.

As your wax on/wax off assignment, we challenge you to write a newspaper story or magazine article about your future success. Imagine you're a reporter chronicling your success in a positive news story. Take off your realistic thinking hat and stretch your imagination to wild extremes. How can you succeed *beyond* your wildest dreams if you haven't thought of what those wild dreams might be?

"So you had Lisa lie to me?"

Michelle flipped the sign in the front window to read Closed. "If you'll just give me five minutes to explain, I'm sure you'll—" Before Michelle could finish her sentence, Francie saw Kanisha exit the stockroom with a box of books. Without saying a word, Francie moved to the front doors.

"Francie, please."

"Good-bye, Michelle."

Not knowing how else to get her to stay, Michelle blurted out, "I know what's going on. I saw the letters in your Filofax, Francie. I'm sorry, I probably shouldn't have looked, but it was right there on the counter." Francie froze.

Michelle continued, "I've been there and it's not the end of the world. You don't have to go through this alone."

"Go through what alone?" Lisa asked, clearly puzzled. "What's going on?"

"Francie, it's only the beginning," Michelle said, stepping closer.

Francie was like a deer caught in the headlights of an approaching car. Standing in the doorway, with all eyes on her, she was speechless.

"I can help you get out of this," Michelle said softly. "You just have to trust me."

In an icy voice, Francie replied, "How dare you presume to know anything about me?" Her voice shook slightly from the anger raging inside her petite frame.

"It's not like that," Michelle returned softly.

"Leave me alone," Francie said, and stormed out.

After a tense beat, Lisa joked, "Okay. That went well."

"Be quiet, Lisa," Michelle said exasperatedly.

"What are you getting mad at me for?" Lisa said defensively.

KA-CHING THINKING:
FILL YOUR BANK ACCOUNT TO THE BRIM

Suppose your bank account was directly linked to your thoughts. Every fearful thought costs you a hundred bucks, which gets automatically sucked out of your bank account every time you hesitate to move toward your dreams due to an imagined fear—a rejection, an imagined loss, a painful outcome. You check your savings account in the morning before you go to work. The balance is $2,500. When you come home that night you go online to check it again. It's down to $200.

"What? What happened to my money?"

What happened is that your thoughts are no longer just thoughts. They are things. They have value. They have an immediate benefit and consequence. When you think a negative thought it immediately deducts money from your bank account.

"What? I didn't agree to this. This is absolutely *terrible!*" you exclaim.

You hear a sucking, slurping sound and your balance is reduced to $100 in front of your very eyes.

"*Unfair!*" you scream at the screen. "This is terrible!"

Sluuurrrp. Sluuurrrp. Another two hundred bucks is deducted: your balance is -$100. You're in overdraft.

"Hey, you can't do that!"

Sluuurrrp: -$200.

You're still fuming as this question pops into your head: "What happens when I think a positive thought?"

You hear the sound of a cash register: *ka-ching!* And $100 gets redeposited into your bank account, which is now at -$100.

"Do I make a hundred bucks every time I think a positive thought?"

Michelle hung her head in defeat. The plan to get Francie to join the financial Mastermind Group had backfired.

Francie's black Prada high heels were moving fast down the sidewalks of Main Street. She crossed the street toward her Jaguar, which was parked on the corner of Seventh and Main. She was a proud woman, and she didn't want anyone to see her like this. She was embarrassed. "If I can just make it back to my car, I'll be fine. Just keep walking," she said to herself. "Don't look back and don't you start to cry. Not now. Not here." She was determined. "Just a little further and you'll be fine," she said, coaching herself through the mental chaos.

"Francie. Stop. Please, just stop for a second," Michelle called, running after her, but Francie only sped up.

"Please stop. Allow me to explain."

When Francie continued to ignore her requests, Michelle finally grabbed her arm. "I didn't say that to embarrass you."

Francie ripped her arm from Michelle's grasp and kept moving toward the safety of the car. Why was this happening to her? She just wanted to be left alone. Was it too much to ask?

"Francie . . . He's gone. It's been over three years and he's not coming back."

Francie's heels skidded to a halt, but she didn't turn around. She knew her husband was gone, but she didn't want to hear it said out loud. Not now. Not ever, in fact, and especially not from someone who was younger than she was. Who was Michelle to tell her about her life?

"I lost my husband and I was left with a pile of debt," Michelle said softly. "I lost my house and I almost lost my kids. Foreclosure is a scary thing, but there's a way out, I promise you."

Ka-ching! You're at $0.

You wonder how quickly you could you learn to think more positively. *Ka-ching!* Another $100.

You start to dust off your dreams, the ones you've buried beneath your fears for all these years. *Ka-ching!* You connect to the feeling of living your dream lifestyle. *Ka-ching!* You get up the next morning a half hour earlier to put together your plan. *Ka-ching, ka-ching, ka-ching!* You're watching your bank account out of the corner of your eye. It's back up to $2,500 and climbing. You pat yourself on the back for learning to think positively. *Ka-ching. Ka-ching.*

Every once in a while you notice that your account has dropped a few hundred dollars. It's so easy to fall back into the pattern of negative thinking, listening to your critical voice, or blaming others for your problems. Every time you notice that, there is an immmediate consequence.

You learn to think more positively every minute of every day. When something that appears to be negative happens, you learn to immediately ask, "Where is the good in this? What can I learn from this?" *Ka-ching. Ka-ching.*

This is your future bank account. It's hidden from your awareness, but it is as real as your current bank account. Every less-than-positive thought deducts value from your future. Every positive thought adds value. Some people arrive in the future to find abundance everywhere and bank accounts full to the brim. Other people arrive and find that their accounts have been looted, their safety deposit boxes open and empty, their vault plundered. The hardest part is when they're told that they themselves are the culprit. They embezzled their own money. They did it. It was an inside job. They squandered their own money—their own future—one thought at a time.

At that very moment, standing in their empty vault, they still have a choice. They can curse themselves or the heavens for a lifetime of wasted thinking: "What an idiot! It's too late for me!" And then they hear giant sucking sounds. *Sluuurrrp!*

Or they can start from that very moment and say to themselves, "What can I learn from this?" *Ka-ching.* "I wonder how fast I can fill this vault back up?" *Ka-ching.*

"I'm fine, Michelle," Francie said, digging into her purse, looking for her car keys as if she'd just turned down an invitation to the movies.

"No, you're not, and I'm sorry to keep on you like this, but if you're going to walk away from me, I want to know I did everything I could to try to help you."

"Who said I needed your help?"

"Francie, you came into the store today because you didn't know what to do."

"How do you know I don't know what to do?"

"Because you're out buying books on foreclosures, which is something I've already been through. You have to know that we met for a reason . . . and that young girl in there, she's part of it. You might not think you need any help, but I'm certain she could use yours. Hell, what else have you got to do?"

Francie shot her a nasty glare, so Michelle softened the message.

"Imagine if you'd had someone as smart as you offering you guidance and mentorship when you were her age. You have to ask yourself whether or not you'd be in the situation you're in now."

"I don't owe that girl anything," Francie said.

"Why, because she's black?"

"Don't be ridiculous," Francie quickly shot back.

"Or is it something else?"

"I don't know, Michelle. You tell me. You seem to have all the answers about how to fix my life."

Michelle paused for a beat. "Okay. And this is just a guess, but . . . maybe it's because you see a woman who's homeless and broke, and it scares you to death because you think maybe her situation could happen to you."

Francie said nothing, but her face showed that Michelle's guess had been dead on.

That's the choice that each of us has. The lesson is to have a faster disaster. Get over it more quickly. Learn from it more rapidly. Laugh about it as fast as you can.

Learn to laugh faster whenever there's disaster.

That's the way to live.

Every moment

Of every day.

Here is your wax on/wax off assignment.

Count the number of times you say *ka-ching* in your mind today.

More than likely, there will be moments in your future when all will appear lost. Your critical voice will want to beat you up (if you let it). Your past failures might loom around you. Your mind might be full of low-energy words. It is at this precise moment when you need to turn off your critical voice. Remember and reexperience your past successes. Think only positive thoughts. Fill your mind with the sound of Ka-Ching!!!

Turn the page for a story that will show you the power of your thoughts. Copy the page and share it with others!

"Come on, Francie. You can do this," Michelle said after a moment.

"Do what?"

"Start over."

Francie opened the car door and placed her purse into the car.

"Running away won't solve anything," Michelle said urgently.

"I'm not running away."

"Then what would you call this?"

Francie didn't answer.

"I'm forming a money Mastermind Group for women, and we're going to focus on making money, fast money. Right now that's your only choice to turn this foreclosure thing around. The bank will take the house and you'll have to file bankruptcy. But I can help you. This group can help you. You just have to trust me."

Another long silence passed between the two women.

"Being in debt and running away from your life is no way to live. I've been there, but someone taught me the way out. When I thought my life was coming to an end, she taught me it was actually just beginning. After thirty-three years, I finally discovered what living really was. The way you're feeling right now, Francie . . . I know the other side and it's beautiful." Michelle waited to see if Francie had anything to say. She didn't, so Michelle kept going. "Tell you what: if you don't like what I have to say, I'll leave you alone. But if there's anything I've learned in this life, it's this: what *has happened* does not define what *will happen*. The final chapters of our lives haven't been written. All of this is happening for a reason."

"And what reason is that?" Francie finally said.

"So you can begin to forgive," Michelle offered softly. "Forgive your husband for leaving you behind. Forgive your parents for what you think they didn't give you." Michelle stepped closer now. "But most of all, Francie, forgive yourself."

THE STORY OF THE WISH-FULFILLING TREE
How to Guard the Self-Sabotaging Mind

In a small village far away from anywhere and with no access road to the nearest town lived a poor Farmer. He had nobody. No family to help him farm. He was all alone.

In the heat of a scorching summer's day he had to go to town to buy seeds for his next crop. He had to walk there while the sun beat down on the parched earth and on him. It was hot.

Half way to town the Farmer saw a beautiful Tree with long and strong branches, still filled with green luscious leaves. Under the Tree at the base of the trunk it was cool and the shade defiantly challenged the scorching Sun. He decided to rest there for a while.

As he was dozing off in the cool of the shade resting under the Tree he thought if he would have a cold glass of water it would be great. He did not realize that he was sitting under a Wish-Fulfilling Tree. Before you know it, he saw a very cold and refreshing glass of water before him. He quenched his thirst and wished if only he could have some sweets and some food. Lo and behold he saw a banquet before him.

After having had the meal of his life he wished, if only he would have a bed to take a nap. He was lying on a most comfortable bed before he could even speak his thought out completely. He immediately thought if only he had a house to sleep in on this comfortable bed and the house was there before you know it.

The fulfillment of one wish led to larger and larger wishes. Before you know it, he had wanted the most beautiful woman for a wife and had plenty of children to help him in the farm, and there he was surrounded by family and wealth.

When he saw what he got just by wishing, he got a little worried. No, as a matter of fact he got a lot worried. He thought, "What will happen if now a ferocious man-eating tiger comes out of the jungle and eats me up?"

A ferocious man-eating tiger appeared and ate him up. He was still sitting under the Wish-Fulfilling Tree.

From Tulshi Sen, *Ancient Secrets of Success for Today's World* (Toronto: Omnilux Communications, 2006), 65–67.

Francie stood there for a minute, looking Michelle in the eyes. She somehow found a smile, but there was something different about the smile this time. It was a distant smile. She was lost.

Kanisha joined Lei Kim and Lisa on the couches as the front doors of the Heartlight opened. Michelle walked in alone.

"What happened?" Kanisha asked Michelle.

"Michelle, what's going on? What was in her Filofax?" Lisa asked.

"She's in foreclosure," Michelle told them.

"What? Francie?" Lei Kim said, surprised.

"I thought she had tons of money," Lisa added.

"Did you ask her to join the group?" Kanisha put in.

"Yes."

"She didn't go for it, did she?" Lisa sat back, almost as if she knew the answer to the question.

"Nope. I thought I had her, but she just drove away. Left me standing right there on the curb."

"Was it because of me?" Kanisha asked shyly.

"No, honey. It's not because of you. It's because of her."

"Why?" Lei Kim asked.

"Because I'm guessing she'd rather live her life in fear. And you know what? That's her choice. This goes for everyone, by the way. If you don't want to be part of this group and learn about how to make some real money, then there's the door . . . and take your poverty mind-set with you."

"Wow. That's kind of harsh, don't you think?" Lisa asked.

"You want harsh, Lisa? Try waking up one day and realizing you're out of money and you aren't sure if you can feed your kids

9

VIBRATIONS:
HOW TO WOW YOUR NOW

Voices. Visions. Vibrations. These are the languages of your mind.

Voices: What you say to yourself—and how you say it—has an enormous influence on your thinking right now. And your bank account!

Visions: What you envision from your past and in your future—and how you envision it—has an enormous influence on your thinking right now. And your cash flow!

What kind of influence are we talking about? What you say and what you see now have an immediate impact on how you feel right now.

Our word to describe these feelings is *vibrations*.

Vibrations: From such a positive space, you just vibe in the right kind of future. Whether you are attracted to the future or the future is attracted to you is not important. You are just attractive . . . like a magnet.

As Napoleon Hill states in his book *Think and Grow Rich:* "Our brains become magnetized with the dominating thoughts which we hold in our minds, and, by means with which no man is familiar, these 'magnets' attract to us the forces, the people, the circumstances of life which harmonize with the nature of our dominating thoughts."

In other words, you become a literal magnet for the things you want. If you want money, money literally can't say no.

Brian Tracy, in his classic book *Maximum Achievement,* refers to it as the Law of Emotion.

The Law of Emotion states that 100 percent of your decisions and subsequent actions are based on emotion. You are not largely emotional, or 90

that day. You don't want your kids to know what's going on, so you play it like nothing's wrong. But deep down, you're in pain. You're in the kind of pain that doesn't go away, no matter how many glasses of wine you have. I'm telling you this because I've been there and it's not pretty. How's that for harsh?" Michelle gathered her notes from her briefcase, frustrated.

"Let's drive over to her house and get her," Lisa suggested.

"If she doesn't really, really want to be here, it won't happen. We don't have time for whiners. You don't want someone like that around you. If you want success, you have to surround yourself with winners," Michelle fired back. "If you want to stay, we'll get started in a minute. If you don't . . . then good luck." Michelle went to her office.

A somber mood quickly fell over the group. Michelle had thrown down the gauntlet, but she was right and all of them knew it.

Lei Kim took a deep breath and tried to lighten the mood.

"So, Kanisha. How are you feeling, sweetie?" Lei Kim asked.

"Other than this big fat belly, I'm fine," Kanisha replied with a laugh.

"Don't worry, that will go away," Lei Kim said.

"At your age, I'm guessing you'll be back to normal in a month," Lisa offered.

"And Faith? How is she?" Lei Kim asked.

"Hungry. All the time," she said with a laugh before getting serious. "Thank you for all that you did. Michelle told me about . . ."

"The incredible mess you made in the office?" Lisa said, laughing. "Looked like a war zone in there. Don't worry, I took care of it. Should've been a commercial for Resolve carpet cleaner. So you had a baby on your carpet? Use Resolve carpet cleaner. It's one tough baby,'" Lisa said in her best advertising voice. Lei Kim and Kanisha laughed out loud. The mood was light again.

percent emotional and 10 percent logical, as has been assumed. You are completely emotional. Everything you do is based on an emotion of some kind. . . . There are only two main categories of emotions: desire and fear. Most of what you do, or don't do, is determined by one or the other. And the things you do, or refrain from doing, because of fear greatly outweigh the number of things you do because of desire. . . . The more you desire or fear something, the more likely you are to attract it into your life. A thought without an emotion behind it has no power to influence you one way or the other. An emotion with no thought to guide it causes frustration and unhappiness. But when you have a clear thought, positive or negative, accompanied by an intense emotion of either fear or desire, you activate the various mental laws and begin drawing whatever it is toward you. That is why it is so important for you to keep your thoughts on the things you want and keep them off the things you fear.

What you think causes vibrations of feeling and emotion. These vibrations are picked up by people around you like radio or television signals. Through the force of your mental activity, you bring more wow into your now.

You are in the now. You can never escape from it. It is the only time over which you have any control. You can't really change your past. You can only transform your memories of the past and the lessons you've learned from those experiences. You can't really change your future right now. It hasn't happened yet. You can only change your future memories of what you want to attract into your life.

The field of now is the only place where you have any power to act. You can't act in the past. It's already over. You can only change your perception now of what actually took place back there by changing what you see in your rear view mirror. There really is no past. You can't act in the future. When you finally arrive in the future, it will be just an extension of now. There really is no future. There are just continuously touching moments of now.

"Okay, let's get started," Michelle said, joining them again.

Still a bit preoccupied with Francie's state of denial, Michelle took a deep breath to clear away the negative energy. "Who's ready to make some serious money?"

"I am," Francie said, stepping inside the bookstore. Her eyes were bloodshot and swollen. She said nothing and didn't look at anyone as she took off her coat and hung it on the coatrack next to the door. Michelle quickly nodded to Lisa to scoot over so Francie could sit down. When she did, Lei Kim reached over and patted her hand in support. Francie gathered herself and then locked up at Michelle. "So, where do we begin?"

"Yeah. What's a mastermind?" Kanisha asked.

"A Mastermind Group is based on the idea that when two or more are gathered, a mastermind is created," Michelle replied.

"Kind of like two heads are better than one?" Kanisha asked.

"Exactly. When one person stumbles, the others are there to catch 'em, stand 'em up, and get 'em movin' again. The biggest thing to understand here is this: you can't do it alone, no matter how smart you think you are. If you really want to make some serious money, you're going to need a team. Some of you will pick this up right away, because there's always at least one thoroughbred in the group. One snap of the whip, and they're off and running, making money, and living a happier life in no time. For the rest of us, it takes a little longer, but don't give up. Don't be shy to face your problems, because as you will learn, your problems are your solutions."

"Hey, I'm not shy. I could stand to make some money," Kanisha said.

"It's not just about money, Kanisha. Focusing on money alone will create a disturbance in the balance of your life. If you aren't happy, what does it matter how much money or things you can accumulate?"

THE SUN-DIAL AT WELLS COLLEGE

The shadow by my finger cast
Divides the future from the past:
Before it, sleeps the unborn hour
In darkness, and beyond thy power:
Behind its unreturning line,
The vanished hour, no longer thine:
One hour alone is in thy hands,—
The NOW on which the shadow stands.

—HENRY VAN DYKE

It's all about now. How you act in the now has a direct impact on the next, contiguous moment of now. If you learn to wow every moment of now, it will infuse the very next moment with wow.

The way you think about your past and the way you think about your future are all happening right now. If you think your past was bad, it infects your now with fear. If you learn to tweak your past to experience your positive memories and observe your not-so-positive moments, then it makes you feel more positive right now. If infuses your life with "up." Maintain this way of thinking and there is an endless vista of "up" as far as you can see in your future nows.

In fact, by thinking now about the way you want your future to be, it sends a signal off into the future and prepares everything and everyone in the future for your arrival. If every negative thought deducts $100 from your future bank account immediately, then every positive thought sends an electronic message to your future bank accounts and deposits $100 there immediately.

In this way, your past and your future can empower your now.

"Are you saying there's something wrong with making money?" Lisa continued.

"Absolutely not. I want you to make lots of money—piles of money. So much money you need a dump truck to take you to the bank."

"This sounds good to me," Lei Kim said to Francie.

"But how many times have you used the phrase 'Money is the root of all evil'?" A few hands shot up.

"What about 'Money doesn't grow on trees'?" Lei Kim suggested. That opened up the rest of the group for suggestions. Michelle could barely keep up writing them onto her yellow legal pad.

It takes money to make money.
I'm too young to be rich.
I'm too old to start over.
All the good ideas have already been taken.

"This is what is known as the *critical voice* inside your head," Michelle told them. "It's the voice of the ego, and it talks you out of stretching beyond your comfort zone."

"Why?" Kanisha asked.

"Because your ego doesn't want you to change. All these lies we've written down here have been driven into our heads by this critical voice ever since we were young girls. That keeps us from making serious money. Sure, we make money here and there, but when was the last time we got a check that made us say 'Wow'? That's what I call money."

"So, you want us to think about ways to make money?" Lisa asked.

"Exactly," Michelle replied.

"How?" Francie wanted to know.

YOUR SECRET SPOT

Another way to empower now is to step into the most idealized now and carry it with you throughout the day. We call it your Secret Spot.

Imagine a spot at your feet just in front of you. Ask yourself these questions:

> What if there was an imaginary spot that I could step into at any time to give myself a surge of positive energy?
> What shape would that spot be? Circular, oval, rectangular, square?
> What would be its dimensions? Three feet across? Four? Five? More?

Since it's in your imagination, it's invisible to anyone else except you. It's your secret.

> What if I could infuse my Secret Spot with the ingredients of confidence, happiness, excitement, power, peace, and so on? What other attributes would I like to add to this spot?

Since you really want to fully experience this spot, make sure you add all of your senses.

What sounds would you like to include? The sound of applause? The sound of your favorite music? The sound of people laughing with you, not

"There are infinite ways to make money. There's long money . . ."

"Long money?" Kanisha asked.

"Long money means the work is all front-loaded and the money arrives later. Like creating a product or even writing a book. If you started writing today, your book won't reach the shelves for another year at the minimum, and that's if you get it published. But you *should* write a book if you feel the calling. Likewise, you should always be on the lookout for new product ideas, even though obtaining a patent can take up to eighteen months. You can sell the product with a patent pending, but you still have the design phase and the manufacturing phase, and then finally you have market entry. There's no guarantee your product is going to take off, but if it does and you're able to hold on to a majority of the rights, you could do well. The profits for creating products are spread out over time, which is why I call it long money. The key is to make enough money from your endeavors so when the unexpected arrives, you can handle it. Emotionally and, most of all, financially, you'll be ready." Michelle looked around at the faces of the women in the group and continued.

"The other kind of money is fast money. You lose your job, you face foreclosure, or you're a victim of a natural disaster like Hurricane Katrina, and you need money right away. If you don't have the cash on hand, you need to find a way to make it fast. One of the best ways to make fast money is to start with your problem," Michelle said, energized.

"Wouldn't it be better to start with the *solution* to the problem?" Lisa asked, confused.

"No, and we'll talk about this at great length as the weeks progress. But in short, your problems *are* your solutions. When something happens, it's leading you to something better. If you ask anyone who's seen the other side of a problem, they often tell you

at you? The sound of positive experiences of all kinds? Perhaps you hear the sound of your imagined success mentors advising you: "Be strong. Have faith. You can do it." Step into that spot in your imagination and notice what kinds of sounds make you feel even more empowered.

What kind of tastes and smells would you like to add?

Imagine stepping into your spot and hearing, tasting, and smelling the sweet sounds, tastes, and aromas of success. Let your imagination run wild.

What kind of feelings would you like to insert? What kind of scenes would you want to be accessible to you in your special spot? What spiritual messages or prayers would you be accessing? It's *your* Secret Spot. You can imagine it any way you choose, even like this for example:

Now, your critical mind might try to tell you how silly all of this seems . . . after all, you're an adult with serious responsibilities and pressures. This sort of playful thinking certainly can't lend any support to your ongoing activities!

Yes, that's a reasonable assessment. Yet scan forward in your mind to a future pressure-filled situation. Imagine preparing to make a presentation to your boss about a project you've been assigned to do. Just before you enter her office, you take a moment to step into your Secret Spot. You allow yourself to breathe deeply and center yourself. You remember a day from the past when you were particularly confident. You bring that memory to now and step into it. You scan forward into your future and access a future memory of you being the boss of your own enterprise, living an amazing lifestyle. You populate your spot with your imaginary mentors whom you've selected. You hear them encouraging you. You smell a garden of fragrant flowers that makes you feel calm and peaceful. You imagine a

the problem showed them something about themselves that they weren't able to see before the problem."

"I understand what you're saying, but how do I—" Francie started to say.

"Yeah, how do I make fast money from my problem?" Kanisha interrupted. Francie gave her a look.

"When I lost my kids in a custody battle, I looked for help and found nothing online whatsoever. I wrote an e-book called *Money Loves You* and generated over $400,000 in a week," Michelle said.

"You published it yourself?" Lei Kim asked.

"Yes. You can do it all by yourself—publish it on your website, put in a shopping cart with PayPal, or go with YouPublish.com. You can start making money tomorrow," Michelle said.

Francie started making notes in her Filofax.

"I've never written anything longer than my return address when I pay my bills, plus I don't have any money to start a project," Lisa said.

"You don't have anything?" Michelle asked.

"I think that's what I just said."

"It doesn't take money to sit down and write an e-book, does it? The thing I want you to know is that it doesn't take money to make money—it just takes a great idea and the recognition that when a problem arrives, the problem is trying to lead you to something better. You can worry about finding the money later," Michelle replied.

"You don't get it—I don't have any money to spend right now," Lisa told her.

"The goal of our money Mastermind Group is to come up with great ideas. If the idea is good enough, *I'll* lend you the money," Michelle told Lisa. "It doesn't take a lot of money to launch a great idea. I made my first million with my mentor on a few thousand dollars, and recently I've been inspired by a guy they call the 'banker

cylinder of light that emanates from your spot. This light virtually vibrates with enlightened energy that reaches high into the heavens and descends deep into the earth. You draw from the deep well beneath you the wisdom of Mother Earth. You attract from high above you the wisdom of the Universe. You silently whisper a prayer to bring to your awareness whatever words or thoughts you will need at the exact right moment.

All of this might take less than a minute. Now you are ready. You enter your meeting and maintain your presence in the spot. You exude positive vibrations and you glow with positive anticipation. Who wouldn't want to be in your presence? You have the power within you to rally your immense internal forces and conquer almost any obstacle, like getting a bank loan, meeting the most influential and important person alive, or asking for a giant piece of business.

Of course, your boss is not in that space herself. She might just be burdened with pressures, responsibilities, and problems. Your energy will most likely be a welcome change to the swirling challenges she faces every day. But whatever her response is to your higher energy—whether positive or negative—choose to respond with positive answers. Refuse to be drawn into the vortex of any downward spiral. Remain firmly situated in your Secret Spot, linked clearly to empowering experiences from your past and future that expand your now. The person with the highest energy usually controls every situation. Therefore, start your day by virtualizing yourself as being such a person, in each and every situation.

How does this experience seem to you? Do you think you'd be more prepared to enter your boss's office if you were walking in your spot?

Or would your previous way work better?

By the way, what was your previous way? Were any of the following thoughts flooding your mind as you prepared: worry, negative self-talk, fear of stumbling like previous times, fear of the worst-case scenario looming in the future, doubt that you'll say the right thing at the right time, concern that your hair or clothes might not look just right, a nagging critical voice like a loudspeaker telling you that you're not up to this?

Your new Secret Spot would certainly be better than that!

to the poor.' He won the 2006 Nobel Peace Prize because his bank has lent money to over a hundred million poor women to launch their small businesses."

"Who is this guy?" Lei Kim asked.

"His name is Muhammad Yunus. He's a Bangladeshi banker and economist. Once we get through what it takes mentally to become a millionaire, I'm going to loan each of you some money to help get your projects off the ground. If you need it."

"How much money?" Lisa asked.

"Anywhere from $1 to $500 will help foster the start-up of any great idea or project."

"What project?" Francie asked.

"That's up to each of you to decide. And we'll get to all of that, but right now, let's go back to the mental chatter that goes on inside of your head when you are looking to make chunks of money.

"In addition to the critical voice that tries to talk us out of success, there's another voice," Michelle continued. "It's a voice that cheers you on, pulls you to your feet and dusts you off when you fall. That voice is called the *true voice* of your soul. This is the voice of your Inner Winner. It's this voice that reminds us that when you are in step with something that is connected to your soul, the money is a by-product and that work is no longer 'work.' This is the voice that causes you to leap out of bed in the morning, excited to go to work."

"I don't think I've ever leaped out of bed excited to go to work," Lisa said jokingly.

"That's because you haven't found something you love. When you do, you won't ever work another day in your life."

"Are you saying I'm unhappy?"

"I'm saying there's something deeper to consider. When you find something you love, you make a difference in the world, and that's

So now, with a newly transformed past and a clearly imagined future, plus your special spot to precede you wherever you go, consider that your now has been wowed.

Wow Now. For the past few chapters, we've been explaining the importance of the first ingredient in the recipe for riches—Wow Now. We hope you're now beginning to agree with us.

Your wax on/wax off assignment for this chapter is to continue building your Secret Spot. Add more details to this imaginary source of power that you carry invisibly with you everywhere you go. Practice stepping into your Secret Spot several times today. Notice how it makes you feel more positive, more empowered, more creative, more confident. Add your own ingredients to your Secret Spot. What could you add that would make your spot even more effective? A special song? An important quote? A unique, awesome memory? An exciting future opportunity?

Visit us online at www.cashinaflashthebook.com and learn how to play the Prosperity Game.

---

what this group is all about—discovering how we can help each other find our greater purpose in life and, yes, make lots of money while doing it."

"I'm sorry, I like my life just the way it is." Lisa shook her head.

"I'm not saying you don't like your life, Lisa."

"Then what *are* you saying, Michelle?"

"Do you like living paycheck to paycheck?" Michelle asked, but Lisa didn't answer. "I seriously doubt you want to work here forever, right? No, you want what everyone should want, residual income to fund your endeavors. You want to make money while you sleep. You want money to show up in the mailbox each day. That's what financial freedom is all about. Creating multiple streams and chunks of income so you can do *what* you want *when* you want."

"Chunks?" Lei Kim asked.

"Real big checks, Lei Kim. I'm talkin' about windfalls of cash. This is no different from creating a new recipe in your kitchen, only now the ingredients for this new recipe are all of you. By working together, you have the ability to create the results you've all been dreaming about." Michelle turned to Lisa. "Lisa, right now you're tethered to your job. I give you, what, two weeks off a year? Two weeks a year? Is that what your free time is worth? Lei Kim, what about you? When was the last time you took a vacation?"

"A long time." Lei Kim laughed. "Too long."

"All I'm saying is if we help each other expand our vision to what is possible, we can achieve greatness and make lots of money in the process."

"How?" Francie spoke softly.

Michelle smiled. "First you have to learn to take risks."

"Haven't you read the newspapers, Michelle? I really don't think it's a good time to be taking risks," Lisa said.

PART TWO

The Second Key Ingredient: Inner Winner

"Why not?" Michelle asked.

"Um, hello? The economy is in the dumper."

"Do you think God reads the newspaper? All you get from the newspaper is the evidence of a world lost in translation."

"What do you mean?" Lei Kim asked, leaning forward in her chair.

"The newspapers are filled with stories of greed and fear. If it bleeds, it leads. When you read this kind of stuff, all you do is react to the bad news. That's why the concept of the Mastermind Group, the team, is so important. We focus on the good news we want to create in—"

"I don't think burying your head in the sand and ignoring what is happening in the world is a very good concept," Lisa put in.

"You know, every time you interrupt me—"

"It's annoying to everyone else." Francie finished her sentence for her.

Lisa snorted. "Well, if you would make some sense, maybe I wouldn't have to interrupt."

Michelle stalled for a second because she suddenly realized that the look on everyone's face was the same. She was dropping down too much information too soon. As she stared at the framed painting of the Rocky Mountains hanging over the fireplace, she wondered what her mentor Samantha would do, but quickly dismissed the thought. She knew she couldn't think about Samantha right now. This was her group. She had to do things her own way. What was *she* going to do right now?

The painting seemed to be calling out to her. It was oil on canvas, and if you stared at it long enough, you felt like you were standing in the middle of a meadow. It was that kind of painting. The shading was so perfect it was almost three-dimensional. Michelle smiled and turned to the group.

10

FOLLOW YOUR HEART:
ACCESS YOUR INNER WINNER

Follow your heart—your intuition.
It will lead you in the right direction.
—FROM "INTUITION," A SONG BY JEWEL KILCHER AND LESTER MENDEZ

Let's review before we forge ahead. The first few chapters in this book are about Wow Now. These are the strategies for focusing the mind. They are "thinking" techniques designed to prepare you for action. If aerobics is the science of exercising your body, then neurobics is the science of exercising your mind—how to think more positively, how to keep your mind unrcluttered of unwanted past memories and looming future fears. Neurobics is the science of how to direct the voices, visions, and vibrations of your mind. The result: single-minded focus, confidence, excitement.

In a word: *conviction*!

When you practice Wow Now, you feel what it feels like to be living your dream lifestyle. This feeling permeates your every cell. This then radiates out to everyone you meet. If Wow Now is how you focus your mind, the Inner Winner is how you tap into your heart. You are reactivating your inner guidance system and giving back control to the part of you that instinctively knows what is best.

Many who read this book are looking for ways to earn quick cash to solve an immediate need. They assume that once they've solved their pressing financial problems, they can then resume their search for the ideal source of income. They put their dreams on hold temporarily, waiting for a more convenient time. They stop listening to their heart. But

"Tonight's a full moon, right?"

"I think it was last night," Kanisha said.

"Why?" Francie asked.

"Because I have an idea . . . it's something that might help explain things better. Who's up for a little adventure?" Michelle said, looking at the women like they were all twelve years old again. One by one, they nodded.

"Great. Lisa, you grab the flashlights from the storage room. We're going out. Francie, we'll have to swing by your house so you can change your clothes."

"I'm not dressed appropriately?" Francie asked, sitting up.

"Well, I don't think you want to go hiking in those heels."

"Hiking?" Lei Kim asked.

Kanisha stood up. "I can't go."

"Why?"

"I've got to be home . . . I mean, at your house," she said, correcting herself midsentence. "My baby. I can't leave her."

"I wouldn't worry about her," Lisa said from the hall closet.

"Why not?"

"Because your babysitter Justine is studying to become a teacher. If she can handle our three kids, she can sure handle a cutie like Faith." Lisa returned with the flashlights.

"She's right," Michelle added. "And we'll only be gone for an hour or so. I know how important it is for you to be with Faith. Grab the flashlights—we're going hiking."

the signals from the heart are often the fastest path to cash . . . and wealth.

So, how do you recognize the most profitable signals from the heart?

THE LANGUAGE OF THE HEART

Now, let's talk about a power that is deeper than mere thinking. We want to talk about a feeling that is more profound than excitement. Let's discuss your heart of hearts—your inner heart. We call this your Inner Winner.

Beneath all of your memories of the past and future, barely below your awareness, there is a part of you that knows all the answers you need to succeed immensely.

Have you ever had a hunch—a gut feeling—that something good (or bad) was about to happen? Have you ever had a sense of certitude that a decision you made was right or correct?

Some people refer to these impressions as your intuition. Others call it the sixth sense. We call it the Inner Winner.

If you want to be more successful—wealthier, happier, and healthier— you need to heed the signals from your Inner Winner. It may be the most important success tool in your tool kit. If it's so important, why do we receive almost zero training in it in school?

Remember a time when you had a strong hunch about something or someone. Scan through your memory banks to find a good example. Access the memory of your hunch and go back to that time as if you were reliving the experience. In other words, remember what it was like to be in your body at that time and to experience the hunch all over again. Rewind to the place in your memory just before you had your hunch. Now, play the scene forward until the moment when the hunch happens and then freeze the frame so you can isolate the intuitive experience. What were the clues you received that let you know that this kind of knowing was special, was true or real? How would you describe it?

You knew it at a deeper level. You just knew it, didn't you?

But how did you know it? More specifically, where did you know it?

6
The Adventure Begins
The Art of Changing Your Perception

As they gathered in the damp parking lot at the trailhead leading to Mirror Lake, Michelle began to notice the tone of uncertainty trickling throughout the group. One by one, the women's eyes shot into the dark shadows of the trail before them. The scraggly limbs of the giant pine trees hanging overhead only enhanced their fears that something bad was about to happen. They all liked the idea of a spontaneous adventure, but hiking at night?

"This is crazy. What if someone gets hurt?" Lisa said.

"What if we get lost?" Lei Kim muttered.

"What kind of animals they got up here?" Kanisha added.

Michelle quickly reassured her that there were very few bears in the area.

"Very few?" Kanisha said as as her eyes grew wide.

"Bears? Nobody said anything about any bears!" Francie said, standing up from tying her shoes. She was dressed in a black workout suit with silver trim and her shoes were fresh out of the box.

Lisa handed out the three flashlights she'd brought from the bookstore.

"Where's mine?" Francie quickly asked.

"We only had three," Lisa replied.

"Three flashlights will be more than enough. Trust me, your eyes

Heighten your awareness to notice what was going on. What kind of signals did you process? Were there any visual clues—flashes of insight or images of future possibilities? Were there any voices—verbal messages or whisperings? Did you notice any specific feelings or impressions?

Where did that inkling come from? How did you know it?

Deep inside each of us—beneath our fears, anxieties, and worries—there is a bedrock of wisdom, insight, and good sense that we all possess. It came with our operating system at birth.

Throughout your life, you add to your store of knowledge and experience. You fill up your data banks with more information. Everything you've ever learned, studied, read, or assimilated is just a blink away. You access this vast store of information through one simple method: questions.

When you ask yourself a simple question, you activate your wisdom retrieval system, which searches for the right answer.

Women are reported to be very intuitive. They just know things. Men are also intuitive, although reportedly not as sensitive as women to their hunches. Men seem to be more in their heads and women are more in their hearts. It's just the way it is.

Your first wax on/wax off assignments were designed to make you aware of the voices in your mind. As we learned in chapter 5, this voice—your critical voice—is not your friend. We call this your Inner Whiner—because it's always whining about something. We showed you how to turn the volume down on this voice so that it doesn't affect you as negatively.

Don Miguel Ruiz, author of the international best seller *The Four Agreements*, has written another book called *The Voice of Knowledge*. In this book he describes the critical voice as "the liar who lives in your head . . . Every time we judge ourselves, find ourselves guilty, and punish ourselves, it's because the voice in our head is telling us lies." He continues:

> When I was a child, I used to watch Walt Disney's Donald Duck cartoons. On one side of Donald Duck's head was an angel, and on the other side of his head was a devil, and both were talking to him. Well, this is real. . . . You have a voice that is telling you why you are not good enough, why you don't deserve love, why you cannot trust, why you will never be great or

will adjust and you won't want a flashlight," Michelle said, closing up her car.

"No, I want a flashlight," Francie said.

Michelle saw that Francie was serious. She wanted a flashlight. "Okay, Francie. We'll take turns as we move up the trail. Will that work?" Michelle replied, but Francie was like a child. She wanted a flashlight all to herself. She stood with her arms folded.

Either I get a flashlight or it's time for me to go home," Francie said.

Kanisha extended her flashlight toward Francie. The older woman didn't like Kanisha, and the kind gesture only seemed to annoy her, but she took the flashlight anyway.

The smell of the damp soil wafted upward as their feet hit the trail and the adventure began. Walking without a flashlight, Michelle took the lead. She turned and smiled. She knew getting them this far was an accomplishment in itself, but bigger hurdles lay ahead.

To keep their minds occupied so they wouldn't think about turning back, Michelle told them the story of the great Colorado explorer Sir Walter Kennington. While he was famous for his expeditions and photographs of the Colorado Rockies, the discovery of Mirror Lake was legendary by the mere nature of the discovery. While following a mountain lion and her cubs for *National Geographic* magazine, Kennington got turned around and became lost in the wilderness for five long days. It would turn out to be his finest hour.

Disoriented and on the verge of severe exposure, Kennington stumbled upon Mirror Lake simply by accident. Mirror Lake became one of his greatest discoveries, and although the governor of Colorado at the time suggested the lake be named after him, Kennington explained the discovery was not about him but about the majestic beauty of the Rockies. To this day, however, nobody could

beautiful or perfect. That voice is lying, and the only power that it has is the power that you give it.

He goes on to explain that the other voice is the *voice of the spirit, our integrity, the voice of love.*

If you sit quietly, you can often notice a deeper, heartfelt voice. We call this your true voice or your Inner Winner. This is the part of you that knows the truth. This voice is sending constant signals also. Most people miss these signals because they are so subtle, so sensitive. It's hard to notice them while your critical voice—"the liar who lives in your head"—is chattering incessantly. Once you turn down the volume of the nagging voices in your mind, you can learn to listen to your Inner Winner.

YOUR INNER WINNER VS. THE INNER WHINER

Let us ask you a question: when your critical voice speaks to you, where is it? Point to that spot right now.

When your true voice speaks to you, where do you notice it?

When we ask audiences worldwide these questions, the members of the audience predominantly point to very different spots. For the critical voice they point to their head. For the true voice they point to their heart.

Where do you doubt things? Generally in your mind.

Where do you know things? Generally in your heart.

Each of us has a flickering flame of truth in the center of us. We just know what is right and not right for us. It's our conscience—our inner guidance system. We can just feel it. On either side of this flickering flame of truth are two big bullies trying to blow that flame out.

One bully is the Bully of Fear. He tries to blow that flame out. He

talk about Mirror Lake without telling the story of the great explorer of the Rockies who got lost.

Coming up the last section of the now well-traveled rocky trail, the women were tired and walking in silence. Kanisha's left heel had a blister forming, Francie was out of breath from the elevation gain of the hike, and both Lei Kim and Lisa were dragging behind, ready to turn back whenever anyone suggested this was far enough. Suddenly the women stopped in unison. They heard something . . . something in the distance.

"What is that?" Francie asked with hushed concern.

"It's nothing. Come on, we're almost there," Michelle said, continuing up the trail without fear.

"Almost where?" Lisa said, struggling to keep up, but Michelle didn't answer. As Michelle began to disappear in the darkness before them, the women looked at each other for guidance. There was none. So, with no other choice, they pressed on.

The low rumble grew even louder. "What could it be?" Lei Kim asked herself as she tried to catch up with Michelle, but something was wrong. She suddenly grew dizzy. "It's nothing, keep going," Lei Kim coached herself, but she stumbled and fell to her knees.

"Michelle," Francie called out.

Michelle turned around and saw Lei Kim on the ground. The others rushed to her side.

"I'm okay. I'm okay," Lei Kim assured them. "Just got a bit dizzy there for a second."

"You sure?" Michelle asked, concerned.

"Yes, I'm fine."

"Have a drink of water," Lisa said, pulling out the water bottle.

"Thank you," Lei Kim replied, and took a swig. "Really, I'm okay."

doesn't want you to win. He wants you to retreat, to back away from your dreams. If he can get you to procrastinate, he wins.

He usually works through one of the five major fears:

Failure Embarrassment Abandonment Rejection Success

If you ever find yourself in the grip of one of these fears, it's often evidence that the Bully of Fear is working hard to keep you from finding your true path.

The other bully is the Bully of Greed. He wants to fan the flames of inappropriate desires—to lure you from your true path in life. He appeals to your ego. If he can distract you with shiny trappings, he wins.

Your task is to find your true path and follow it.

What is the language of your Inner Winner? It uses the same types of voices, visions, and vibrations that are used by your thinking mind—generally in your head, from the neck up. Yet the voices, visions, and vibrations of your Inner Winner are centered more in your heart area—from the neck down to the belt.

Have you ever heard someone say, "I just had a gut feeling that this was the right thing (or the wrong thing) to do"? Or "I had a flash of insight and it just looked right to me"? Or "I told myself that I'd better act before it was too late"?

Often, you'll have several different manifestations of truth—a voice, followed by a flash or insight, followed by a peaceful feeling. Or any combination. Some people only feel an impression. Some people only hear a wise voice. Some people only have a flash of visual insight. How do you do your hunches?

Sometimes you just know what do and what to avoid.

A SPIRITUAL CONFIRMATION

Intuition is a good indicator of truth, but it's not infallible. It's been our experience that a more profound confirmation of your intuitive decision is very helpful. It's the difference between intuition and inspiration.

"We can go back if you aren't," Michelle said, but Lei Kim stood up on her own.

"Really, guys. I'm fine," Lei Kim replied, so the group continued. Michelle kept a close eye on Lei Kim, who she thought looked pale, but Lei Kim smiled back at Michelle and even picked up the pace a bit.

As they came around the last of what seemed like a million switchbacks, they were treated to an amazing view of a waterfall, aptly named Kennington Falls. The full moon glinted off the water as it crested the top of the eighty-five-foot waterfall. Tumbling like a ribbon in the sky, the water landed on the jagged rocks below. This was the same stream Sir Walter Kennington had followed down to safety into the small Colorado mining camp of Idyllwild. Michelle explained to the group that this was one of the last times the falls would be visible until spring. Winter was on its way and the entire area would soon be covered in six feet of snow. There was a moment of silent appreciation.

"Great. Can we go home now?" Lisa finally asked.

"Not yet. We're almost there," Michelle replied without breaking stride. "Just around the next switchback, I promise you."

Cresting the trail, the group quickly fell silent, for before them stood Mirror Lake.

"Turn off the flashlights," Michelle ordered. One by one, the beams of light winked off. Their eyes quickly adjusted, and with the full moon, they could see the entire lake and the massive mountain range behind it. The night air was crisp and the smell of pine trees was strong.

"Now, imagine being lost in the wild for five days and then discovering this. What a gift." Michelle looked around at the immense beauty surrounding them. The moonlight shimmered across the still lake, and one could understand why Kennington had named this discovery Mirror Lake. It was a mirror for all the beauty that surrounded

Oprah Winfrey, at a recent California women's conference, taught a profound lesson about spiritual guidance. She calls it the Whisper.

God always first speaks to you in the Whisper. So right now . . . the Universe is whispering to you about your job . . . is whispering about your children . . . is whispering to you about your relationship. If I were you, I'd take it in the whisper. Because after the whisper, you get a little thump on your head. . . . A thump on the head is a message, trying to get through to you. If you don't pay attention to that, you end up in a big old problem. That's a brick falling up-side your head because you didn't hear it in the whisper. And if you don't pay attention to the brick then you get a whole wall of bricks falling down. Now you don't have a problem, you've got a crisis. And if you don't pay attention to the brick wall falling . . . the whole house caves in and you're in a full-blown disaster. So what I try to do is get it in the whisper. Get it in the whis-per. Your life is whispering to you right now. What is it saying?

All successful people have learned to be more attuned to the Whisper. All great successes can be linked back to following these initial spiritual nudgings or peaceful feelings. If you're not attuned to them now, we hope you will be more so before you finish reading this book.

We hope your awareness is expanding. Yes, awareness. Awareness of what? Awareness of how a Higher Power is prompting and influencing most of your decisions. We are being nudged and prompted daily. Success is learning how to recognize those promptings. The first step is to learn how to turn off the critical voice and listen to the true voice. Then make your decision guided by your intuition. Heighten your sensitivity to a spir-itual confirmation. Do you notice a whisper? Or does it just feel right? If it doesn't feel right, don't do it!

If these promptings are happening inside you, then become aware that they are certainly going on in other people around you. Some people are so tuned in to critical voices, they miss constant subtle signals that are urging them to the green pastures of a better life. Sometimes they notice their whispers. Sometimes they don't. Become aware that many of our prayers are being answered by other people who are being prompted to help us.

it. Michelle was right. It was a gift, and the women looked in every direction, taking it in. It was a magical moment, a spiritual awakening of sorts. Even Lisa was silent, and that was a miracle in itself, Michelle thought.

Gathering the women in a clearing, Michelle convinced everyone to find a place to sit down. Kanisha found a fallen tree. Lisa sat directly on the ground. Lei Kim joined her. Francie looked unsure what to do but, with a few swipes of her hand to clear away the dirt, she finally perched on a large rock as Michelle finished the tale of Sir Walter Kennington: "Sometimes in life, you need to get lost to find your way." The women just sat there and absorbed the profound thought. Michelle then directed their attention to the lights of the town in the valley below.

"Kind of gives you a sense of perspective as to what's important, doesn't it? All those lives going on down there, rushing about, fighting with each other, falling in love, falling out of love . . . And it's all up to us. We get to choose how we want to live. Which is the reason I brought you up here. Have you considered what you want?"

"I have a clear idea of what I want," Lisa cracked.

"Lisa, please. I'm serious. When was the last time you stopped reacting to life and actually asked yourself the question 'What do I want?'" The group didn't respond. They all remained silent until Michelle continued. "It's something to think about. Life is about claiming the thoughts in your mind. If you don't choose these thoughts directly by asking yourself questions like this, uncertainty will rule. That brings about frustration and anger because at the end of the day, you *know* you should've chosen a direction. So, if you would, I'd like everyone to close their eyes."

"Close our eyes? What are you talking about? Look at that moon. Turn around, look at that lake," Lisa said to Michelle. "You want me to close my eyes and miss all this?"

A well-known scripture says it best:

Trust in the Lord with all thine heart;
and lean not unto thine own understanding.
In all thy ways acknowledge him, and he
shall direct thy paths.

—PROVERBS 3:5–6

Here is your wax on/wax off assignment for today.

After you've turned off your critical voice, intensely focus for several minutes several times today on trying to notice your Inner Winner. Remember the times in your past when you had a hunch about something. Notice the process that works for you in how you know things.

Try to remember which came first: the voice, the vision, or the vibration. Did you hear a whisper, followed by a feeling of peace? Or did you have a flash of insight followed by a whisper and then a feeling? Were all of these components present in your hunch? Or did it just feel right and then the voice said, "You can do it"? Maybe you didn't notice a whisper. Just a feeling.

Ponder how you know things. Then notice your personal knowing pattern. Then find someone you trust and share with them how your inner guidance system works.

Let's talk tomorrow.

"Yes. But you're not missing anything. What I want you to do is to look for that kind of beauty on the inside. I want you to stop worrying about money. Don't think about your to-do lists or how you're going to get out of debt. We can think about all that stuff later. Right now, I want us to look for . . . well . . . for whatever shows up."

"You're serious?" Lisa asked.

"What am I looking for again?" Kanisha asked, opening her eyes.

"That's the thing. You're not looking for anything. When you're busy looking for something, you're missing the point. Clear your mind so you can receive the message from your soul and stop worrying about your problems. Problems are good. They make you stronger, wiser, and more courageous. See yourself fully funded in all of your endeavors by imagining a life where all your dreams are accomplished. What does that feel like? What does it look like? Have you thought about it lately? Don't you think it's time you started living the life you dream about? Why not begin right now? I want you to transport yourself virtually, because you are explorers of the undiscovered territories in your mind. This virtualization process helps you clear out the chaos in your mind and learn how to accept greater things, things you thought were reserved for other people. Well, guess what, ladies? You are other people, and it's time you start getting what you want from life. And listen up, because this is the most important part of this virtualization process: *do not* think about *how* you'll achieve the things you see. Thoughts like that are just your ego adding more chaos in your mind. Your recipe for your new life is free of any mental activity that keeps you from knowing that all your needs are met right now. So virtually transport yourself to the end result and leave the beginning alone. Trust that if you can see it, you can achieve it."

And so it began. A peaceful silence engulfed the women like a warm blanket. Looking around, Michelle noticed her surroundings

11

YOUR FASTEST PATH TO PROFIT: MAKE MONEY FROM WHAT YOU LOVE

The prime function of the Inner Winner is to help you discover your life's true path—your life's purpose.

We can just imagine what your impatient critical voice has to say about this: "Wait a minute! What does all this talk about whispers and purpose have to do with making some serious money now? You don't have time for this."

Yes, you do have time. It's time for you to decide that the lifestyle of your dreams is not only possible but inevitable. The purpose path is your fastest path to enlightened cash. Everything else is prostitution—doing what you don't love just to earn some money. Don't make love for money. Make money from what you love.

Earlier we encouraged you to imagine a virtual place five years in the future where you are living your dream lifestyle. What are you doing there in the future? Whom are you surrounded by? What kinds of activities are you passionately involved with? How do these activities bring money in your door?

Starting *now*, decide to find and pursue your purpose path—and to earn a fortune doing it.

Imagine that you inherited $100 million today. What would you do with the money? After you'd paid off the credit card debt, your mortgage, given some money away, done some traveling, gotten the thrill of it out of your system, what would you do with your time? How would you serve the world? If money was no object, where would your heart lead you?

For some, these are easy questions to answer. They know exactly how they'd love to spend their time and money. Cyclist Lance Armstrong had

one more time before she closed her eyes and joined the women in this now sacred moment. As her eyes shut, the sounds of the distant waterfall grew louder. She could still hear the lake lapping lightly against its narrow shoreline. She took a deep breath and could smell the moisture of the pristine lake water drifting toward her as a slight breeze gently kissed her skin.

Several minutes passed in silence. Then Michelle began to take them on a journey into the future. "Imagine the lifestyle of your dreams. How good could it be? That kind of lifestyle is awaiting you, right now." She paused to let this thought sink in. "Where do you live your ideal lifestyle? What kind of home do you live in? Walk up to the front door of your dream home and open the door. Walk inside and notice what kind of life you dream of creating for yourself and those you love. What kind of people do you see yourself sharing this dream life with? Notice the abundance surrounding you. Spend a few minutes wandering through your dream home. I want you to experience everything in all five senses. What do you taste, smell, feel, hear, and see inside your new home? Remember, this is the reward you've earned for actively following your dreams."

Several minutes passed before Francie began to fidget. Struggling with the sounds of night going on around her, Francie finally opened her eyes when she heard an owl hooting. Her gaze quickly shot up to the tree above, and she spotted the giant bird. Its head swiveled toward her, its eyes reflecting the moonlight. Wanting to call attention to the creature, she discovered that everyone's eyes were still shut, including Michelle's. Hadn't they heard the sound too? But evidently they hadn't. It was as if this majestic creature was there, on that branch above, just for her to see. Was this owl trying to tell her something? She began to smile. For here, directly above her, was one of the grandest animals in the kingdom, sharing this moment with her.

all the money and fame in the world from winning the Tour de France seven times in a row. Yet after two years in retirement, what did he want to do? He started to train to ride his bicycle again. That was his passion.

What is your passion?

If you're going to earn some serious money fast, wouldn't it be nice if you tapped into this vast reservoir of the passion of purpose?

The Inner Winner is equipped with a honing mechanism to help you discover your own unique path to prosperity. It begins with the passions, talents, and gifts you already possess. You are already a winner inside—at something.

Are you aware of it yet?

There are hints all around you.

What do you love to do?
What are you good at?
What is important to you?
What feels right to you?
What kind of people, ideas, and/or things are you drawn to?
What fascinates you?
What interests you?
What kind of magazines, books, and movies attract you?
What things do you cherish?
What hobbies do you have?
Where do you spend time?
Where do you spend money?
What is your secret wish?
What are you curious about?
What were you doing the last time someone said to you, "How did you do that?"
Who do you like to hang around?
What place just feels right?

The bottom line of all of this questioning is the discovery of your *why*. Why do you get up in the morning? Why do you do what you do? Why do

A rustling sound suddenly came from somewhere behind her. She jerked her head in reaction. Was it a bear moving in for the kill? A pack of wolves arriving to devour a delicious five-course meal? Remembering what Michelle had said about runaway thoughts, Francie returned her gaze to the owl above. When she did, however, she saw something on the branch behind the great owl. Was she seeing double?

Everything soon made sense when the owl bent to fluff its feathers. Standing behind it was another owl. It must be a male and a female, Francie thought. When the two owls began rubbing their necks together, she realized that she was witnessing a mating dance.

Francie slowly closed her eyes, to internally register the beauty of this moment, but soon she opened them again, because she didn't want to miss anything. When she looked up once more, however, the owls were gone. A feeling of sadness quickly washed over her. She wondered if she'd imagined the entire experience. But what did this mean? Was it somehow a metaphor about her life and the time she'd wasted? And what about the impending foreclosure? She wanted answers.

She felt alone again, and she found herself suddenly missing her husband, Christopher. She wanted to break the silence and ask for help. She was panicking. Her palms were sweaty and her chest grew tight, until finally she took a deep breath. It seemed to calm the thoughts swirling in her mind. Filling her lungs with deep, soulful breaths, she shut her eyes again and returned her mind to a place of calmness. As she released another breath, Michelle broke the silence.

"Slowly bring your attention back to your awareness and gently open your eyes."

The women's eyes seemed to scan the landscape as if they were seeing the lake for the very first time—all except Lisa, who shrugged, stood up, and announced, "Okay, I'm ready."

you behave the way you do? Why do you yearn to find your better self? Why? It's the bottom-line question of your life.

Why?

When you discover your why, it makes sense of everything that went before and everything that goes after. You'll see the reason why you did things in the past, when you were unaware. You'll notice the right things as they come from the future toward your present. They just feel right.

Some people reading these words right now are nodding. They know exactly what we're describing. They're there. Some people reading these words are puzzled: "Who are these guys talking about? The rest of us have to go to work every day. We've got bills to pay."

Yup, we were there once too. We were overwhelmed with responsibilities too. We know the difference between being there and not being there.

We just hope that sooner or later you find yourself. You're worth finding. You're magnificent. Just the way you are.

When we talk like this, some people don't get it. There is a Sufi proverb that explains why:

To one who doesn't hear the music, the dancers look crazy.

It's our hope that you'll hear your own music as quickly as possible. There's a song you were born to sing. It's your song. Write it. Perform it.

You have an inner guidance system that instinctively knows what is best.

Think back to when you were a child. Your inner guidance system is more alert when you are a child; you know what feels right and wrong. As we get older, we become desensitized to our inner authentic voice. Instead of trusting our gut, we rationalize based on our references—good or bad.

Before you go to bed tonight, take a moment and ask yourself the following questions:

1. What is my soul's journey?
2. What is my divine right livelihood?
3. What will bring me from the right place to my true place?

Michelle ignored Lisa's comment. "I'm sure there's a lot you'd like to talk about, but let's remain quiet as we hike back to the parking lot. Listen to the sounds of your feet touching the ground. Listen to your breath moving in and out of your body. Feel your heart beating and stay present. Know that where you have taken yourself in the last forty-five minutes of silence—" "Forty-five minutes? Really?" Francie said, astonished.

"Yes, believe it or not, it has been forty-five minutes since we closed our eyes. As I was saying, know that where you have taken yourself in the last forty-five minutes of silence is a sacred place you can return to whenever you want to. You don't have to be sitting next to a lake, though it doesn't hurt. You can carry that place with you . . . inside of you." She smiled. Michelle liked knowing that her thoughts could become a sanctuary of the mind and that this place was always available, no matter what life was doing on the outside.

"So when we reach the parking lot, I want you to get in your car and drive directly home. Don't turn on the radio. Don't call home before you get there. Just continue with the process of letting go of any attachments you might have about money. About what you don't have, or what you think you should've gotten in life, or the financial pressures bearing down on you. Let it all go now and concentrate on the ideas welling up from within your soul. Then, when you get home, sit down at the kitchen table, climb into your bed, or sit on your couch, and write. Write about what you saw. What you felt. Whatever. Just put pen to paper, fingers to keyboard, and write." Michelle stood up.

Slowly, the women nodded and climbed to their feet as they began the journey back to the parking lot. Lisa seemed not to have gotten anything out of the process, as she led the way and put more and more distance between herself and the rest of the group, who walked in silence. With their minds swirling, the women were so focused they

Let your inner guidance system ponder these questions and see what is revealed to you the next morning. You may wake up feeling refreshed for the first time in weeks. Or it may be more subtle where you find yourself smiling for no particular reason.

Once you become more aligned with your inner guidance system, your level of awareness will increase as well as your energy and ability to generate new ideas—the kind of ideas that give solutions to your current situation.

START WITH THE OBVIOUS

Start with what you know.

Here are some questions to help you think about yourself in a new light:

1. What is something you do well?
2. What is something you do that receives compliments?
3. What do you enjoy doing and for you is not work?

You are probably familiar with the phenomenon known as Crocs. They are those clunky, colorful, clog-like shoes that have taken the world by storm. But do you know the story of Jibbitz, the company that develops the charms that fit into the holes of Crocs?

Stay-at-home mom Sheri Schmelzer and her three children were decorating their collection of Crocs with homemade charms when Sheri's husband saw a unique product with massive potential.

What began as a craft project turned into a home-based business that developed an in-demand product that sold over eight million pieces in its first year.

What Sheri Smeltzer did was take something she enjoyed—doing a craft project with her children—and turn it into a lucrative business.

She believed she could do it and she did.

Another example is our friend and colleague Nora Roberts. A self-proclaimed reader and storyteller, Nora tried her hand at writing almost

forgot to turn on their flashlights. The walk home was a different experience than the walk up. It seemed like everyone, except for Lisa, was now walking with a sense of wonderment and awe. Their step was lighter. Their spirits were lifted, but Michelle knew this was only a momentary experience. She knew trouble lay ahead.

Michelle knew they would fight tooth and nail to remain the same by holding on to their preconceived notions about money. They would fight because it was the devil they knew. The process of becoming awake and aware was not for the fainthearted, and Michelle couldn't help wondering who would break down first. Would it be Francie, who up to this point had been locked in a life of sameness and fear? Was Lisa going to quit the Mastermind Group as if she'd gotten nothing from this experience? Would Lei Kim fall back into a workaholic pattern again, spinning on a treadmill of linear income living? Or perhaps Kanisha would run away altogether. Would she leave the baby behind? Despite all the questions running through her mind about the others, Michelle's thoughts soon began to drift to her own evaluation. Had she been too tough? Not tough enough? Had this hike been a good idea? What would Samantha have done?

The thoughts continued until she finally smiled, let go of her critical voice, and knew that what had just happened was perfect. This was a different group from Samantha's, and she didn't need to spend any mental energy on comparing and competing. This was her group, and right now she was pleased with the first session. Ideas raced about their next gathering. Michelle couldn't wait.

thirty years ago during a blizzard. Her first manuscript was 55,000 words written in longhand. After being rejected many times she finally found a publisher and what followed (and still continues today) was a long and prosperous career as a bestselling author with over 150 books written and 280 million copies sold.

To withstand multiple rejections, do you think she had a strong belief system?

If you believe enough in yourself, it is as basic as asking yourself, "Have I ever thought of making money with this?"

Think in terms of value for yourself, your future, your family's future, and your future fortunes.

BELIEF JOURNAL

We strongly recommend documenting your progress as you embrace awareness as your belief system.

Keep a journal to get clear on your desires so you can rise higher and higher. Each day, when you have a new innovative thought or idea, write it down in your journal. On the same day each week, open your journal, read your ideas, and look for the pattern integrity between all of them.

Oprah Winfrey, considered by many to be the most influential woman in the world, says she journals every day. If you look at her empire, with a net worth of over $2.5 billion, and all that she has accomplished—including her Leadership Academy for Girls in South Africa—is that not reason enough to engage in this daily practice?

There are various types of journals—anything from gratitude to love to dreams—but there are really no rules to it. If you are new to this concept, it may be best to start small. Have you ever heard of daily food logs? This is where you capture what you have eaten for the day so you can track your progress and find your pitfalls.

Why not try this method for your awareness and reinvention? Because you are more in tune with what is happening around you, try logging your

7

Trusting the Process
Knowing You Can Do Anything

During the next week, Michelle handed out copies of *Think and Grow Rich* by Napoleon Hill to each of the Mastermind Group members. She chose the book because it was the bible of finance and spiritual intention. While it taught sound financial advice, it also taught the feeling behind making money, and Michelle knew it was a perfect choice for the group. She delivered the books with the following note:

Thank you again for participating in the moonlight hike last week. I am really excited about our next gathering, which will be Tuesday at 7 P.M. Please read the enclosed book before our next meeting. Again, thank you for being open, and I'll see you all next week.

Kanisha read the book in one sitting and was eager to discuss it at the dinner table, but Michelle told her to wait for the group. As time passed, Michelle was fast learning that Kanisha wouldn't be the one to run from her life. She was embracing change beautifully. Lisa, on the other hand, was back to her normal self and resisted any discussions about the moonlight hike. While she did agree to read *Think and Grow Rich,* Lisa became very busy with other things. Michelle knew this was Lisa's way of keeping herself safe.

daily routine and look for what we call pattern integrity—profitable patterns in your life.

There are three key points to finding pattern integrity.

1. Ask yourself better questions. Where do you spend the most time? What do you enjoy the most?

2. Journal in the morning. Give yourself the thought command before you retire to bed each night: "What is my divine livelihood?" When you wake up, write what first comes into your mind.

3. Share your journal. Your Dream Team may see what you do not see.

THERE IS TREASURE IN YOUR NOTES WAITING TO BE DISCOVERED

When everything finds its place and you actively believe that abundance is your fundamental right, it is time to expand your vision even further.

Everyone has 360 degrees of talent and everyone is born an entrepreneur. As your awareness grows, you get back in sync with your birthright to be anything you want to be—regardless of what you have chosen to believe in the past.

What do you believe *now*?

An inspiring example of a woman living her dream and taking advantage of her talent is Mia Hamm, formerly a forward on the U.S. Women's National Soccer Team. Mia started playing organized soccer at the age of five. Her career high is that she scored more international goals than any other player, male or female, in the history of the sport. Mia's talent was recognized and supported early on in her life and she fulfilled her life's purpose by utilizing her gifts.

So think back again to when you were a child and answer the following questions:

What was your dream?
When did you stop believing it could come true?

In reality, being busy revealed Lisa's desire to remain small in life. Lisa wasn't the type of person who responded well when pushed into a corner. Michelle knew she would have to lead her out of the corner. For now, all she could hope for was that Lisa would read the book.

Pulling into Francie's driveway to bring her a package of herbal tea as a gift, Michelle gazed at Francie's home. With its wraparound porch, the white house with black trim resembled a plantation house from the Old South. The leaves hadn't been raked up, an obvious sign the gardener had been let go, but for the most part the house was in great shape. Michelle knocked on the oversized door.

The door opened and Francie stepped into the sunlight. She looked terrible, like she'd been up for days. She was wearing the same black track suit she'd worn on the moonlight hike, but it looked slept in. Michelle wondered if she had even taken a shower since they last saw each other, and worried that Francie had gone off the deep end.

"Francie? Are you okay?" Michelle asked, stepping forward with concern.

"Michelle! What a surprise! But it's perfect timing. Come in, I need to show you something," Francie said, grabbing Michelle's arm. She pulled her inside and swung the door shut behind them.

This was Michelle's first time in Francie's house. It was beautiful, and immaculate throughout, just like she expected. Michelle thought it looked like something out of *Better Homes and Gardens*. The study, however, was a mess. Papers and opened books were strewn about and the blinds were drawn. With the exception of Francie's laptop computer glowing like a digital campfire in the middle of the floor, the room was completely dark. The book-lined shelves were merely a faint shadow in the background.

"Francie, what is going on?" Michelle said, looking around.

Does that dream still ignite a spark within you?

If you have the means tomorrow, will you pursue it?

How much do you value making this dream come true?

More important, how much do you value making this dream come true and *acquiring new wealth with your existing resources*?

And when we say value we are not talking dollars and cents. We are referring to the deeper meaning, the core of your soul.

Do you value your wealth at the same level of your family, friends, pets, or charitable causes? Do you think that your wealth deserves to be at the same level of importance?

We do.

MIND-SET CREATES YOUR MONEY-SET

Just by having the mind-set, you create the money-set. By making your wealth a priority and treating it with the same caring and concern you would treat those people or organizations closest to you, you foster new growth.

At the beginning of this chapter we asked you to imagine what it would be like to inherit $100 million. Here is your wax on/wax off assignment: Find an old checkbook and actually write out checks to spend or invest the *entire* $100 million of your imaginary inheritance. Let your heart make the decision.

Don't go on to the next chapter until you've done this.

Then join us in the next chapter.

We've got a secret to share.

"It's amazing. I don't know what to say," Francie told her, barely able to contain her excitement.

"What's wrong?"

"Nothing. Everything is great . . . and it's all thanks to you," Francie said, digging through the papers. Suddenly a thought arrived, and she quickly jotted it down. "Yes. I must meet with my lawyer . . . file the LLC. Can't forget that."

"Francie. I don't understand. What is all of this?"

"Yes, well, after the hike last night—"

"The hike was three days ago, Francie."

"Time flies when you're having fun, doesn't it?" Francie smiled.

"I'm worried about you."

Francie picked up her laptop and placed it in Michelle's hands. "Look at this."

Michelle focused on the computer screen showing a very basic website:

FORECLOSURE HELP: *Funding a Way Through!*

"Here, look. Scroll down," Francie said as she tapped the down arrow on the keyboard like someone who's had way too much coffee. From the looks of her, she probably had.

"Eighty dollars for a handbook? I think we might have a cheaper alternative for you down at the Heartlight," Michelle said.

"Honey, there are people out there charging a thousand dollars, if you can believe that, for CDs and DVDs on this stuff, but the thing they don't understand is, someone in foreclosure doesn't have a thousand dollars. I know I don't."

"After the hike the other night—three days ago," she said, smiling at Michelle, "I got home and couldn't stop thinking about what you said. About how if we don't fill our mind with thoughts about

12

SHOW ME THE MONEY:
YOUR FORTUNE IS HIDDEN
IN PLAIN SIGHT

In the last chapter, you imagined inheriting $100 million. Imagine that:

ONE HUNDRED MILLION DOLLARS
$100,000,000

Here's the secret.

That hundred million is not just an imaginary wish. You've already inherited it.

Yes. You're already worth at least a hundred million.

"What?!" you say. "Where is it? Show me the money!"

You already possess it. It's inside you and all around you. *Now.*

Your fortune is hidden in plain sight.

Sound crazy?

Remember the Post-it note game that we learned in chapter 6? Putting yellow Post-its on everything around you? "Important—Forever" or "Stuff—Temporary."

All of the important stuff in your life is priceless—worth far more than a hundred million. The temporary stuff is just that—temporary stuff.

Of course, all of us would like to have a lot more of that temporary stuff. So the $100 million that we're talking about—the fortune that is hidden around you—is not just philosophical. No, we're talking about a

what we want, other things fill it up for us. Well, I thought the only way for me to get out of this foreclosure was to see what I could learn, but every time I read a book or went to a new website, I found maybe one useful bit of information. Nobody seemed to have all the answers. I thought, what if we could put all the answers into one place in simple language so anyone could understand? So I came up with this."

Francie took the laptop back, opened up a PDF file, and spun the laptop toward Michelle once more.

"You wrote all of this?"

"A little. Mostly I assembled it," Francie said, looking at Michelle. "All I did was take all the research you see scattered on the floor and put it into a simple twenty-five-page guide for people in foreclosure to help them understand what they're up against and how to get out of it."

"And?" Michelle asked, scanning the document.

"Then I set up a PayPal account and a website, just like you suggested."

"You built the website too?"

"Don't be silly, dear. I barely know how to get e-mail, but there's this place called GoDaddy.com. They do it for you. I just told the nice young man from California what I wanted and he did everything. The site went live two nights ago. We had a few glitches here and there, but look at that . . . one hundred and thirty-six orders."

Beep. Her inbox chimed with another order.

"I'm sorry, one hundred and thirty-seven orders," Francie said with a laugh.

"Are you telling me you made . . . how much in two days?"

"One hundred thirty-seven orders at $80 each. Eleven thousand dollars."

"Francie, that is great. Will that allow you to keep your house?"

real, monetary $100 million in cash. Maybe you've never wanted to earn that kind of money. Okay. Scale that number down. Strike off two or three zeroes. How much would that leave?

100,000,~~000~~

That leaves $100,000 to $1 million. Notice what you think when we use those numbers.

Did you think, "A hundred million! I could *never* earn that kind of money. But a hundred grand—that would be nice"?

Or did you say, "An extra million. I could go for that!"

Or did you say, "A hundred million. Yeah! Let's go, baby! Show me the money."

Well, look around you right now. Notice everything you own. Scan through your apartment, condo, town house, house, trailer—wherever you live. Make a quick mental inventory of all of your stuff.

Some of it is valuable. Some of it is worthless. Some of it is a garage sale away from moving out of your life. Some of this stuff you bought. Some of it was given to you. Regardless of its current value to you, each of these items was created by someone. Either you or someone else bought it (or made it). In most cases, someone made a fortune selling it. That someone could have been you.

Add up the profits made by the people who sold you the stuff that's in your house right now and you're looking at a minimum of $100 million dollars. Doubt that? Okay. How much profit did the company that sold you your carpets and flooring make in the past ten years? Got to be $5 million to $10 million, minimum. What about the entrepreneurs who sold you the appliances in your kitchen? Tens of millions. Your cell phone? Hundreds of millions . . . just off that one device alone. In fact, if you really tracked it down, the companies that were responsible for creating all of the stuff in your current lifestyle have generated *billions* in profit over the years.

Why can't you peel off just a sliver of that for yourself? Not just imaginary money. We're talking cash! In your pocket. Interested?

We did some of the brainstorming and writing for this book in a

"When you showed up I was just about to go over to the bank to see if they'll take a PayPal transfer."

"Might I suggest a shower first?" Michelle said.

Francie laughed and looked down at herself. "Yes, perhaps."

"The group will need to hear about this," Michelle said. "Will you be there on Tuesday?"

"Certainly. I wouldn't miss it."

"Wonderful. I have to get back to the store, but you have fun at the bank," Michelle said with a smile.

"I can't wait to start paying off those bills again."

"I'm really happy for you."

"Happy for *us*," Francie corrected her.

"Yes, happy for us. Great job, Francie, I'm proud of you," Michelle said as she turned to go. "I'll see you Tuesday."

Lisa was helping a customer with a print-on-demand order when Michelle returned to the Heartlight. They shared a smile of acknowledgment as Michelle made her way to her office. As Michelle set her purse down, her cell phone beeped with a voice-mail message.

She listened to a message from the mayor. Brady said he'd be coming over for lunch and bringing Chinese takeout, her favorite. He also said that he wanted to talk. This was unusual, Michelle thought; a man who wanted to talk? She smiled at her little joke about men and their unwillingness to share their feelings, but soon Michelle began to experience a myriad of emotions, ranging from trepidation and fear to curiosity and wonder. "What would he want to talk about?" she asked herself. They hadn't crossed the bridge to officially dating, so it couldn't be about normal relationship stuff. They hadn't even so much as kissed.

well-appointed conference room. There are dozens of things in that room: tables, chairs, lightbulbs, carpets, glass, light sockets, tiles, paint, paintings, picture frames, art, pens, computers, extension cords, flip charts, and so on. A fortune was spent to design and outfit that conference room. The fortune was sent to dozens and dozens of individual companies and entrepreneurs. Cash traded hands. Hundreds of millions were made as these sellers sold their wares to thousands upon thousands of other customers around the world.

Every single thing you see in your current living space made someone a fortune. You might be barely making ends meet at this time. Maybe you're unemployed. Or deep in debt. But the stuff all around you (even if you live in a cramped apartment) made someone a fortune. It's probably *still* making them fortunes. Hold that thought.

BUT HOW DO *I* TAP INTO THESE GUSHING FOUNTAINS OF FORTUNE SURROUNDING ME?

Well, everything you currently own is one of the clues to your future fortune. Why did you buy it? What caused you to pull out your maxed-out credit card and pile on some more debt to acquire it? Why did it speak to you?

To help you answer these questions, let's assume you have to move to a new place across the country and you can only take half of your current pile of stuff. You literally must throw away, give away, or sell half your stuff in the next seven days. Take some yellow Post-it notes and mentally label each item in your life on a scale of 1 to 10 as follows:

0	3	7	10
Worthless	Sell it at the next garage sale	This stuff is cool	Highly prized stuff
I don't need it	Give it to Goodwill Industries	I'm hanging on to this	This makes my heart flutter
I wish I hadn't bought it	Dump it for whatever I can get for it	Put it in storage	An heirloom
What a waste of space	Give it away and take a tax write-off		Priceless

Whatever his intentions were, he was on his way over. With a quick check of her watch, Michelle realized he would be there any moment. How did she look? Did she have time to freshen up? Pulling out a small compact mirror, she made sure her lip gloss was okay. It was, as usual, perfect.

As she snapped the mirror shut, the mayor cleared his throat in the doorway. He was fifteen minutes early, holding a spring bouquet of flowers and two bags of Chinese takeout.

"Szechuan beef, kung pao chicken, brown rice, and flowers . . . which are for you."

Wondering what he was up to, since he'd never brought her flowers before, she rose and thanked him as she placed the flowers into the empty vase next to her filing cabinet. The vase hadn't seen a bouquet of flowers for more than a year and a half, when Nicky and Hannah had picked wildflowers on a school field trip.

Her eyes moved from the flowers and met his, gazing down at her from his six feet four inches. His blue eyes seemed to make her stomach do flip-flops, like she was on a roller coaster at the county fair.

What was she waiting for? He was good-looking, smart, and a better-than-average dancer. Plus he liked kids. Perhaps her standards were too high, or perhaps she was afraid of commitment after losing Gideon. Michelle snapped herself out of her momentary daze.

"Shall we eat?" she said, sitting in her chair.

The mayor didn't say a word. Instead, he set the bags of food onto the desk and moved his chair next to hers. Brady took her hand and looked deep into her eyes. Her heart stopped.

"Relax, I'm not going to do anything stupid," he said, watching as the color drained from her already pale-skinned face. "I just want to talk about a few things before we dig in."

"What do you want to talk about?" she said, clearing her throat.

"Do you like me?" he asked.

You'll become aware through this exercise what you value. You valued it enough to spend hard-earned cash on it. You understand why someone like you would part with so much cash to get it. Where did you buy it? How much did you pay for it? Did you get a bargain price or pay top dollar? What would you accept for someone to take it off your hands?

Your highly prized stuff is very valuable to you. Still makes your heart flutter.

Did someone sell this stuff to you? Or did you search it out to buy it? Most of the things you value were obtained when an internal desire of yours was activated and you went seeking to get it. You Yellow-Paged it or Googled it. You were on the prowl.

Millions of people just like you are on the prowl to buy things they are attracted to. They love to buy. As an entrepreneur, you're on the prowl for things that you can sell to people. If you're going to sell anything, sell only what you love. If you don't love it, find someone else to sell it for you. The first fundamental is to notice what you've already bought. Then sell stuff like that.

The fortune you want to create on the outside must flow from the fortune inside you. There is a fountain of fortune inside you waiting to be tapped. Here's how you tap into it.

THE CACHE OF CASH

Do you know what the word *cache* means? The dictionary describes the word as follows:

1. A hidden storage space (for money or provisions or weapons)
2. A secret store of valuables or money

You have a secret cache of valuable resources already inside you waiting to be monetized.

What if we were to scan your brain and your heart to determine which assets are most cashable? What would we discover about you?

Just for fun, we've imagined a portable pair of spectacles similar to a CT scan, which we call Cache Scan glasses. They look like this:

"Do I like you?" Michelle echoed, letting out a nervous laugh.

"Yes. Do you like me? It's been over six months since we . . ." He searched for the words. "Exactly what would you call what we've been doing here?"

"Getting to know each other?" Michelle offered.

"Right. For six months," he offered with a deadpan look on his face.

"And?"

"And I'm starting to feel like Switzerland over here."

"Switzerland?"

"Yes. Neutral. You. Me. It all feels so neutral, and I don't want to be neutral with you. I like you, Michelle. I like spending time with you, and while being friends is nice, I want . . ."

"Something more," Michelle said, finishing his sentence.

"You make it sound as if that were a bad thing."

"Not at all."

"But?"

"There's no but." She paused as she gathered her racing thoughts. "But sometimes things should just happen organically. What I mean is, if we need to have this kind of conversation, maybe—"

Before she could finish, he leaned in and gave Michelle the kind of kiss that would have buckled her knees on the spot if she'd been standing. It was a passionate kiss and spoke volumes about the kind of lover he would be. It wasn't an overly aggressive kiss, but rather an invitation to something special. Michelle and Lisa had often talked about relationships and the countless bad kisses they'd had to endure in life. While they disagreed on many things, like whether or not a woman should ask a man out, they both agreed that everything came down to the kiss. If a man couldn't kiss, nothing else mattered. But, Michelle realized, as Brady released her, this man knew what he was doing.

"Something like that," he said, looking closely into her eyes.

Each lens identifies valuable assets that can be converted into fast cash. The left lens (from your perspective) deals with the assets in your mind. The right lens deals with assets in your heart. Imagine if you put these glasses on and, instantly, you were able to scan a willing participant to help that person uncover his or her hidden cache of cashable assets.

The process includes asking the subject ten questions around the central core of who he or she really is. There are five mind questions and five heart questions. The answers to these questions help you counsel the individual on where to invest time and effort toward the highest-probability monetary endeavor—in other words, how that person can generate some fast cash.

The Cache Scan glasses focus on five specific assets of your mind:

Knowledge
Skills
Successes
Failures and fears
Challenges

When it comes to a Cache Scan of the heart, the five hidden chambers are:

Desires
Passions
Talents
Wisdom
Connections

Here are the ten questions. Answer each question with your top three choices.

Michelle couldn't move. She couldn't talk. All she could muster was a smile, which grew ever so wide.

The silence between them seemed to last forever. Then Michelle moved in for another kiss, just to make sure the first hadn't been beginner's luck. As their lips touched for the second time, and Michelle began to feel the same electricity she'd felt in the first kiss, Lisa walked in unannounced.

"Oh, geez, I'm sorry," she said, backpedaling into the hallway.

"No, it's fine," Michelle said, collecting herself.

"I can come back."

"Lisa, it's okay. What's up?"

Lisa slowly appeared in the doorway again with a giant grin on her face. "I was just going to step out and grab something to eat and was going to see if you wanted anything, but . . ." She smiled, enjoying the obviously uncomfortable moment Michelle was having. "It seems you have everything you need."

Michelle shot from her chair. "No. Hey. Here. Grab some plates from the kitchen. You can join us. You love Chinese food, don't you? Of course she does." Michelle looked back at Brady. "Everyone loves Chinese food. Why would I think you wouldn't, right?" she said to Lisa.

"Oh, I don't want to be a bother," Lisa began with a wry smile.

"Don't be silly. I'll help you get the plates," Michelle said, grabbing Lisa's hand.

"We're getting the plates," Lisa said to Brady before Michelle ripped her from his view. He smiled.

In the kitchen, Michelle looked back to make sure Brady hadn't followed them. She whispered to Lisa, "You can't leave me alone in there."

"You're not alone in there, girl. Mr. Hunkalicious is in there with you."

MIND CACHE	HEART CACHE
Knowledge: What do you know?	**Passions:** What are your passions?
(Specialized knowledge, schooling, education)	*(Fascination, intense interest, hobbies)*
1.	1.
2.	2.
3.	3.
Skills: What can you do?	**Desires:** What do you want?
(Skills, know-how, street smarts)	*(Things, experiences, or feelings you desire)*
1.	1.
2.	2.
3.	3.
Confidence: Where have you been successful?	**Talents:** What are you good at?
(Money, relationships, organization)	*(What you're really innately talented at)*
1.	1.
2.	2.
3.	3.
Failures and fears: What have you failed at/feared?	**Wisdom:** What are your life's top three lessons?
(What did you do that hurt? What don't you want?)	*(Lessons learned through problems, disasters, troubles, accidents, sickness, and struggles)*
1.	1.
2.	2.
3.	3.
Problems: What are your three biggest problems/challenges?	**Connections:** Whom do you know?
(Current dilemmas, difficulties)	*(Name three successful friends)*
1.	1.
2.	2.
3.	3.

"Would you stop messin' around? I'm serious."

"Oh, stop. What are you so afraid of?"

"I'm not afraid. I'm just not sure I'm ready to jump right in and make out with the mayor in my office like a couple of horny teenagers."

"The way you two were goin' at it, I thought he'd just asked you to the prom."

"Stop!"

"Would you go back in there and kiss the man already!" Lisa ordered.

"Great advice, Lisa. What if the kids walked in?"

"The kids are in school."

"You know our kids. They could get expelled."

"Right, and then Nicky could steal the principal's car keys and drive everybody down here because they know you're making out with Brady Wilson!"

"You think this is funny, don't you."

"No, I think it's great—and about time," Lisa said, grabbing an apple from the fruit bowl next to the refrigerator.

"So you'll stay?"

"I didn't say that," Lisa replied as she took a big bite out of the apple.

"Lisa!"

"Calm down, I'm kidding. Of course I'll stay."

"Great," Michelle said, relieved.

"If I can have a raise."

Michelle spun around, but Lisa was obviously kidding. She took another bite of the apple and watched Michelle work things out.

"Okay. This is good. This is good," Michelle said, straightening her blouse. "All right. We better get back," she said, moving into the hallway.

Many of these inner assets come with your programming the day you are born. Why do some people love to fish? To travel? To do genealogy? Eat ice cream? Some of these things come ready to use right out of the box. Some of them need to be developed. Regardless, there are enough inner qualities that everyone possesses to fuel success—if they just don't get talked out of it (by their critical voice or the critical voices speaking through the mouths of other people).

In addition to these interests, desires, and passions, we come pre-gifted with amazing talents—gifts, abilities, tendencies—that are our unique combination of strengths. Some of these talents are obvious: being seven feet tall, being a parent of ten children, winning eight gold medals in one Olympics, winning the national spelling bee. Other talents we discover or uncover over years of experience.

One of the most famous stories in the Bible is the Parable of the Talents (Matthew 25:15–19). A man called his three servants and gave them each five talents, three talents, and one talent, respectively. The first two servants doubled their talents. He rewarded them richly. The final servant hid his talent because he was afraid of losing it. His lord summoned the "unprofitable servant" and rebuked him.

Your goal is to become a profitable servant, doubling your investment as quickly as possible. To be a profitable servant is to find something you love or are good at and to sell it profitably to other people who are searching for it in such a way that they feel served.

When you sell this way, it's not selling. It's serving. You love it. They love it.

Here's the bottom line. All talents are cashable! You can turn any talent into money.

Most people have hobbies. Most hobbies are simply heightened interests fueled by latent talents. They could become sources of short-term cash and full-time cash flow.

There are a million ways to earn a million dollars, but only a handful of ideal ways for you to earn your "right livelihood." What is your right livelihood? It is your purpose path—earning money doing things that you truly

"Michelle?" Lisa asked, leaning against the counter with a big smile.

"Yeah?"

"The plates?"

"Yes. Right. The plates," Michelle said, obviously still flustered. Lisa couldn't help laughing.

"Don't laugh. It's not funny."

"Yes it is."

"So, you think he's cute?" Michelle asked, leaning in like a high school cheerleader talking about her quarterback boyfriend.

"Are you kidding? He's gorgeous. And hey, an added bonus—if you ever get into trouble with the law, he's not a bad guy to have around, ya know. He can bail ya out."

"Yeah, like I'm going to start knocking over banks."

"You're the one who wanted us to start thinking about money. I could drive the getaway car, Francie could be the bag girl . . ."

Michelle wasn't amused. This was serious business—she hadn't kissed anyone besides Gideon in over fifteen years. She wondered if she'd done it okay. Maybe she was out of practice. She hoped Brady would want to kiss her again, because her body was alive and her mind was racing with all sort of possibilities.

enjoy to serve all of humanity. The secrets to your right livelihood are already planted inside you.

HIT THE GROUND RUNNING

If you look through a catalogue of business opportunities, most of them will require study, training, and experiential learning. This will mean hours of assimilating information and acquiring new knowledge. Then you'll be required to practice applying this knowledge until it becomes a skill. Like learning a new tennis grip, it will require the unlearning of old skills and relearning of new skills (i.e., getting worse until you get better), as with all skill training.

The quickest money is from what you already know, love, and do. Why? Because you're familiar with it. You enjoy it. There won't be a long learning curve. You're at the starting blocks. You're ready to run.

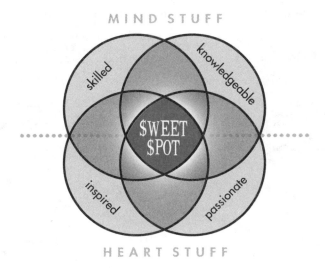

The overlapping of these four concentric circles is almost always a pure vein of gold. It's when you use your current knowledge, skill, and passion to create products, services, and/or information that you're inspired to

8

The Great Mental Debate

Yes I Can, No I Can't . . . oh, but I Really Want To!

Still energized from the kiss, Michelle all but ran up the steps of the bank to make the store's weekly deposit. As she opened the doors, Francie came out with a huge smile on her face.

"Hello there. Fancy meeting you here," Francie said cheerfully.

"How'd it go?" Michelle asked with a smile.

"PayPal takes three days to deposit, but it will go directly to my account and I will be officially off foreclosure."

"That's wonderful, Francie."

"Yes it is, and I'm glad I ran into you. I need some advice. On the way over here I saw a piece of property over on the north side of town, just off Van Ness."

"Nice area. What shape is the house in?" Michelle inquired.

"Beautiful," Francie quickly replied. "I think somebody should buy it."

"Ever think that somebody should be you?"

"Michelle, I just got out of foreclosure, I don't think—"

"Oh yes. You should think about it," Michelle said, cutting her off. "What are the particulars of the property?"

"About twenty years left on a thirty-year mortgage, a balance of $255,000 at 6 percent. The owners are about four months behind on their mortgage payments. They're scared because they just got a

create. That's the sweet spot. That's what we call leverage. All four of these attributes don't always need to be present, but the more the better.

The process of acquiring knowledge, skill, and confidence can take years. You don't have years. You have less than ninety days from now.

Wouldn't it be much quicker if you didn't have to learn any new knowledge or skill but could convert what you already know—and what you already know how to do—into cash?

We call this "low-hanging fruit." This is the easy stuff. You already know it. You don't have to practice to learn how to do it. You're already good at it. You can pick the ripe fruit that is hanging right at eye level. It's ready to eat, right now.

That's where you start. What are you ready to implement now? No start-up time. No getting ready. Forget ninety days. You could do it in ninety minutes from now.

A little higher up the money tree are those fruits that are a little harder to reach—just beyond your fingers. You'll need a short stepladder. This fruit refers to assets in your cache related to your innate yet undeveloped talents and gifts. You may need to learn more or study about those things you don't know but have always been interested in. Go to more classes, courses, seminars. Then you'll need to practice to turn that knowledge into skill. This will take longer than ninety days.

At the top of the tree, where few dare to climb, are the richest, largest, untouched fruits. You'll be climbing in riskier places. This takes more knowledge and skill. The fastest route to profit is to be mentored by some-one who already has the knowledge, skill, confidence, and track record of success for you to emulate. Let that person take you to the highest branches until you are skilled and confident enough to go there alone. Even as you become an expert, you should always work in teams. It could take months. Even years.

The focus of this book is the low-hanging fruit—making money faster. So the questions we ask you are these:

What do you do?
Who are you?

notice of default from the bank. It should take about ten thousand plus costs to assume."

"Any appraisal?"

"Three hundred and twenty-five thousand," Francie replied. "But there's a problem. The owners are such a sweet couple—I don't feel right taking their house like this and putting them on the street."

"If you don't, the bank will."

"Yes, I understand that, but this was me just seventy-two hours ago. I felt so scared, and I don't want anyone to feel the same way. I just want to help if I can."

"And make money in the process?" Michelle reminded her.

"If there a way to make it work and not put them out, yes."

Michelle smiled. "This is what it means to be an enlightened millionaire, Francie. Making money while doing good for other people. I will say this, though. It's hard to extend a line of credit to someone who can't make the payments on the loans they already have. Sweet couple aside, this is still business. You'd be throwing good money after bad. What you could do is take over the loan and then negotiate a lease with an option to buy. That will keep the bank off their backs and they get to stay in their house. Hopefully they can weather the storm and buy it back when they get right side up, but you have to know that at the end of the day, you're the owner of the property. If they're delinquent just once with the payments . . ."

"Yes, I understand. See? I knew you'd know what to do," Francie said with a smile.

"Question is, do you know what *you're* going to do?" Michelle asked.

"That depends."

"On what?"

"On how well my e-book does in the next few days," Francie said.

How do you bring money in the door living your ideal lifestyle?

What magnetizes the fortune to flow toward you?

Why would anyone want to send you money?

Because you're going to do something for them that they couldn't get done any better, anywhere else in the world. Because that's just what you do. That's who you are.

Be that person.

As fast as you can.

THE MICROCREDIT MOVEMENT

But how is this done? How can you convert your internal "stuff" into money?

Our model for this is Muhammad Yunus, the 2006 Nobel Peace Prize winner and founder of the Grameen Bank. He has been working with beginning entrepreneurs for over thirty years, starting in Bangladesh—one of the poorest nations on earth. He shows poor women all over the world—over one hundred million of them—how to earn cash quickly. He shows them how to get above the poverty line so they can take care of themselves and their families.

Their need for cash is dramatically different from most of us in North America. They either earn money or starve to death. They don't have ninety days. They don't have nine days. They have real *dead*lines—they've got to bring money in the door *tomorrow* or their babies die.

His approach seems counter to everything we learn in this hemisphere about education. He teaches tens of millions of poor women "how to fish" so that they can become self-sufficient.

Yunus says, "We give loans to the poorest women in Bangladesh. They take the money and start tiny, little businesses with $30 or $40. They're so small people feel reluctant to call them businesses. I say that's a business no matter how you look at it. Just because the size is small doesn't make it less of a business in her opinion. She moves from one level of business to

"Well, keep me posted."

"Indeed I will. See you Tuesday," Francie said, continuing down the steps.

Michelle smiled. This was a good day.

On Tuesday the wind decided to rest for the evening. The glow of the setting sun outlining the distant Rocky Mountains had faded as night fell. Main Street was empty.

Kanisha opened the front door of the Heartlight and quickly stepped inside. Checking the time on the antique grandfather clock sitting next to the front register, she exhaled a sigh of relief as the old clock began to strike seven. Kanisha was on time. Before shutting the door behind her, she took in the harmonic strikes of the clock as it gently filled the room. The music it produced demanded a smile, like an hourly wind chime. Michelle said she liked this because she felt it made customers feel at home. The truth was, Kanisha thought, the sounds of the old clock made Michelle feel at home, and that was all that mattered.

As the clock finished echoing throughout the store, Kanisha closed the door and moved to where Francie and Lei Kim sat on the soft couches.

"Hello," Kanisha said, sitting down. "I thought I was late."

"Right on time," Lei Kim said with a smile, but Francie didn't even look up to acknowledge Kanisha's presence. She was too busy penciling something into her Filofax planner.

Kanisha didn't let Francie bother her. She asked Lei Kim, "Where's Michelle and Lisa? Are they coming?"

"In the back. Michelle told us to wait in the bullpen," Lei Kim answered.

the next level of business to the next level of business, until she is out of poverty."

What does he teach these women? Much *less* than you'd expect. Counter to the many educational programs that teach valuable knowledge and skills to poor people in underdeveloped countries, Muhammad Yunus teaches them *zero* information about how to earn money.

When we first learned this, we were shocked. Doesn't a person need to learn to earn? People think the answer to success is to learn how. That's why there are so many how-to books. It's probably why you bought *this* book. Then, why do Yunus and his microcredit organizations teach so little how-to?

He has discovered that the more his clients learn, the dumber they feel. That might sound counterintuitive, but that is the nature of knowledge. Knowledge is addictive. Often, the more you know, the more you think you need to know in order to get started.

Yunus doesn't want any of his borrowers to be stopped by having to learn new knowledge and new skills. He starts them *now* with what they already know how to do.

There is one main requirement. Each woman must have enough self-confidence to attract four other like-minded women into a team of five. They become the support group for each other. The women in these groups brainstorm each woman's cash-generating idea. Then, with only this infrastructure of social support, the Grameen Bank lends each woman enough money to start her business. The women have no other collateral for their loan other than a team to support them. The loans must be repaid with weekly payments, and 98 percent of these loans are repaid—a rate far exceeding that in traditional commercial banking.

These poor women start where they are with what they have.

In an interview, Dr. Yunus explained how it works:

Formal learning is threatening to our borrowers. People learn better, more easily, and more comfortably from each other. A poor person has lots of capacity, skill, which is unused—like making baskets, raising poultry, raising

"The what?" Kanisha asked.

"This couch area is known as the bullpen." Lei Kim leaned closer. "Clearly a baseball reference she picked up from her late husband."

"The rules?" Francie said to Lei Kim.

"Ah yes, the rules. There are two rules of the bullpen: don't ask small questions and don't engage in small talk."

"That's right!" Michelle said, coming down the hallway. "We want this place to be filled with large thinkers who choose to live large lives."

"Rah rah," Lisa said, carrying a whiteboard and a large wooden easel.

"What's the motto, Lisa?"

"I'm busy setting up the easel. Why don't you ask Francie?" Lisa said.

"Francie?"

"I'm sorry, what?" Francie said in a lackluster tone. Michelle didn't repeat the question. She just carried on.

"How we do anything is how we do everything."

"That's kinda cool," Kanisha said in response.

"*Kinda* cool? This is super cool!" Michelle said with enthusiasm. She truly believed it too. If you weren't asking big questions about your life, you weren't looking for big answers. Michelle had found a way to use the problems she d faced in her past to form the solutions of her future. This was the secret she wanted to teach the Mastermind Group, and Francie's foreclosure was a perfect example of this ideal.

"What's the whiteboard for?" Francie asked.

"Yeah. Are we going to play Pictionary?" Lisa asked, kicking off her shoes like they were about to have game night.

"Before you can go anywhere, you first have to know where it is

any other animal, or whatever thing they do in a family way. Once given a chance, whatever their favorite thing is, they can transform it into a business.

They do what they enjoy and at the same time they earn money. Women do sewing and make beautiful dresses; they love making dresses. They love seeing the dress they made bought by somebody who's living in their village. She can say, "This is the dress I made." She can prove to other families that she can do better than her friend in designing and coming up with new ideas in fashion. These things happen naturally. You don't have to set up training schools for everything. Attending a school is good, but it's only needed after you've exhausted your first level of skill—what you have after you have used up all your existing skill. Then they can learn new skills. But their basic skill is so much more immediate. They don't need training.

Each human being has tremendous potential locked inside. We never give them any chance to find out what they know—what they have inside of them. Microcredit allows them to reveal themselves to themselves.

That's our advice to you. Start with what you have, where you are. That is your low-hanging fruit. That is your "first level of skill," as Yunus calls it.

Yunus is an example of an enlightened entrepreneur. To learn how you can make a fortune and make the world a better place through principles we call Blessonomics, visit www.cashinaflashthebook.com.

LET'S PICK SOME FRUIT

What is your low-hanging fruit? What are you already good at?

So go back to your Cache Scan list of cashable assets.

If your life depended upon generating some immediate cash, what one resource would you draw from in each category?

you want to go," Michelle answered, setting up the whiteboard at one end of the couches.

"What?" Lisa replied, tilting her head in confusion.

"In order to achieve what you want, you have to become clear on what it is you want. What do you want? Do you know? Have you asked yourself the question? '

Lisa looked back at her with a blank stare. Michelle then turned to Francie.

"Francie, maybe you could help us out here and tell the ladies what you came up with after our hike."

"Well, I am in foreclosure—"

"*Was* in," Michelle said, correcting her.

"Thank you . . . I *was* in foreclosure, and I made a website that took off."

"A website?" Lei Kim asked.

"What kind?" Lisa inquired.

"On what to do when you receive a foreclosure notice from the bank," Francie explained. "I put together a twenty-five-page guide of information that helps you see through the mess of foreclosure."

"Tell them why," Michelle prodded.

"Because when I got the notice in the mail, I was so scared, I didn't know what to do," Francie admitted.

"But how did you know to write the guide and make the website?" Lei Kim asked.

"Lei Kim, I honestly don't know, but it has something to do with what Michelle said the other night, and the hike." She smiled, almost apologizing. "I don't know—something just happened."

"Come on, Francie. Tell 'em the good part. Tell 'em how much money you've made," Michelle said, smiling widely.

"Does it matter?"

"A number with four zeros after it is a lot different from a number

Combine the ten ingredients into one great idea. If you had to create something in the next ninety minutes that could be generating cash in the next ninety days, what would it look like?

Bring that idea with you into the next chapter. We'll show you how to form a Dream Team who can help bring your ideas to life.

with only three," Michelle said, noticing how Francie shifted her weight. She seemed uncomfortable—completely different from the woman Michelle had heard explain how the idea came about and how excited she was about paying her bills.

"So, how much?" Lisa prodded.

"Before I left the house, the PayPal account was up to about fifteen thousand."

Lisa jolted upright. *"Dollars?"*

"Yes," Francie said, half smiling. "In ten days, if you're in foreclosure, I can teach you to be stress free, debt free, and walk away without owing a penny."

As the women clapped and carried on, Michelle caught Francie's eye. Something was indeed amiss. She'd just gotten herself out of foreclosure, but she wasn't fully enjoying this moment. Maybe she was just tired, Michelle thought, and moved on with the discussion.

"Fifteen thousand dollars in just a few days. While this is great, Francie, the thing you need to start thinking about now is how to have supplemental products to support the popularity of your initial product. You always want to think of new ways to monetize the popularity of your website traffic."

"I don't want to be greedy," Francie said.

And there it was. Michelle now realized what was wrong. Francie was having trouble with making money. She could confront her about this, but she knew there would be opportunities for Francie to discover it on her own, so Michelle decided not to press it.

"I want to know where she found all those people to buy her book," Lisa said, thoroughly engaged in the conversation now.

"There's a website that gathers e-mail addresses of people in foreclosure. I'm assuming they get them from the county clerks' offices. Anyway, I gave this website my credit card number and they

PART THREE

The Third Key Ingredient: Dream Team

did a blast to a couple hundred thousand people all over the country. I started getting orders the next hour."

"How come I can't find something like that?" Lisa asked, sitting back into the cushion of the couch.

"The easiest way to answer questions like that is to become single-minded in your intention. Your attention has to be on your intention. If you are engaging in back-and-forth, 'yes I can' 'no I can't' self-talk, you are simply playing mental ping-pong. Discernment is good, but back-and-forth is a waste of time. The universe is a friendly place and abundance is available for everyone, no matter what you might think. Did everyone get a chance to read *Think and Grow Rich?*"

"Yes. I loved it," Kanisha erupted first.

"Yes, very good," Lei Kim said.

Francie nodded, but Lisa missed the question altogether, preoccupied with arranging the cushions behind her. Looking up, she noticed that all eyes were on her.

"What? Sorry. The pillows," she mumbled.

"Did you read the book, Lisa?" Michelle asked.

"Yeah. It was cool, from what I read. I mean, I could tell it was good," she said, looking away.

Michelle thought about Lisa's reaction. While Lisa was a good employee, her personal life was a mess. She was chronically late and oversubscribed, but she wasn't willing to do the work. That was her problem—by keeping "busy" with a life of chaos, she was able to continue the drama. This would soon change, Michelle thought.

"I encourage you all to review it as often as you can. If there's any book out there that captures what it takes to be an enlightened millionaire, it's *Think and Grow Rich*. Okay, let's move on." Michelle said, moving to the whiteboard.

13

YOUR DREAM T.E.A.M.: TOGETHER EVERYONE ACHIEVES MIRACLES

Your mind is convinced that you are on the verge of unprecedented prosperity. Your heart is fully engaged. You want it. You're passionate for it. It feels *so* right. The final ingredient is to form a mastermind alliance.

What is a mastermind alliance?

We believe it is the way to unlimited results in business and in life.

A mastermind alliance is two or more individuals voluntarily coming together to accomplish more than either could alone.

Masterminding uses blended mind power and action to obtain infinite results in all realms of life. None of us can be totally successful alone; we need other people to energize our outlook and find the best that is in us. We need others to work with us, support us, encourage us, and empower us in ways that we have yet to see for ourselves.

When two individual candles, both lit, are brought together, you get a brighter, more powerful flame. The same is true of a mastermind relationship. As Napoleon Hill taught in his book *Think and Grow Rich*, two or more individuals come together to create a third more powerful creative, intuitive, and synergetic mind.

No one mind is ever complete until working in harmonic, purposeful relationships with others. It is these relationships that foster growth and opportunity for each individual.

"Hold up. We're not even gonna discuss the book?" Kanisha questioned.

"No, and I'll tell you why," Michelle said, picking up Kanisha's highlighted copy of *Think and Grow Rich*. "There's nothing in here that you don't already know on a soul level."

"Soul level? I thought we were here to learn how to make money," Lisa asked.

Michelle moved to the financial section in the bookstore and gathered an armful of titles. Returning to the bullpen, she dropped them onto the coffee table one by one.

"There's a million books out there on the ABC's of making money, but unless you carry a consciousness of wealth, you will always be just over broke . . . which is another name for a j-o-b. The work we're doing here is deeper because what we want to do is cultivate a foundation of wealth."

"I don't understand," put in Lei Kim.

"When we're born, we already possess all the knowledge and instinct we'll ever need to get through life. The things you read in any of these books are simply reminders of what we already know. It's great to absorb what other people have said. Absolutely, you should attend seminars and you should read books. Take in as much as you can handle. But at some point, we must begin to rely on who *we* are. What *we* think. It's that kind of self-reliance that propels us toward self-mastery and our greatest yet to be."

"Question," Francie interrupted. "That phrase, 'greatest yet to be.' What does that mean?"

"Your life, fully expressed."

While this sounded great to everyone else, Kanisha was hung up. She was still snagged by the thought that the hours she'd spent studying the book were wasted. She was shaking her head, looking away from the group.

YOUR DREAM TEAM

In *The One Minute Millionaire*, we referred to your mastermind relationships as your Dream Team. We said that instant solutions exist in Dream Teaming. This process helps you to take your ideas and expand them into greatness.

To become a great person, entrepreneur, leader, artist, speaker, or author, you must have a Dream Team. Read any biography or autobiography and you will find examples of these mastermind relationships.

Your capacity to be, do, and have will inevitably increase through your Dream Team and you will become a better individual. Assuming your association is with like-minded people who live in truth, honor, and integrity, the possibilities are endless.

Enlightened millionaires have Dream Teams!

I SAY MASTERMIND, YOU SAY BROAD SQUAD

Our friend, our agent, and a contributor to this book, Jillian Manus, has graciously allowed us to share the term she uses for her Dream Team—Broad Squad. This is a title that excites and drives her and articulates the experience for her and her group. We use the terms Mastermind Group, Dream Team, Broad Squad, and Guy Tribe interchangeably, and you will also want to come up with your own term that suits you and your group.

Your Dream Team does not have to be formal. In fact, it may be that you are in such a group and just have not yet given it that type of title.

Are you already participating in a group of some kind where you offer support, talk about ideas, or provide a safe space for sharing? Are you part of a book club at your local library? Perhaps you are a member of a military family support group or a new mothers' group. All of these preexisting groups may be easily transitioned into something even more powerful if given the right focus and direction.

If you do not see one of these groups as an easy progression into a Dream Team, there may be some members who belong with whom you could team up with outside of this cause.

"Kanisha? Is there something wrong?" Michelle asked.

"No, I . . . well, yeah. I did all that studying like you asked, and we ain't even gonna discuss it?"

Before Michelle could answer, Francie snapped, "I'm sorry. I can't do this. Surely there should be a requirement for us to speak in proper sentences," she said, as if Kanisha wasn't even in the room.

"Excuse me? I'll talk however I damn well please."

"Then you talk like a tramp," Francie shot back.

"Whatever, Grandma. I *ain't* here to impress your droopy ass."

"All right, that's enough," Michelle said.

"What? The bitch came at me." Kanisha slammed her notebook onto the coffee table.

"Kanisha, stop it."

"Me? You should be talkin' to Ms. High and Mighty 'I made fifteen G's' sittin' over there. I ain't done nothin' wrong except stick up for myself. The woman been throwin' dirty looks at me since we started this thing."

Suddenly everyone felt uncomfortable.

"I think it's time we talk about the rules," Michelle said, finally breaking the silent tension.

"Rules? For a book club?" Lisa said.

"Yes, the rules. And this isn't a book club, Lisa. This is a Mastermind Group, and you're here to do big work and think even bigger. The first rule, like it or not, is that we always support each other, no matter what."

"I don't wanna be friends with her," Kanisha said, indicating Francie, who sat with her arms folded across her designer blouse like a pressure cooker waiting to explode.

Michelle addressed Kanisha. "Well, that's good, because I don't want to be friends with you either, Kanisha."

We always say to start with the obvious and look at whom you know already and where you are spending your time. This way you do not feel overwhelmed by starting from scratch.

If you truly feel that you do not have any people to pull from and bring into this experience, it is even more important to expand your thinking. What about your coworker in the cubicle four spots down? Your accountant? Your pediatrician?

Another area where masterminds are showing up is online, through virtual mastermind groups. Type in "mastermind groups" on Google and see what you find. Try local community websites or even place your own ad!

START WITH WHAT YOU KNOW

We are saying that everyone is entitled to and has access to a Dream Team. Right away. Today.

You do not have to have advanced degrees, an executive position at a major corporation, or a network of high-worth investors. All you need to do is start with what you know.

Have you ever felt like the more you learn, the more you realize you do not know?

What we have found is that many of our students have been hesitant to form a Dream Team for fear that they do not have enough knowledge or skill to offer any value to the other members. They set themselves up with a prerequisite to-do list before they will start or join a group.

The idea of a Dream Team is tempting, but the fear of not being or knowing enough overrides the excitement.

It does not have to be that way.

Start with what you have and what you know. Start taking action right now . . . even though you might feel that you don't know enough. The truth is you'll *never* know enough. You just have to have faith to get started and figure it out as you go.

As we mentioned earlier, Dr. Muhammad Yunus is a Nobel Peace Prize winner for launching the microcredit movement that has gotten over a hundred million people out of poverty in his home country of Bangladesh

Kanisha's jaw dropped in astonishment. "What'd I do to you?"

Michelle didn't answer her. Instead, she addressed the group with authority.

"Ladies, we aren't here for friendships."

"We're not friends?" Lei Kim asked quietly.

Michelle's shoulders grew heavy. This wasn't how she'd seen things unfolding. She'd thought for sure the excitement and success of Francie's foreclosure idea would energize the group with more moneymaking ideas, but that wasn't the case. Somehow she was losing control.

As the women began to bicker back and forth, Michelle finally smiled, because she knew this was the beauty about life. It had a way of unfolding perfectly no matter what it looked like on the outside. She knew this firsthand, but she needed to do something. She needed to lead this group past the mental roadblocks they had before them.

"Quiet! That's enough!" Michelle ordered. "When we're in session, I am not here to be your friend. If you want a friend, go buy a dog. This is business, and if you can't hack it in here, you'll never make it out there. We're here to learn how to make money, and we can't do that if we're stuck in the quicksand of old thought patterns and bad habits, like bickering about nothing. We need cooperation from each other. We don't have time to compare and compete with each other."

"There's nothing wrong with friendships, Michelle," Lisa cut in.

"I never said there was, Lisa. I said *inside this group*, we have no time to worry about the delicate nature of friendships."

"Why not?" Lisa continued.

"Because friends buoy you up. Friends hand over approval like change at a fast-food restaurant. Why? Because when you're friends, you don't want to hurt anyone's feelings by telling the truth. I'm

and throughout the world. When asked what strategy made his bank, Grameen Bank, so successful that the poor pay back 98 percent of their loans, he answered: "Whatever the banks do, I do the opposite. Banks lend to men; I lend to women. Banks are in the cities; I am in the rural areas. Banks require collateral; I require no collateral. Banks are literate-friendly; I am illiterate-friendly. Banks need paperwork; I need verbal agreement."

Most important, Yunus says, "I do not want you to know more. Go out and do what you know." You don't need a new skill; you have all of the skills you need already. Yunus's program is so successful because instead of wasting time teaching the poor new skills, he helps them maximize their existing skills—anything from weaving to raising cows to peddling a rickshaw. Borrowers also have the opportunity to assist each other and share what they know because they are involved in what he calls solidarity groups—five women in a group that meet once a week.

We in North America should be inspired and motivated by the example of these solidarity groups because they have been so amazingly successful in the lives of the extremely poor. They give proof that Dream Teams do work.

According to Yunus, in his book *Banker to the Poor*, "When we discovered that support groups were crucial to the success of our operations, we required that each applicant join a group of like-minded people living in similar economic and social conditions. Convinced that solidarity would be stronger if the groups came into being by themselves, we refrained from managing them, but we did create incentives that encouraged the borrowers to help one another succeed in their businesses. Group membership not only creates support and protection but also smoothes out the erratic behavior patterns of individual members, making each borrower more reliable in the process. Subtle and at times not-so-subtle peer pressure keeps each group member in line with the broader objectives of the credit program. A sense of intergroup and intragroup competition also encourages each member to be an achiever."

They have even successfully dealt with the challenge of forming the groups. As Yunus explains, "We found that it is not always easy for borrowers to organize themselves into groups. A prospective borrower first

serious. We have to trust each other to tell the brutal truth. We have to rely on each other, and if we don't, we are wasting our time and we should all go home right now."

"I don't want to rely on *her* for anything," Kanisha snapped, tossing her head in Francie's direction.

"And I think you should go back to where you came from," Francie shot back.

"I ain't goin' anywhere, lady."

"That's enough. What, am I talking to myself here?" Michelle was upset now. The tension was thick, the silence even thicker, and it lasted for a good thirty seconds as Michelle processed her next move.

Francie put her purse on her lap; she was certain things were about to end. Kanisha stared at her, but Francie didn't even look anywhere near the end of the couch where Kanisha was. It was a standoff.

"What do we do now?" Lisa finally asked. It was the question on everyone's mind, so all eyes turned to Michelle. She took her time to answer.

"We're going for a ride," Michelle finally said, standing up and gathering her keys.

"Another hike?" Lei Kim wondered.

"No. We're just going for a ride," Michelle said.

"Where?" Lisa asked.

"Will I need my purse?" Lei Kim asked.

"No. You can leave everything right here. We'll be back in ten minutes, tops. We can take my car."

Not sure what they were getting themselves into, the women stood up and followed Michelle down the hallway.

Michelle waited at the door as Kanisha went back to retrieve her sweater from the couches. Francie was not happy.

has to take the initiative and explain how the bank works to a second person. This can be particularly difficult for a village woman. She often has a difficult time convincing her friends—who are likely to be terrified, skeptical, or forbidden by their husbands to deal with money—but eventually a second person, impressed by what Grameen has done for another household, will take the leap of joining the group. Then the two will go out and seek out a third member, then a fourth, and a fifth."

If this system works so well for these women, with seemingly limited resources and knowledge, there is no reason why it will not work for you! So start with what you know. Regardless of your economic or social standing, you need to find the common thread that weaves through your group and brings you the outcomes you desire.

DREAM TEAM AT A GLANCE

If you are doing a formal Dream Team, you definitely want to have a structure, especially for inviting and accepting new members.

Before a Mastermind Group, Broad Squad, or Guy Tribe can grow, each candidate should complete an introductory application or eligibility questionnaire.

A sample of eligibility questions:

1. Are you willing and able to commit to helping others reach their goals?
2. Are you committed to yourself and your goals?
3. What has happened in your life to allow this commitment at this time?
4. What is your greatest passion?
5. Are you willing to do what it takes to achieve your ideal life?
6. Do you have short- and long-term plans or goals?
7. Will you commit to weekly meetings at the same day and time?
8. Is recognition important to you?
9. Are you thankful?
10. If you had a million dollars, what would you do?

"That girl needs to learn some manners."

"Don't we all," Michelle said. "So, did you make a decision on the Van Ness property?"

"Yes, I did," Francie said as she headed into the back parking lot to join the others. "I decided it's not a good time for me to buy property."

Lisa sat between Lei Kim and Kanisha in the backseat while Francie sat in the passenger seat. Michelle was behind the wheel and driving faster than normal. The drive to the edge of town took longer than the promised ten minutes, but Michelle didn't care. She was through playing around and was ready to draw a line in the sand.

When she pulled onto a dirt road, the Range Rover bounced from one bump in the road to another.

"You think now would be a good time to tell us where we're going?" Lisa asked. Michelle didn't answer. She kept her eyes on the twisting road ahead. The trees became more and more dense, choking off the moon, which had begun its slide from full to crescent. The Range Rover finally slowed in a clearing.

"Okay, we're here. Everyone out," Michelle said with her foot on the brake.

"Michelle? I have heels on," Francie said.

"That's okay."

"Very *expensive* heels," Francie said to clarify.

"That's okay. It's not another hike. We're just going to gather in the lights of the car so we can see each other. I'll explain everything."

As Francie and Kanisha stepped out first, Michelle turned to Lisa in the backseat. "Shut the door."

11. What are your three most important assets, talents, and skill sets?
12. Who are the ten best make-it-happen people that you know?
13. What are your three greatest weaknesses? (Someone else in the group may be strong where you feel you are weak.)
14. What skill have you acquired that will benefit the group?
15. What skill do you need that someone else may be able to offer?

While you may come up with your own decisions or mandates for your group, there are a few standard guidelines that you will want to follow.

The average group works best with no more than six individuals. Muhammad Yunus limits his microcredit groups to only five. It takes time to share, and keeping the group numbers relatively low allows time for everyone.

You will want to meet each week either live, by phone, or by teleconference. If you are meeting live, find somewhere comfortable, well lit, and spacious enough for everyone to be able to interact with ease.

During the meeting, have each member update the group on what has happened since the last meeting, including any problem or opportunity the member has experienced. Have each member ask for whatever resources he or she may need at this time.

One of the first tasks in forming a group is to come up with guidelines and bylaws. Here are some sample Dream Team ground rules from a sample North American group.

1. **Mission statement**: The group must establish a related objective/purpose/goal/ mission—a reason for its existence.

2. **Invitation**: To invite a higher source to be a part of the group.

3. **Acceptance**: No group member at any time will disrespect or put down another member's shared ideals, thoughts, or opinions. Members are to be polite and courteous toward each other while sharing their thoughts. No interruptions or other discussions while one member is speaking.

4. **Support**: Individual group members are to provide support and encouragement, and lift each other up. They are to be positive with one another, not negative, and provide constructive comments.

"Why?" Lisa asked, staring back at Michelle.

"Lisa, shut the door."

"You're going to leave them here, aren't you?"

"If you'd like to join them, now's your chance," Michelle said with a steely gaze.

Lisa didn't move and she didn't shut the back door of the car either. It was another standoff, but Michelle wasn't in the mood for Lisa right now. Her eyes narrowed, and without so much as a word to Lisa or a look forward, she jerked the car into reverse and stomped on the brake. The back door slammed shut. Michelle quickly hit the auto-lock button and jerked the Ranger Rover forward. Francie and Kanisha stepped out of the way and Michelle rolled the window partially down. The dust from the dirt road drifted past the headlights like a San Francisco fog.

"You can't leave me here with her!" Kanisha said to Michelle.

"Michelle? What is this?" Francie demanded.

"This? This is a Broad Squad road trip."

"A broad what?" Kanisha stepped closer to the window, which was rolled down only halfway.

"Broad Squad. It's the new name of our group. Kind of catchy, don't you think?" Michelle replied. "And a road trip is reserved for members who aren't willing to communicate with each other. So if you two can't work together to get back home, then we'll have to reconsider the membership of the Broad Squad." Michelle turned to Lei Kim for effect. "I sure like the new name."

Lei Kim smiled, looking a bit confused as to what she should say, if anything.

Michelle turned back to Kanisha and Francie. "So, ladies, we'll be meeting tomorrow night. If you don't kill each other in the meantime, we'll see you at seven o'clock at the Heartlight. Have fun," she said as she rolled up the window and drove away.

5. **Communication:** Each member must be open and honest and fully communicate his or her wants, needs, and desires in order for the group to help the member meet his or her goals.

6. **Organization:** Establish the following:

Facilitator. The group must designate a group leader whose job is to be the spokesperson for the group, to facilitate the meetings and provide guidance and direction for a set term determined by the group.

Recorder. The group should designate a note taker or secretary who will record notes from each meeting. This person will e-mail them to each member.

Missing-in-action caller. The group should designate a person who will call any missing members on the day of the meeting.

Scheduler. The group should designate a separate person to schedule the weekly conference calls and reminder on the day of the meeting by e-mail or phone.

7. **Closer synergy:** In order to create faster bonding, the group may experiment with one-on-one calls with different members and face-to-face group meetings.

8. **Monetary commitment:** No significant money is required to join the group. If money or costs are incurred for operating the group, strict, clear guidelines as to the use of the money and who will be accountable will be formed.

What will be the rules that you come up with for your group?

The guiding principle behind any Mastermind Group is that you can believe for others what they cannot fully believe for themselves.

After a meeting the members will feel an elevated sense of well-being, a feeling of being connected to a higher spiritual source. A new energy will flow through their minds and hearts.

Try this virtualization now to get into your heart space and imagine your ideal Dream Team.

I have a dream.
I have attracted my ideal right team.

"Michelle, you can't do this!" Lisa exclaimed.

"Do you think they'll be okay?" Lei Kim added with growing concern.

"That's up to them."

Lisa turned and watched the bewildered faces of Francie and Kanisha disappear in the distance as the car drove away.

In my mind, I am attracting always the best and the brightest dream
members. Together they make my life and everyone else's better
and better and better.

I have a team.
We meet regularly live, by phone, by webinars.

My Dream Team helps me make my dreams come true.

My T.E.A.M. means Together Everyone Achieves Miracles.
We are excited and delighted to get together.
Our every encounter stimulates breakthroughs.
We discuss problems and "plus" them into moneymaking opportunities.
We bolster each other's spirit with feelings of what's possible.
No matter what the mountain-like problem is, we feel we can conquer
it and make it a molehill.

With my Dream Team's support, I feel like David fighting my Goliaths.
I know I will win when I begin.

Together, we will help make our individual world and the collective
world work ever better, now and into the future.

THE BROAD SQUAD

Once you form one successful group you will probably form others.

We both travel extensively and are involved in several Mastermind
Groups around the world. As you learn and practice procedures you will
form alliances with other successful individuals in specialty fields. They
will work with you and together will guarantee future success from the beginning of every one of your endeavors.

Jillian's Broad Squad is composed of women in various fields across
the globe. She has invited women who are in the fields of real estate, law,
medicine, education, the arts, politics, finances, philanthropy, fitness, and
family, just to name a few.

9

The Road Ahead

You Never Know What You Might Discover About Yourself

Francie and Kanisha glared at each other as the fading taillights washed over their faces. Both were wondering how they were going to get out of here—and why this was happening to them.

Kanisha's eyes searched her surroundings. Darkness, everywhere she looked. There was the moonlight, of course, which at this point was just a distant glow because of the trees that lined the small dirt road. She was in the middle of nowhere. While her concern for her situation was obvious, her mind began to drift to her daughter. Surely Michelle would handle things, she thought, but Kanisha couldn't get Faith out of her mind. The predicament before her somehow caused her love for her daughter to grow even greater than it had been before, if that was possible.

Francie, on the other hand, wasn't thinking about anyone but herself. Her mind was racing. She looked down at her shoes, wondering why she'd chosen these particular shoes to wear tonight. If she'd known she was going hiking again, surely she would've chosen something more appropriate. Francie took pride on making good wardrobe choices, but this had to be the worst choice to date. Her eyes lifted to the trail ahead, where the red taillights were now mere dots in the far-off distance. Suddenly the dots began to glow; Michelle had braked. Perhaps Michelle was satisfied that she'd made her point and

Her Broad Squad has a mission statement with some very clear guidelines, including a 24/7 rule.

She gives a very personal explanation of the 24/7 rule below:

One night, I was confronted by the rising fever of one of my children. As many of you know, this happens often in small children, so I didn't really become alarmed until it reached 105 degrees at 2:00 A.M. I couldn't reach my doctor, the pediatric nurse was not returning my calls, and the ER at our hospital was spilling over with victims from a massive fire. So what's a mother to do but to call the medical branch of her Broad Squad? One in particular: the pediatrician in New York City.

Out of bed she popped, and had me download the symptoms (which were not only just a fever, but also some other odd things); she then got on the line with her pediatric Broad Squad (as she too had formed her own due to my constant encouragement). Thirty minutes later I had a conference call going with two other pediatricians and two Broad Squad members. You should always set up an outside conference call number regardless of whether you are in business or not. It has become invaluable to me.

After many different theories were batted around, one of the doctors told me to scour my son's entire body, looking for what might be a tick.

Though I thought this a bit far-fetched, she was right! I found a tick behind Nick's ear. She then told me to get some toothpaste and suffocate the tick by covering it completely in the goo. It worked. The tick fell off. Within hours Nick was doing better and his own pediatrician put him on some medication early that morning. The good news is that the tick had not been fastened on him for too long, which could have manifested into full-fledged Lyme disease! There's nothing that a little toothpaste and a handful of some broads can't fix.

We shared this story with you because it is important to note that your Dream Team, Broad Squad, Guy Tribe, or whatever you end up calling it is crucial to your entire well-being. It is not just about finding funding, closing the next deal, or making your million dollars. There is more at stake.

would be coming back for them. But when the lights disappeared to the left, Francie knew Michelle wasn't coming back. Without saying a word, Francie started down the trail, her heels crunching on the trail.

"I wouldn't walk in those shoes if I was you," Kanisha said, following after her.

"You aren't me."

"I said if I was!"

"Do me a favor—don't talk to me."

"Suit yourself."

"I will."

"Good."

"Good."

If they weren't so physically different, one would have to guess these two women were somehow long-lost siblings, catching up on years of much-needed arguing.

"Why are you such a bitch to me?" Kanisha blurted out.

"Because I don't like people like you," Francie shot back, snapping more than talking as she struggled with a rocky section of the trail.

"Oh, so you have a problem with black people, is that it?"

"Why is it that you people think if someone has a problem with you, you immediately draw the conclusion that it's because you're black? I don't like you because I don't like people who use other people, and you are obviously using Michelle!"

"You people? See there, you said it again," Kanisha said, laughing. "Wow, that's kind of funny. I didn't take you for being a racist, but you *are* white, and you *are* from Texas."

"And I didn't take you for having a victim complex either. Honey, if that's the case, that's your problem, not mine."

"I ain't got no problem," Kanisha said defensively.

Your Dream Team is the missing link in a life of optimum abundance—mind, body, and heart.

As Jillian's Broad Squad helped her son avoid severe illness and Yunus's solidarity groups save the poor, your Dream Team can be the determining factor in matters of life and death.

For Jillian's complete Broad Squad Mission Statement, visit www .cashinaflashthebook.com.

And one other thing to note: since your Dream Team is about maximizing your relationships and growth, negative, selfish, critical, and demanding attitudes will destroy your Dream Team. Do not settle for less than your highest standard.

We grow from the people and the projects that we encounter. The better and bigger the projects are, the more we transcend ourselves.

MONEY SOUP

There is an old Grimm fairy tale about travelers who arrive at a village and are not well received. They begin to boil a soup in the center of the village with a large stone in the soup kettle and nothing else. When curious villagers pass by and inquire about the soup, the travelers let on that it is not quite ready and could use some more flavor. One by one, the villagers begin to bring different things to season the soup. The end result is an overflowing pot of soup for the travelers and the villagers to share.

We want you to create Money Soup.

Consider your Dream Team as the pot for your Money Soup. Each of you can bring a little something—a skill, talent, resource, credential, or belief—to the soup that, when combined, produces something fabulous.

Before you start dropping ingredients into the pot, invite everyone to put on their Money Soup glasses. These glasses will allow all of you to

"You ain't got?"

"Yeah, that's right."

"When are you going to learn that if you talk like an idiot, people will treat you like an idiot? Didn't your mother teach you that?"

"No, lady, my mother taught me how to sell drugs. Is that what you want to hear? Does that somehow make you feel superior to me now? Sorry I wasn't born with a silver spoon in my mouth. Oh wait, that's right. You married money, which makes you worse off than me. Least I know I come from the ghetto. You aren't sure where you come from, *ain't* that right?" Kanisha quickly moved past her on the trail.

Francie remained silent. She hadn't expected to hear so much information from Kanisha. She didn't want to feel sorry for her. "What a nightmare," Francie muttered under her breath. "I'm sorry," Francie finally called out. "I didn't know."

"You didn't know? Gee, I thought you knew everything," Kanisha fired back.

"I never said that."

Kanisha stopped, turned, and walked right up to Francie. "Well, that's how *people like you* make *people like me* feel. You walk around with your nose in the air. Why, 'cause you got money? You're just an old lady with expensive shoes she can't afford."

Francie was actually trembling. She was afraid of Kanisha right at that moment.

As the silence hung between them, a low grunting sound suddenly emerged from the darkness behind Francie.

"What the hell was that?" Kanisha whispered.

Francie stood frozen in her tracks.

The grunting sound came again, but this time it was closer. Francie wanted her feet to start moving, but when she told her legs to step forward, nothing happened. Kanisha's mouth was wide open in fear. She too was unable to move.

see things with a different perspective—one of awareness and abundance.

Align yourself with people whom you want to work with to make a profound difference and let them watch the pot boil over with possibility!

Be purposefully on purpose for something greater and grander and more terrific than yourself.

If you want to observe firsthand the dynamics of a successful Dream Team, enjoy watching one of Mark's early mastermind meetings at www.cashinaflashbook.com/mastermind.

For more tips on developing your own mastermind, download the free e-book *Team: Working Together to Get It Done* from www.cashinaflashthebook.com/gift.

It is our fervent dream to get every person who wants to be motivated, awake, and fully functioning enrolled in a Dream Team or Broad Squad. It will make the world a better, safer, richer, healthier, happier, and more meaningful place to live.

Here is your wax on/wax off assignment. Make a list of twenty people you know who might be interested in forming a Dream Team with you.

Suddenly a dark shadow appeared behind Francie. In the dim moonlight bleeding onto the trail, Kanisha saw a huge black bear, grunting and snorting as it scratched the trail beneath its massive claws. It wasn't happy.

"What is it?" Francie whispered. "Kanisha, what is it?"

Kanisha's lips moved, but nothing came out.

"Kanisha. What is it?" Francie repeated.

"BEAR!" Kanisha finally blurted out as she spun around and ran in the other direction. Francie didn't look back as she followed, her high heels barely touching the ground.

Suddenly, Francie went down hard, turning her ankle in the high heels.

Hearing Francie go down with a thud, Kanisha skidded to a halt and spun around. The bear slowed. The massive beast began to stalk Francie, who was too scared to turn and face her assailant. Kanisha's heart jumped through her chest when she got a good look at the huge animal. "Oh my God, what am I going to do?" she whimpered as the bear moved in even closer. Grunting and huffing, it was a nightmare realized.

With her knees bloody and her legs tangled beneath her, Francie slowly turned her head as the large bear rose onto its hind legs, announcing its superiority with a loud roar. Amidst the fear rushing throughout her body like a raging river, Francie felt sure this was the end. Her vision blurred for a second and the images before her slid into slow motion.

Kanisha screamed for her to get to her feet, but Francie couldn't hear anything over her own heartbeat. She turned back to the bear and watched it open its mouth. Saliva slid from its jagged teeth like a monster in a horror movie. But this wasn't a movie. It was real life.

PART FOUR

Rapid Riches

Suddenly, Francie wasn't afraid anymore. Faced with the situation before her, all she could feel was a sense of peace. Time seemed to slow nearly to a stop.

Out of nowhere, the giant bear suddenly began to flinch, again and again. It landed on all fours and bellowed. Finally snapping back into real time, Francie looked up and saw Kanisha firing rocks at the bear like Cy Young winner Greg Maddux striking out batters. Picking up rocks and throwing in one motion, Kanisha moved closer and closer toward the bear, which finally turned and scampered into the cover of darkness.

Firing a few rocks into the darkness for good measure, Kanisha bent down next to Francie and ripped off her high heels. Kanisha quickly found a large rock and hammered the high heels like a blacksmith shaping a horseshoe. In two lethal strokes, the heels broke off at the base of the sole, transforming the expensive shoes into a pair of flats. Kanisha dropped the rock to the ground.

"Are you okay?" Francie asked her.

"Am *I* okay?" Kanisha repeated with a shaky laugh as she put Francie's shoes back on her feet.

"Yes. Are you okay?" Francie asked again.

"I'm cool, but we gotta get moving. That thing's bound to come back," Kanisha said, keeping an eye over her shoulder. She finished putting Francie's shoes on her feet. "There. That oughta be easier."

"Thank you," Francie said.

"Can you walk?"

"I think so."

"Good, because it's probably the time for us to get outta here as fast as possible," Kanisha said, helping Francie to her feet. Kanisha turned to start down the trail, but Francie halted briefly and took Kanisha's hand.

14

YOUR PERSONAL WHEEL OF FORTUNE: CONVERT YOUR IDEAS INTO CASH

Everyone can be great, because everyone can serve.
—MARTIN LUTHER KING JR.

Imagine yourself standing in the Wealth Kitchen. You are ready to cook yourself one of the recipes to riches. You have the three major ingredients in the proper amounts in front of you ready to be combined:

Generous portions of Wow Now. You have an image of the richer lifestyle you're trying to create for yourself. You put a copy of that picture in front of you to remind you constantly of what you're trying to cook. You remind yourself of your past successes. You know you can do this.

Ample quantities of Inner Winner. You just know that this recipe is the right one for you at this time in your life. You're ready. More important, you are passionate about accomplishing it. You can hardly sleep at night. You want it. Nothing is going to distract you.

A well-selected Dream Team. You've brainstormed with your team a handful of business opportunities based upon your current knowledge, skills, talents, gifts, and passions. You're ready to narrow this list down to the *one* high-profit, high-probability cash-generating idea.

You're anxious to become a *very, very* profitable servant.

Profitable servant. That's not an oxymoron. The words *profit* and *servant* go together magnificently. A motto for the Rotary International organization for the last hundred years says it all: "They profit most who serve best."

We heartily agree. How do you profitably serve best?

"What's wrong?" Kanisha asked quickly.

"Thank you."

Kanisha smiled. "You'd've done the same for me."

"No. I'm embarrassed to say I wouldn't have," Francie said with great humility.

"That's okay. I'm used to taking care of myself."

"No. It's not okay. And I'm sorry about that. I'm sorry for being a bitch."

"Hey, it's your nature."

"Yes. I guess it is," Francie said with a laugh as another moment of recognition passed between them. Kanisha smiled and leaned forward a touch.

"While this little kumbaya moment we have goin' on here is cool and all, we still got us a bear out there wantin' to take a bite outta your ass."

"My ass? What about yours?"

"Girl, I don't know if you noticed or not, but that bear didn't seem to like the dark meat."

For the first time since they met, the two women laughed together. There was a new look between them. Despite what Michelle had said about there being no room for friendship in the group, the look between them was one of a beginning friendship. It was still very different and volatile, but they were now friends nonetheless.

"How'd you learn to do that?" Francie asked.

"Girlfriend, when you spend time on the streets, you learn to adapt quickly or you die. Gotta throw whatever you can get your hands on to keep away the bad guys."

"No, I mean, the shoes."

"Same reason. Gotta take what life gives you."

There are two primary ways to profit: (1) find value, and (2) create value.

In the movie *The Sixth Sense*, Haley Joel Osment said, "I see dead people." Enlightened entrepreneurs can just "see opportunity." Hidden. Everywhere. In this world, some people are good at sports. Some are good at music. Some are good at managing other people. And some people are good at spotting ways to profit.

They're good at spotting value—how to improve existing products, services, and information. They find it easy to come up with ways to make things cheaper, faster, more exciting, or more interesting—more valuable. They make everything they touch better and carve out a slice of profit for themselves by improving things.

The billionaire Sir Richard Branson wouldn't be a billionaire today if he hadn't spotted some hidden value and exploited it. The genesis of Virgin Records, Virgin Atlantic airlines, and now over two hundred other Virgin companies worldwide was a small student magazine, called *Student*, run by the cash-strapped young entrepreneur. As he describes it in his book *Screw It, Let's Do It*:

> *I do keep my eyes and ears to the ground and saw how teenagers spent most of their disposable income on records. When the [British] government abolished the Retail Price Maintenance Agreement—the cartel that fixed prices—record shops didn't cut prices. I instantly saw a gap and ran an ad for cut-price mail-order records in* Student. *The response was incredible. I didn't know it, but that was the launch of Virgin. We handed out leaflets for mail-order records and almost overnight, we were getting sacks full of orders containing checks and even cash.*

What Branson did is called "finding value."

Other "profitable servants" are especially gifted at creating value. They think up unique, different, new ways to serve people. They invent products. The billionaire Steve Jobs created a whole new industry of personal computers that has blessed the lives of millions. Back in 1976 when he and Steve Wozniak were launching Apple in their garage, all

"I think maybe it's time we change that. What do you think?" Francie asked.

"Sounds good to me."

They began to make their way down the trail.

"What should we tell the others about our little adventure?"

"I have an idea about that," Francie said with a smile.

they had was their passion for electronics and the dream of creating something "insanely great." It's that same passion that has created a new digital music industry with the iPod and iTunes. He made another fortune by finding value with the iPhone.

Have you ever had a profitable idea? Even a million-dollar idea? Do you ever wonder what it would be like to turn your ideas into cash? Have you ever had an urge to flip a piece of real estate (find value), or come up with a unique product (create value)? Whether you help make incremental improvements to the stuff around you, or whether you create brand-new stuff to bless the world, you're a profitable servant.

WHAT DRIVES ENTREPRENEURS TO FIND BETTER WAYS TO PROFIT?

You love to create products/services/ideas because it's who you are. You don't need to be motivated to do it. You can't *not* do it! It's why you breathe. It's why you get up in the morning. It's deeper than desire. It's your essence. It's your *why*.

If you want to be a profitable servant, find something you love to do—that is part of your ultimate why. That is the center of your business. That fuels your business.

For example, Allyson Ames has been making pastries since she was five. In her late teens she started Wonderland Bakery with her mother, Sondra. They're passionate about it. If you have any doubt, just go to their website: www.wonderlandbakery.com. The treats look so delicious you want to order them immediately. In three short years they went from zero to selling millions of dollars' worth of "wonderlicious" baked goods! They'll be doing this for the rest of their lives—and make a fortune doing it. That is the heart of their business.

THREE DELICIOUS RECIPES FOR RICHES

As an entrepreneur, you have three major categories of things to create and sell: products, services, and information.

10

The Beginning

"Getting Up from Here!"

From the looks of the dark puffy clouds that began to form over town just before lunchtime, the storm moving off the Rockies was no longer a rumor. It was indeed coming. "High winds and buckets of rain" was how the local weatherman described it during the morning forecast. Raincoats and rubber boots hit the sidewalks just after four-thirty as people began to head home early. It wasn't like there was a hurricane approaching or anything; people just liked to be off the roads when the Rockies delivered the weather, because you never knew what you might get.

The energy of the three kids running around the store almost knocked Lisa and Michelle over, but it was a good energy, the kind they needed in the group—the energy of youth and the joy of being at play in life. Michelle knew she would have to reel them in a bit if they were going to have a productive Broad Squad meeting tonight, but as long as they weren't breaking anything, she let them carry on.

Every so often the kids would accompany Michelle and Lisa to the Heartlight for book club meetings and gatherings. Michelle liked the idea of having the kids in the store for adult gatherings. She thought the kids' energy was a great reminder for everyone to not take life too seriously, and the kids benefited by watching how adults interacted in a social setting. She felt this was an important element to becoming a well-rounded kid. Hannah said it was like show-and-tell when

Products

Products are physical objects such as cars, shoes, pencils, and so on. You get the idea. It's all about buying and selling material things—or, as someone once said, the hard, lumpy objects such as the things that occupy a home, including the house itself. In other words, stuff. Comedian George Carlin used to have a monologue about stuff. He would say, "Your house is just a pile of your stuff with a cover on it. . . . Your house is just a place to keep your stuff while you go out and get more stuff." Fortunes are made by selling "stuff" to people.

Services

A service is when someone does something *for* you. A service is when you rent someone else's know-how, time, talent, or skill and your product gets improved. For example, you have a car—a product—but your car is dirty

Michelle brought them anywhere because Michelle often bragged about them. The reason they had to come for tonight's Broad Squad meeting was because Justine had biology class and wasn't available for babysitting duties.

Michelle was worried, though. When she'd woken up this morning, there was no sign of Kanisha, and Faith was gone too. And it was five after seven and Francie wasn't there yet, either. She couldn't help thinking that her road trip idea had backfired, but if that was the case, so be it. The group had to learn how to work together despite their differences. It would be a group of unconditional support or nothing at all.

Nicky had been filming his mom and her friends secretly, from behind the shelves of the kids' section of the store. He'd started out thinking it'd be like a mix of surveillance footage and music video, but he was getting bored. There wasn't enough action. Grown-ups' meetings were often like that. So he turned the camera onto Hannah, sitting behind him in the middle of the floor with Lisa's son, Russell, playing a board game. While this shot wasn't a chase scene or something dramatic, it was better than a bunch of old people sitting around talking, he thought. As Russell hammed it up in front of the camera, Hannah secretly moved her game piece two spaces forward when Russell wasn't looking. Nicky lowered the camera.

"Hannah, what did Mom say about stuff like that?"

"I didn't do anything," she said, acting innocent.

"Do you wanna go to the videotape evidence?" he asked, flipping open the viewfinder of the camera. "Mom said that how we do anything is how we do everything."

"I thought you were making your new movie," she replied as she moved her game piece back to its original spot.

"This is boring," Nicky said, lying back on the floor to stare at the galaxy system Michelle had painted on the ceiling.

so you take it to the car wash. They wash your car and provide you with a shiny, clean car. They applied their know-how (skill) plus time (labor) and gave you a clean result.

If you were a service entrepreneur, you would use your skills to do things for other people that they can't or don't want to do for themselves. For example, in our homes, we hire lots of people to do services for us— from the maid, the landscaper, and the pool cleaner, to the pest control guy. When things break, we call up repair people of all varieties—AV technicians, appliance repairmen, handymen of all sorts, locksmiths, telephone answering services, electricians, carpet cleaners. Delivery people bring things to the door of our house—flowers, FedEx and UPS packages. When we need to be delivered to the airport we can call a limo driver. People do services for each other and get paid for it such as accountants and travel agents.

One form of service is entertainment. We watch skillful people perform—sports, music, humor. We pay for this service. The more skillful you are, the more money you make. Politicians are service providers. When you get paid to use your skill, you are providing a valuable service. What skills do you possess that someone might want to hire you for? One of the fastest ways to earn profit is to find someone who needs your skill and to sell your skill to them for immediate cash flow.

But this also creates a serious problem: you have to be there to provide the service. For example, an attorney or doctor can earn a large income, but if that person stops working, the income also stops. We like businesses where you can earn money when you aren't there—residual businesses where you earn money while you sleep.

In addition, service businesses are also very employee-centric. A service business is a people business, and you can only scale up by hiring and managing more people. We prefer owning businesses where you can make multiple sales quickly and easily. I can sell ten thousand widgets with one telephone call. But it's more difficult to sell ten thousand carpet cleanings.

Because of these restrictions, we won't be spending much more time in this book about this form of entrepreneurship. Only seriously consider this option if it's your purpose in life to render this type of hands-on service. If that's where you get your buzz, then go for it. God is smiling on you. You've

"You can say that again," Russell agreed.

"We could spy on 'em," Hannah said, sitting up.

"Okay," said the boys, perking up with excitement. One by one, they crawled around the row of shelves to get into position.

Nicky turned on the camera, thinking about whether he would give Hannah a producer credit for the film if something interesting happened. He decided to wait to see the footage, because if he said something now, Hannah would probably want to direct, and that he couldn't allow. "Everyone thinks they know how to direct," he said under his breath as he crawled up closer with the camera, like a soldier moving into position for a shot at the enemy.

Lisa was confronting Michelle about her choice to leave Francie and Kanisha the night before. "What if they got hurt out there? Did you think about that? You're going to be responsible, you know."

"Lisa, we could sit here all night and argue about this. What happened last night was supposed to happen. We have to learn how to work together, or this group will never work. And I refuse to put my attention on the fear of anything going wrong."

"Why?" Lei Kim asked, sitting up.

"Because when you do that, you call forth the very thing that might go wrong."

"They sure aren't here, so something isn't right. Aren't you worried in the least?" Lisa fired back.

Just then there was a knock at the front door of the Heartlight. Thinking it was Francie and Kanisha, Michelle spun her attention around to the doors, but it wasn't them. It was Mayor Wilson, smiling from the sidewalk outside the locked doors.

"Oh shoot," Michelle said.

found your right livelihood. The two of us earn income from public speaking and training. It's part of our purpose in life. Thus, we spend a lot of personal time on these activities—even if doesn't create residual income.

Information

You buy information when you pay for someone else's knowledge. That person teaches you how to do something. You study knowledge that someone else has organized for you to learn.

Information products generally deal with packaged how-to information. How to start a business. How to keep a marriage together. How to lose weight. How to do anything. This information can be shared in books, seminars, special reports, websites, teleconferences, mentoring, one-on-one coaching . . . the list is endless. Everyone has an internal bank account of knowledge and skill. What do you know that others might be willing to pay you to teach them? By sharing this knowledge and skill with others, you can earn substantial profit—sometimes very quickly, as we'll show you in the next chapter.

YOUR PSIs

The first step is to take an inventory of your marketable products, services, and information. In other words, what products, services, and information

"What's he doing here?" Lisa asked.

"I forgot, we had a date tonight. Give me a second," Michelle said, crossing to the doors. Smiling at him through the glass of the antique doors, she turned the lock and stepped onto the sidewalk to join him.

"Am I early?" he asked with a smile.

"No, Brady, you're right on time. I'm sorry, I know we had a date tonight."

"You okay?"

"Yes. And I'm so sorry, but something came up. Something good, but . . . I meant to call, but the day just got away from me."

Gesturing to the group in the bookstore, he said, "I thought you only had meetings on Tuesday nights." He was obviously disappointed.

"We do, but . . ." Michelle said, offering an apologetic smile. "The girls wanted to keep going."

"That's okay, I understand."

"Yeah?"

"How's it going?"

"Well," Michelle said with a slight laugh, "I took a pretty big risk last night, and I think it might've backfired."

As she said this, Michelle saw a pair of headlights round the corner up the street. They slowed and parked under the streetlight at the end of the block.

"Nothing ventured, nothing gained, right?" the mayor said, taking her hand.

When the headlights shut off, Michelle recognized the car. It was Francie. She always parked her car under the streetlight, Michelle remembered. Stepping from the car and setting the alarm, Francie walked toward them.

"Francie," Michelle said, acknowledging her as she approached.

do you possess right now that you can sell? These are your *own* PSIs . . . not someone else's. In other words, if we were to send you out into the world either face-to-face or online, what do you have that you could sell? What skill do you possess that you could sell? What information do you possess that you could sell?

As an entrepreneur, problem solver, and creator, you're looking for people who have problems that you were born to solve. You can hardly wait for one of your creations—your PSI solutions—to be of use to someone else. The profit you earn is nice . . . but the reason to create it wasn't solely money. That's just the side benefit. You're an entrepreneur and you love to create solutions.

ROBERT ALLEN: I first bought real estate for myself as an investment. Real estate was the *product* product. I loved it. Couldn't get enough. Then I became a Realtor and learned how to sell real estate to other people. Selling was my *service* product. I didn't love it as much. So I created my own real estate investing seminars to teach other people how to do what I knew how to do. Teaching was my *information* product. I'm absolutely passionate about it. I've made money in all three areas. But teaching is my passion.

MARK VICTOR HANSEN: I started a company marketing geodesic domes (*product* product). I loved it and was doing well until the oil embargo of the late 1970s. The business went bust. I came up with an idea for a book (*information* product) and sold twenty thousand copies as I spoke to audiences as a public speaker (*service* product). I still earn enjoyable profits speaking to audiences all around the world. Then, with Jack Canfield, I came up with *Chicken Soup for the Soul* (*information* product). Fantastic!

If you open up the Yellow Pages, you'll find thousands of businesses. Most of them can be categorized as products, services, or information:

"Michelle, Mr. Mayor," Francie replied, going inside the store without another word.

"Everything okay?" the mayor asked.

"Hard to tell with Francie, but . . . she's here. That says something," Michelle said. "I'm really sorry about this. Can I take a rain check?"

"Of course," he said with a smile. She stared fondly into his eyes like she wanted to say something.

"What is it?" he asked.

"Why are you so understanding?"

He laughed. "Is that a bad thing?"

"No, it's just . . ." She paused for a second. "It's been a long time since I've experienced that."

He smiled and took her hand. "We have plenty of time. Not to worry."

"How about I check with Lisa and see if she can take the kids tomorrow night? We can make dinner and—"

"Sounds wonderful," he said before she could finish.

Although he had yet to say the words, she could tell he was in love with her. Normally, this would cause Michelle to run in the other direction, but she knew deep in her heart she felt the same way about him.

"Then it's a date?" she said.

"A date. Sounds official," he replied with a smile as he dug for his keys in his pocket.

Michelle kept looking deeply into his beautiful blue eyes. There was a longing in her soul for a feeling like this, and she now knew why she had resisted dating for so long after Gideon died. It wasn't just out of respect for Gideon or a need to mourn the loss. It was the right choice because she'd felt something special coming her way. It was this anticipatory feeling that assured her everything was going to be

PRODUCTS	SERVICES	INFORMATION
(Stuff)	*(Doing stuff for you)*	*(Teaching you how to do stuff)*
A Automobiles	Automobile detailing	Automobile driving school
B Beauty products	Beauty salon	Beauty college
C Computers	Computer repair	Computer training
D Dental floss	Dentist	Dental assistant school

Go to the Yellow Pages yourself and see if you can complete this chart.

E _____   _____   _____

F _____   _____   _____

G _____   _____   _____

WHO WILL BE THE END USER OF THE PRODUCTS, SERVICES, AND INFORMATION THAT YOU CREATE?

Will your PSI be sold directly from you (as a businessperson) to customers? That's called B to C, business to consumer.

Will you sell your PSI to other businesses? That's called B to B, business to business.

Will you become part of the network marketing industry and market products directly to consumers with the opportunity to have your customers become business partners with you? That's called B to B², business-to-business marketers. (You're not only selling nutritional products, you're selling nutrition businesses.)

Perhaps your PSI will be sold to philanthropies to assist them in raising money—business to philanthropies. Our friend Wayne Dyer sells his information products through PBS and helps them raise money for their ongoing programming such as *Sesame Street*.

B to C	Business to consumer
B to B	Business to business
B to B²	Business to business marketers
B to P	Business to philanthropy

okay. The man standing before her was the evidence of that feeling. She finally leaned forward and kissed him. While it was only their third kiss, Michelle packed what seemed like a year's worth of romantic dates into the kiss. He wrapped his strong arms around her, pulling her in close. In his arms, she felt safe . . . comforted and loved. She could spend hours in his arms, something she looked forward to very soon.

The sound of heels clicking on the sidewalk pulled her attention from their passionate embrace. It was Kanisha. She was wearing a stunning black dress with red high heels. Faith was in the small carrier Michelle had given her the day she came home from the hospital.

"Hello," Kanisha said, offering a confident smile. "I hope I'm not too late."

"Not at all. You're right on time," Michelle said, her mouth hanging open.

"You okay?" Kanisha asked.

"Yeah, I'm great," Michelle replied.

"That's good."

"You look very nice tonight, Kanisha," Mayor Wilson said with a smile.

"Thank you, Mr. Mayor," Kanisha said, and went inside.

"What's going on?" the mayor asked Michelle.

"I'm not really sure, but I should get inside and find out." She turned to face him again. "Thank you for supporting me in this. It means a lot."

"Haven't you figured it out yet?" he asked. She looked at him with an inquisitive smile. "I'd do anything for you," he said, kissing her lightly on the cheek. She wasn't sure how he did it, but every time he kissed her, she felt giddy as a schoolgirl. She liked the feeling. In fact, she loved it.

So your wheel of fortune looks like the illustration below. This is the why, who, what, how, when, and where of your business:

Your goal as an entrepreneur is to scan your own mind and heart and find opportunities to create profitable PSIs from the things you're passionate about. However, one of the richest caches of profit from your own experience is often in the least likely area—problems.

Before you choose your PSI path, let's make sure you realize how many millions are found in the problems that have been plaguing you for perhaps your whole life.

Here's your wax on/wax off assignment before you turn to the next chapter. Make a list of the ten greatest challenges in your life at this time.

CASH IN A FLASH

Locking the door behind her, Michelle turned around as Kanisha crossed from the office.

"She sleeping?" Michelle asked Kanisha as she looked at Faith.

"Yes. She'll be out for a while."

"It's really good to see you," Michelle said, smiling. "You look amazing."

"Shall we get started?" Kanisha replied. Michelle could see Kanisha was purposely keeping her in the dark as to what exactly had happened last night, but Michelle was game to play along. Whatever it was, Michelle thought, Kanisha was a different person somehow. Sure, the dress did a lot for her appearance, but there was something different about her. She stood taller. She walked with confidence. Somehow, overnight, Kanisha had grown up.

When everyone was settled on the couches, Michelle immediately turned to Francie and Kanisha.

"So?"

"So?" Francie echoed.

"Anything you two want to talk about? About last night, I mean?"

Kanisha and Francie simply smiled at each other like two Cheshire cats.

"Nope," Kanisha said, straightening the folds on her dress to cover her knees.

"What did we miss?" Francie asked.

Smiling at the obvious success of the road trip idea, Michelle stood up and addressed the group with revived enthusiasm.

"I was explaining to Lisa that with adversity comes enlightenment, and I was about to say how we are either pulled or pushed by

15

TURN YOUR PROBLEMS INTO PROFITS

An entrepreneur is a creator. He/She loves to create. Create what?

Solutions.

Solutions to what?

Problems.

Entrepreneurs love to create and to market those creations to bless the world by solving the world's problems. It's what motivates them. It's their why. It gives them ways to help the world with their talent while, at the same time, generating profits to fund their favorite social causes. That's where the word *profit* comes from—the Latin word *profectus,* as in *pro* (in favor of) + *facere* (to make or to do). You're in favor of making or doing. In other words, you love to create!

Sometimes the quickest way to spot the most profitable problems is to look at the problems you have in your own life. You are on your way to an enlightened future of awareness and wealth. But then something happens. You hit a bump in the road. You know that awareness of yourself, your surroundings, your relationships, and your resources is paramount for you to fulfill your dreams. But there is another level of awareness we need to discuss: problems.

It has become common knowledge that problems are a sign of life. The same could be said for opportunities. What if you started seeing your problems as opportunities? Opportunities in work clothes, maybe.

Easier said than done? We would have to disagree.

Norman Vincent Peale emphasized the importance of problems. He said, "How you think about a problem is more important than the problem itself." Consider that for a moment. How would a slight shift in thinking affect your response to the unexpected?

a vision. I was defending my choice last night because the way you two were going at each other, there was no way a vision could find its way in without a little help. I'm sorry if it was—"

"And I was about to ask Michelle," Lisa interrupted, "why she thought she could play God with other people's lives. What if they'd gotten hurt? Did you ever think about that?"

"Francie? Kanisha? You both seem . . . better than okay. Anything you'd like to share?" Michelle asked, but the two women simply smiled at each other again.

"Oh great, so now we have to sit here and watch the smarmy smiles back and forth like we're back in high school?" Lisa spat.

"Does that make you uncomfortable, Lisa?" Francie asked.

"No."

"Sure seems like it," Kanisha added.

"I was just saying," Lisa muttered defensively.

Lei Kim shook her head.

"Lei Kim? You want to add something here?" Michelle asked her.

"No, it's fine."

"Ladies, I want to reiterate that dialogue is a good thing. Feel free to speak your mind. Nobody's feelings will be hurt, because we all agree this is a place to learn. This is a place to grow, and if the truth hurts, well, then that's something we need to take a look at."

Lei Kim cleared her throat. "I was about to say, and I mean no disrespect to Lisa," she said, turning to face Lisa, "but now you're fighting with Francie because she's smiling? Isn't that what this is about? To find a way back to happiness?"

"I thought this was about making money, and I wasn't fighting with anyone. Why is everyone ganging up on me here?" Lisa replied, now in full defense mode.

"Because you worry more about what other people are doing than what you do."

Go back to your virtual space, where you are clear in your thoughts and intentions. In this realm you are aligned in mind, heart, and body. You are aware and willing to look at things with fresh eyes.

Picture your awareness as a ladder. At the first rung of the ladder is a problem. Problems as problems are negative energy that shut down your spirit. They hold fear, doubt, and anxiety. They stop and stifle your imagination.

A natural reaction to a problem is to seek out comfort. You go and talk to people who will commiserate with you. If this is your usual pattern, it has to stop now.

RISE ABOVE

Do not stay at the level of the problem. Being stuck in security consciousness will not serve you, and you will never create the sustainable income and financial freedom you desire.

We are not saying to take the emotion out of your experience. In fact, emotion often fuels us to make change. But we are saying that your emotion does not need to rule your response. Your feeling nature protects you, but your creative mind will lead you to action.

The goal is to rapidly climb to the top of the ladder. You want to be visionary and create the solution.

Imagine a firefighter who has arrived at the scene of a fire burning in a building, seven stories up. What would happen if she stayed at the bottom of the ladder, unable to act because she was so distraught over what was happening? The fire would continue to burn and possibly spread to more areas.

Would the outcome be significantly different if instead she came up with a plan, sprang into action, and aggressively climbed up? She would save the day!

So why not follow her lead? Be your own hero!

Twenty-five years ago, Teri Gault took matters into her own hands when her family's finances got too tight. As a stay-at-home mom, she got

"That's not true," Lisa retorted.

Lei Kim reached over to Lisa's folder. "May I?"

Lisa shrugged, and Lei Kim opened Lisa's folder. She pulled out two celebrity magazines tucked behind a stack of notes Lisa had taken from their meetings. "Why do you care what a celebrity is having for lunch?"

Lisa scoffed. "You're kidding, right? It's an entertainment magazine. What's the big deal?"

"It's escapism," Michelle pointed out.

"Gee, thanks, Freud. Appreciate the help," Lisa said. "Okay, Michelle, if these magazines are so bad, why do you sell them here in your 'sanctuary,' as you call it? Doesn't that make you something of a hypocrite? I'm tired of sitting here taking all the criticism."

"Selling them and reading them are two different things, Lisa. But you know what?" Michelle thought for a brief second. "You're right. We should stop carrying them altogether."

"Just to make a point? That's stupid. They sell, and correct me if I'm wrong here, but aren't we in the business of selling things? And isn't that the point of this group? Making money, not psychoanalyzing whether or not someone wants to read a magazine? What do you do for fun, read the dictionary?"

"I'm not saying the magazines are bad, but you make a great point."

"Glad to help. Now can we talk about something else?"

"Actually, we're right on topic. Let's stay on you," Michelle answered.

"Let's not and say we did," Lisa said, amusing only herself.

"Let's talk about why you came to work here in the store. You were fired—"

"I was *laid off*, Michelle. We wouldn't want you to spread gossip,

into the habit of cutting coupons for fun when things were comfortable and then, unfortunately, for necessity when her family's situation changed unexpectedly. Realizing there were other people just like her who would appreciate the savings that she worked so hard to find, she opened her own business.

Now running a $12 million business called the Grocery Game, Teri helps other people around the world save time and money and better support their own families through a subscription service that supplies lists and coordinating coupons to maximize savings in stores. She has tens of thousands of members who each save hundreds of dollars a month on their groceries.

Her problem was her solution. And yours can be, too.

When faced with adversity, get with your Dream Team or someone you admire who has an expanded awareness. They will not see your problem as a problem and will help you up the ladder.

Solutions will arise through creativity and enthusiasm, not frustration and aggravation.

IT MAY BE LONELY AT THE TOP

Be prepared, because the higher you climb on the awareness ladder, the fewer people you will find. Many people, even some friends and family members, will stay at the first rung, in security consciousness, because it is safe.

The more success you have and the more you move closer to sustainable wealth and freedom, the more problems and opportunities will surface.

It is incredibly essential for you to rally around your Dream Team during your time of rapid acceleration. Celebrating even minor victories will help balance out the glitches that may arise.

If you feel your personal peer group is not quite as strong as you would like, with the exception of your Dream Team or Broad Squad, you can find higher consciousness in an extended peer group—books, audio programs, online seminars. This way you have access to innovative thinkers and doers whenever you want.

now would we? Being laid off and being fired . . . there's a big difference there." Lisa was feeling the heat of the spotlight.

"Fired, let go, laid off, whatever you want to call it. It's not the point."

"Then please tell me the point."

"The point is you lost your job, which was the universe showing you a new path. Just because the external appearances might not fit into your comfort zone, that doesn't mean that you aren't being led to something higher."

"What does this have to do with what the group is about? My back is up against the wall. I got bills to pay, okay? I thought this was about making money, not whether I read a frickin' magazine or *Think and Grow Rich*. Really, what is the difference?"

"You can't look at it as if your back is against the wall," Michelle said.

"What would you call it, then?" Lisa said, getting emotional, but instead of giving in, she grabbed her purse and started for the door. "I'm outta here."

"Honey, wait," Francie said, rising to stop Lisa. "Running away won't make this any better."

"It's . . . just . . . when you say this stuff, it makes me take a look at my life, and I don't want to." Lisa was crying now.

"And that's a good thing," Francie said. "We've wasted too much time hiding. . . . Please stay."

Drying her eyes, Lisa gathered herself before sitting back down on the couch with the others. She folded her arms. She would stay, but she would be ready to strike back if attacked again.

"Sometimes life can make us feel hopeless," Michelle said, to make Lisa feel at ease. Deep down, she knew that life couldn't do anything to us we didn't allow to happen, but she continued anyway. "We feel helpless, like we have no place to turn. When I was broke

PROBLEMS ARE OPPORTUNITIES;
PROBLEMS ARE SOLUTIONS

What awaits you at the top of the awareness ladder is your true, future fortune. When you are at the first rung, an unexpected problem, it comes down to two critical questions:

1. How will you react and respond?
2. Whom will you talk to for solutions?

Before moving on, take some time to think about how you have handled problems in the past and whom you turn to for advice.

1. What is your usual response to a problem? What is your first reaction?
2. Whom do you go to for comfort/help/ideas? What do they say?
3. How has this strategy served you?

If for some reason a problem appears to be too much for you to handle, use the following exercise to come up with a plan.

1. Write out the problem.
2. Write three outrageous solutions/opportunities.
3. Evaluate each one for practicality and effectiveness.
4. Run your solutions by your Dream Team or a mentor.
5. Pick the best one and set a date to put it into place!

Life provides us with adversity to give us our future abundance, assuming we are aware and paying attention.

Use the following virtualization to help you prepare for and solve any problem.

and about to lose my kids, that's exactly how I felt. But when I look back on it now, I realize that my back wasn't against the wall at all. I was standing in a doorway, a doorway to riches, and all I had to do was change my mind—change my perception of what was happening and what was possible." She paused for a beat. "I guess what I'm trying to say is, our problems are the doorways to our solutions. Francie, if you hadn't faced foreclosure, do you think you would've come up with your idea?"

"No. I would've bought more shoes," Francie said jokingly.

"What's the number this morning?" Michelle asked, eager to hear the latest on Francie's idea.

"Another twenty-five hundred," Francie said with a smile.

"No way." Lisa was amazed at Francie's good fortune. Truth was, however, she was jealous, though she'd never let on. This is how most people looked at rich people, with a sense of jealousy or wishing harm would come to them somehow. Instead of putting her mental energy toward what *she* would do, Lisa was jealous.

"That's great, Francie. And it's good to see you smile about this. You seemed very different yesterday," Michelle said, hoping Francie might finally tell them what had happened last night.

"That's because I was different." She smiled at Kanisha.

"How do you mean?" Michelle asked, sitting down.

"I was ashamed of making the money."

Lisa interjected, "Hey, give it to me. I won't be ashamed."

"Lisa, please. This is a good example for us to talk about. It sounds crazy, but sometimes people think they don't deserve wealth."

"That's because it's . . . embarrassing." Francie took a deep breath. "Not only do I now believe I have been bitter for much of my adult life, I feel like I caused this foreclosure to happen. I was angry. Not at Christopher for dying. I was angry because before this week,

My problems are good.

Saying my problems are good gives me the perspective to solve them and beat them rather than let them beat me. I did not always know or believe that, but I do now.

I realize my problems are a sign of life.

My problems are solvable by me and my Dream Team.

My problems make me stronger, wiser, and more courageous.

My problems and their solution are going to become my future stories. They will help everyone who hears them.

The way to conquer a little problem is to give myself a bigger problem. Seems crazy, yet it works—every time.

Problem solving excites me at the core of my being.

The only people without problems are in a graveyard.

Therefore, I cheerfully accept my problems.

I understand that if everyone could put all their problems in a pool, each of us would ultimately take our problems back. We chose them and are uniquely qualified to solve them.

I like my problems and my problems like me.

I am solution-oriented. I have my mind in the quietude of virtualization knowing that it will find original solutions for me. Every time I go into the state of quiet reverie I know that I am self-sufficient.

I have the answer inside of me. I go inside the secret place of the most high. In here alone, I give myself time to be and comfort to know that every question I ask myself will inevitably get answered.

I ask myself, "What is my most effective way to dash for the cash? Where is my low-hanging fruit? What is tomorrow's moneymaking goal? What multiple sources of income can I most ably pursue? Where are my millions now?"

I cheerfully lull myself to sleep every night repeating one of the above questions or a better question to solve all my problems.

Problems guarantee my future earning power and my results. I am thankful for my problems. I am thankful for my ever-expanding problem solving capabilities. I will vaporize problems. I love turning trash (my problems and others') into cash.

The more I make, the more I make. It feels and is great.

all I really cared about was shopping, the great American pastime, and for what? So I could fit in? So I could own the finest things money could buy?" She paused for a moment. "Last night I realized I've never really done anything with my life. I didn't have to, because Christopher handled our finances and I spent the money. That was our agreement."

Michelle wondered for a moment whether Francine might start crying, but she didn't. While it seemed like a perfect time to let go, Francine's letting go came in the form of empowerment. She was excited for her tomorrow.

"And now how do you feel?" Michelle asked, smiling widely.

"I'm looking for every way possible to monetize my situation. I want to add a zero to each bank deposit," Francie said proudly.

"Problems are our solutions. I'll have to remember that," Lisa said.

"So the problem I have been experiencing with food . . . that might apply here too?" Lei Kim asked, eager to join in.

"Unwrap that for us a bit," Michelle asked, sensing what Lei Kim was trying to do.

"Unwrap?" Kanisha said, looking for help.

"Fancy way to ask someone to explain something further," Francie clarified.

"The problem with my stomach has changed my cooking," Lei Kim began slowly. "And . . ."

"And?" Kanisha prompted her.

"And . . . I have been thinking . . . maybe other people might like the goodies I've been making. I don't know if I could sell them . . . maybe I will try to see if anyone likes these raw food bars before I get too excited."

"No. You should get excited," Michelle quickly put in.

GET OUT OF A LITTLE PROBLEM
WITH A BIG QUESTION

We have said that as you accomplish more and move higher on the awareness ladder there will be fewer people up there with you, but problems (and opportunities!) will increase.

Do not get discouraged.

As you fully surrender to awareness, yes, you will have bigger problems. But with bigger problems, the little (and more frequent) problems will not matter as much.

Why?

It is because *you* have become bigger! You are more equipped to handle anything that comes your way. You have the state of mind, heart, and body along with your Dream Team. You are set.

Bigger problems (and opportunities!) require a different strategy.

We cannot make any presumptions about your current financial situation. But if you are in a state of crisis, where you feel you do not have any resources, we want to give you reassurance that you do have support.

While you may be emotionally stretched due to circumstances outside of your control, mentally you always have the wherewithal within you to move forward.

In 1998, after years of fertility treatments, manicurist Rosie Herman was $75,000 in debt. With the need to make extra money but also stay at home with her newborn twins, she developed an organic nail and hand product in her own kitchen. After six months, she knew she had the right formula when she used the lotion to treat and heal her own dry and damaged skin.

While the business was growing, Rosie used her sister's credit cards to purchase supplies, worked through the night, and traded food for use of her neighbor's computer. All of her efforts led to the creation of the One Minute Manicure and a multimillion-dollar success story.

Remember: your creative mind is there to solve any problem.

So as you juggle the multiple responsibilities, allow yourself the time and space to get centered and rely on your creative mind to lead you.

"It's *your* job to get excited," Francie joined in, "don't you think?"

Michelle got up and wrote two words on the whiteboard:

WOW
NOW

"What's that?" Lei Kim asked.

"Wow Now is the mind's ability to discern what it is we want to do. It's the mental activity, which we often refer to as an idea that wows you. What we want to do is direct that mental energy, the *wow,* and bring it into the *now.* The right now of our lives."

"Wow now?" Lisa asked quietly, more to herself than to anyone else.

"That's right," Michelle said. Just as she was about to continue, out of the corner of her eye she caught a glimpse of the kids spying from behind the bookshelves.

"All right, kids, that's enough. Come in here. I want you all to hear this." Like the expert spies they were, they froze, refusing to surrender their position. But, being the mom that she was, forever engaging her children's desire to be at play, Michelle tiptoed around the shelves and surprised them from behind. They screamed with laughter as she tickled them Then Michelle picked up Hannah and carried her into the group like a sack of potatoes. The boys followed like two thieves walking to a perp lineup.

"Mom! Come on, we don't want to study," Nicky said. "It's no fun."

"We're not studying, we're sharing ideas. You guys are good at that, and I need your help." Russell reluctantly found a place next to his mother while Nicky dragged over a zebra beanbag. Lisa put her arm around Russell and Hannah sat next to Kanisha.

Victoria Knight-McDowell was a second-grade teacher who was constantly catching a cold. In an effort to support and strengthen her own immune system, she began researching and experimenting with different herbal formulas. She tested her creations on family and friends, and when she had her perfect product, she began marketing through her home office. Her all-natural product, Airborne health formula, has made her millions and is the number one cold remedy in the United States.

Regardless of where you may be now—age, career, lifestyle—you can make a plan. Do not be disheartened because you did not start sooner.

Start now.

We have given you the tools to begin the process with little or no monetary expense. It all starts inside of you.

Deborah Rosado Shaw's life changed the day she took a sales call at the umbrella company where she worked. Hired to answer phones, she passed herself off as an account executive and sold over $140,000 worth of product. This massive sale earned her a legitimate sales position, where she continued to excel. She went on to start her own successful companies, Umbrellas Plus, LLC and Dream BIG! Enterprises, and has since become an award-winning entrepreneur and advisor to Fortune 500 CEOs.

You can do it, too.

We want more for you than the status quo. We want you to channel your genius and be, do, and have all that you desire.

GO BIG

There are four currencies that you can use to help you avoid future problems or navigate through them more smoothly.

Relationships

Be in the people business—for, through, and by people—because markets are people.

"I like your dress," Hannah said, looking up at Kanisha.

"Why, thank you, Hannah," Kanisha said, pulling the little girl closer to her.

"What are we doing?" Hannah whispered.

"Right now, we're listening to your mommy. She's really smart."

"I know," Hannah said with a smile.

"Okay. If the Wow Now, the mind, is our mental energy behind an idea, then the Inner Winner, the heart, is the feeling tone of the idea." Michelle began to illustrate on the whiteboard again. "You can have an Inner Winner, the heart energy behind the idea, or the Inner Whiner, which is the energy you expend talking yourself out of an idea."

"Example?" Hannah asked.

"It's like when you say, 'It's too hard. I can't do it. Nobody will like me if I do this,'" Michelle replied.

"Like when I don't want to go to school," Russell piped up.

"Absolutely," Lisa said with a smile.

"That's very good, Russell. The Inner Whiner will defeat us, but the Inner Winner will give us power, propelling us to the success, to the riches, we know in our heart we are deserving of.

"Francie and Lei Kim have tapped in to something that applies to this Inner Winner philosophy that I want us to talk about for a second," Michelle went on. "And that's the hunch, the gut feeling, you get when you feel something good or bad is about to happen." She looked at the kids and rephrased it for their sake. "When they got their ideas, they knew for certain that the decision they made was right." She returned her attention to the adults. "Some people refer to these impressions as your *intuition*." She wrote the word on the board. "Others call it the *sixth sense*, but we're going to call it the Inner Winner. If we want to be more successful, wealthier, happier, and healthier, we need to heed the signals from this Inner Winner.

People are always buying. Get in tune with where the marketplace is going so you can get there first with the products, services, and information that it wants, needs, and will be demanding.

Always have key people on your radar for referrals and connections. Work every day to strengthen your friendships in the workplace and beyond.

Be likable. Are you someone who goes out of their way to acknowledge others? Do you make an effort every day to reach out and share your gifts?

Mobility

Just as you do not want to stay stuck on the first rung of the awareness ladder, similarly you do not want to lock yourself into a product, service, or information business where you are limited to when and where you can go. Now *that* is a problem.

To all of you superachievers and especially supermoms, how thin can you spread yourself before you are no longer there? If you are feeling like you are working as hard as you can and are not moving, know there is another way.

The future of moneymaking is simplicity, outsourcing, innovating, diversifying, and constantly building passive, recurring revenue so you are in control.

You want to have the freedom to be anywhere you choose, when you choose.

Time

Are you efficient or effective? Efficient means you take a lot of action and may or may not get results. Effective means you take definitive result-generating action and get the rewards almost every time.

Everyone has a to-do list, but the vastly more important and neglected list is the to-be list: "be leading edge," "be in use of my full potential in every area of my life," "be fun," "be joyous." What do you want to be?

Francie just went ahead and fleshed the idea out, and look what happened. What I'm saying is any one of you could have a product idea that may reap financial rewards. If you don't try, you won't discover. This may be the most important success tool in our tool kit."

Michelle turned to Nicky on the beanbag. "Nicky, have you ever heard one of your teachers talk about something like this in school?"

"You know they only talk about problems and homework, Mom," Nicky replied.

"That's right. School is all about solving problems. There is little or no focus on teaching us to tap in to our creative expressions. But what I'm saying is that if we want to be successful, everything starts with a mental focus on what *isn't* written on that chalkboard in school.

"Everyone close your eyes for a moment. I want you to think back to a time when you had a strong hunch about something or someone."

"Like wanting a golden retriever?" Nicky said with a laugh.

"Yes, kind of like wanting a golden retriever, Nicky. As if you knew having a dog was going to somehow bring you closer to happiness. Which is not far off from what we're talking about here." Nicky beamed from the attention.

"I want you to scan through your memory banks and look at the moment your hunch or sixth sense kicked in. Go back to that time as if you were reliving the experience in real time. In other words, remember what it was like to be in your body at that time and experience the hunch all over again. Now, rewind the memory to the point just before you had your hunch. Everyone have that kind of moment?"

They all nodded.

"Great. Now play the scene forward until the moment when the hunch happens and then freeze it at the moment of the hunch so you

TO BE:
fun!
inspiring!
focused!
wealthy!
grateful!!!

The more you elevate in consciousness, the more time you create and the more freedom you have to do something that is important, meaningful, and makes a difference.

You can either trade time for dollars or get into the results and performance economy, where your time is your own. You want to make every moment count, do more with less, and get bigger results in a shorter time.

Let's add one other list you may not have considered: a to-don't list. "I won't waste time"; "I won't do B- and C-level tasks when I can do money-generating A-level tasks that will advance my business, my future, my finances, and me."

To further your awareness of time and what you can accomplish, download the free e-book *Time for Everything* at www.cashina flashthebook.com/gift.

Money

Money is available to you (fundamental abundance!) and you want it to be residual.

can isolate the intuitive experience. What were the clues you received that let you know that the message was special, true, or real? How would you describe it? Open your eyes. I want us to harvest some of those feelings," Michelle said, sitting down with the group. "Lei Kim? Will you go first?"

Lei Kim nodded.

"Would you mind standing up?" Michelle added.

"Do I have to?"

"In the span of, what, a week, you've had two breakthough ideas, but you still insist on playing small? Lei Kim, if you want to stand in the company of greatness, you have to learn how to accept greatness in your life. And that goes for all of us. We are here to stand tall and move confidently in the direction of our desires, because if we won't, who will? If you don't learn how to consciously accept money, the money will find someone else's bank account to go into. You don't want that, do you?"

Lei Kim got the message and stood up. She cleared her throat. "While part of me is afraid to change the menu at the diner, I wonder if having these stomach problems was showing me a new path, like you said before to Lisa."

"And?" Michelle encouraged her.

"And . . . I wonder if I marketed the bars I made last week . . ."

"If it was made with chocolate, I'd be the first to buy it," Lisa said in support. To Hannah she said, "You should taste it. It's yummy."

Hannah smiled. "I love chocolate."

"Have you looked into manufacturing the bar?" Francie asked Lei Kim.

"A little, but . . ."

"But what?" Nicky said. Lisa gave him a "good for you" nod of approval.

Is your goal to make $100,000? Why stop there? To get to $1 million, all you have to do is add an extra zero. Again, change the way you look at it.

And if the question of how to make $1 million in a year is too intimidating, ask a better question: "How can I make an additional $500 per day?"

Get used to the word *profit*. Without a profit you cannot stay in business, grow, hire and pay your team, live the good life, vacation, be philanthropic, or ultimately retire.

You deserve a fair profit for creating, controlling, contributing, nurturing, and sustaining your business. Yes, we said it: you deserve it.

WHAT IS THE BEST PROBLEM YOU CAN HAVE?

The best problem to have is the one you can solve and monetize at the same time.

When you are on a new exercise regimen, how do you measure the results? You use a scale or you judge by the fit of your favorite jeans, right?

How do you measure your relationships, your time, your mobility, and your money?

If you do not measure your money, you do not get more. If you do not measure your time equity, you do not get to have any time freedom. And time freedom is what opens you up and gives you other freedoms.

See, money freedom gives you time freedom. Time freedom gives you relationship freedom, so you can be with the people you want, when you want. You have to have a currency of mobility so you can go do something that needs to be done when you need to do it. There has never been so much in the world that needs to be done.

You want to increase your money freedom, your time freedom, your mobile freedom, and your relationship freedom; that is all there is to it.

It is time for you to assess your currencies and create your plan for increasing your awareness and wealth in each one.

Lei Kim smiled at the inclusion of the kids. Somehow this made her feel comfortable enough to continue. "With everything that's going on at the restaurant, my husband, my son, the house . . . I just don't know where the time will come from." She sat back down.

Michelle stood and wrote on the whiteboard: "*Whatever it takes.*"

"Whenever we receive a gift of insight, especially when it comes to making money, we have a duty to do *whatever it takes* to see that gift to realization. This is the holographic expression we talked about the other day. There's a part of you that knows if you move forward, the idea will make you money. If you can see it, you can achieve it."

"That all sounds great, but I think what Lei Kim means is that taking on another thing can put your life into a tailspin," Lisa added.

"You can't look at it as 'taking on another thing.' It's all part of one thing," Michelle said, erasing the board again.

"You have the diner here." She wrote the word *diner* and drew a box around it. You have your family here. You have your social life . . . this group . . . your health . . . working out . . . stuff like that. You have cleaning your house, laundry, and other household things on a daily basis. Then you have this . . . we'll call it a meal in a bar, for the sake of discussion."

"I actually like that. Meal in a bar," Francie said.

"Me too," Hannah said, joining in.

"I do too." Lei Kim smiled broadly.

"Maybe that's the name. We can brainstorm names and slogans later. But the point is, you can't look at every single thing in your life as 'another thing.' If you pile all these boxes of things to do on your back, you will most likely topple over. However . . ." Michelle drew a large box on the whiteboard, then drew smaller sections inside the box, which made it look like a Rubik's Cube.

1. On a scale of 1–10 (1 being empty, 10 overflowing), how much currency do you have in:
   a. Relationship
   b. Mobility
   c. Time
   d. Money
2. Put a star next to any of the currencies that are below a 5. These are the currencies that demand your attention.
3. How is not being abundant in these currencies negatively affecting your life? What are you not able to be, do, and have?
4. What are three steps you can take to increase your currency? When can you start? Set a date.
5. How will you measure your growth in these currencies? Name three people who will help keep you on track.
6. How will your current situation dramatically change by taking these steps?

For free audio downloads of *Guided Virtualizations to Increase Your Four Currencies* visit www.cashinaflashthebook.com.

LOOK OUTSIDE OF YOUR BACKYARD

When you are at a place where you can manage your own problems, see them as opportunities, and rise up the ladder, you are now ready to take on problems of a larger scale. Remember, we said your soul is here to serve. You want to take what you know and apply it on a larger scale. We have no doubt in your ability to handle the world's toughest problems.

As we mentioned earlier, Dr. Muhammad Yunus saw a huge problem that needed solving. Armed with his awareness and tuned into his resources, with little money down, he created a system that is allowing

"If you look at all of these things as part of the whole, the one, the one being you"—she turned to face them—"then you have something more manageable. You aren't doing a *number* of things. You are simply doing *one* thing. And that one thing is you. As the authority on you, you are unleashing your talents, your gifts, the things that make up who you are—an enlightened entrepreneur. All of these variables we've listed here are part of the journey into your spiritual awareness, this 'one.' One thing. That's all we have to do." She turned to Lei Kim. "You think you're oversubscribed, but I assure you, if you think of life with this oneness factor in mind, you'll never feel overwhelmed—or alone, for that matter—ever again. Does that make sense?" Though Michelle was addressing Lei Kim specifically, the rest of the women nodded.

Michelle cleared the whiteboard and wrote at the top, "Lei Kim—meal in a bar. Francie—foreclosure e-book." "Okay, who's next?" Michelle asked, looking around, but she realized all the kids were drifting off to sleep. A quick glance at her watch told her it was close to eleven o'clock. "I guess we should call it a night. Is everyone okay with same time next week?"

"Can't we meet again tomorrow night?" Kanisha asked, sitting up.

"I'm free," Lei Kim added.

"Francie? Lisa?" Michelle asked. "We'll have to bring the kids again, but I'm game if you are." Francie and Lisa nodded as everyone climbed to their feet.

women to have a chance at a better quality of life. In thirty-plus years, Yunus, starting with $27, has built a $2 billion bank. He says success comes from the teams of women working cooperatively.

Here is your wax on/wax off assignment.

Take a few moments to answer the following questions to discover which world problem or cause is close to your heart.

1. Have any friends or family members recently gone through an experience where they needed your help?
2. Do you remember a story or situation from the news that greatly affected you?
3. Is there a topic that gets you fired up when others are discussing it?
4. Are there any charitable organizations that in the past you vowed to help once you had the means to do so?
5. What do you think is the biggest problem facing this country and how can you help?

You will always have your own problems. But remember, the little ones will not matter as much when you take on something as meaningful and life-changing as one that makes a difference for others.

Live in the assumption of the wish fulfilled and you imagine new, viable solutions to all the world's problems.

11

Life's Little Emergencies

How We're Pushed or Pulled by a Vision

It was the end of another beautiful day in Idyllwild. The cold October breeze was moving down Main Street like the ghost of Halloween. Lurking. Drifting. Promising the arrival of winter, which was only weeks away. Soon the playgrounds would be covered in snow and kids of all ages would spend hours making snowmen, practicing for the annual snowman contest, held the first Saturday in December.

Lei Kim bolted the large doors of the diner. Built in the early 1900s, the building was a historical landmark, something Lei Kim loved about her diner. Just like the building, most everyone in town had a story, and the lunch counter was their soapbox. Some of the retired customers would tell stories of the "good old days" in Idyllwild, while others complained about city hall, which was just three short blocks away. Having heard most of the stories before, Lei Kim listened intently nonetheless, nodding like a bartender behind the counter of a saloon.

She often thought about staying open for dinner, but the people of Idyllwild seemed to prefer to stay home for dinner. Lei Kim learned this the hard way during her first year in business. She tried dinner specials and free desserts, but nothing worked. People were set in their ways and change took time. But Lei Kim would need

16

SOLVING OTHER PEOPLE'S PROBLEMS: REAL ESTATE IS YOUR MOST PROFITABLE PRODUCT

Since there are almost seven billion people on planet Earth, there are a potential seven billion customers. And new customers are being born every day. The possibilities are limitless.

There is an Ashleigh Brilliant cartoon that explains this perfectly. The caption reads, "I'm not greedy: I'd be quite satisfied with just one dollar from every person in the country."

At $1 profit, to earn $100,000, you'd need to sell 100,000 "widgets" this year. At $10 profit, you'd need to sell 10,000 widgets. At $100 profit, you'd only need to sell 1,000 widgets. Making $100,000 a year in the entrepreneurial world, although not easy, is certainly doable. It could be as simple as doing one great real estate deal. Or marketing a $5,000 yearly coaching program to twenty people. We've each earned $100,000 in a single hour! Of course, it took us thirty years to figure out how to do it.

The first question to ask yourself is "How can I create some product, service, idea, or experience that generates a consistent profit?"

Let's talk about products. How many widgets do you need to sell to earn $100,000?

How about *one*?

The simplest, easiest way to earn profit is by focusing on the primary product—real estate.

something to happen soon, because profits were shrinking. With the exception of last year, when summer seemed to last forever, the restaurant was barely breaking even. She kept the doors open for her older customers who liked to have dinner at four-thirty, but after that, usually around five-thirty or six, Lei Kim would call it a day.

It was almost two years ago now that Lei Kim had become very ill and nearly closed the doors of the diner for good. After flying to the wellness center in Denver, Lei Kim finally learned the source of her cramping stomachaches. Tests revealed that somehow she had become allergic to most everything and her system was rejecting cooked foods. The discovery baffled even the doctors, but Lei Kim thought of it as a sign. Maybe this was a way to get out of the business altogether and do something else with her life. Relegated to a strict vegan diet, consisting primarily of raw foods and juices, Lei Kim had to learn how to adapt gracefully to preparing raw foods.

When she grew tired of salads, Lei Kim began experimenting. To her, eating had always been a social event, which was why she'd opened the restaurant in the first place—to foster community and fellowship. But now, eating had lost its flavor and no longer had the lure of comfort. She found herself wanting to simply "feed the monster," a term she coined to refer to quieting her growling stomach, so she could get back to work. Fortified with all the nutrients and vitamins one could get from a full meal, the bar she eventually created incorporated yummy ingredients like dates, peanut butter, freeze-dried green vegetable powder, and vegan dark chocolate. One bar kept her system happy for nearly six hours. Her husband, however, still wanted a hot cooked meal every night at home. Having lost his leg after stepping on a land mine during the Korean War, Mr. Kim lived off his military pension and disability, which wasn't much at all. Although he had been outfitted with a prosthetic limb by the VA hospital, his confinement was somewhat self-induced. In essence,

OWN YOUR DREAM HOME FREE AND CLEAR

Your primary product is real estate. Regardless of what the media says about declining real estate values, real estate has always been—and, in our opinion, will always be—the fastest way to cash for those inclined to invest wisely. Everyone still needs shelter. You might want a motorcycle or a new piece of jewelry, but if you don't make your house or rent payment that month, you're on the street. It's the number one priority in a household budget, just before food. There are fortunes to be made by buying, selling, and renting the "stuff" of houses, apartment buildings, commercial buildings, land, et cetera.

Real estate is the best product because people live in houses and they understand them. It's low-hanging fruit for them. They already get it. They don't have to learn how to get their product manufactured in China. Or come up with a legally defensible patent for their widget. They already understand houses, so real estate is a natural for them. Shelter is also one of the most basic of human needs. When you match up your most basic human need with what you already know, it's obvious that real estate should be one of your first products. Muhammad Yunus talks about teaching poor women to earn money from their primary skills. In North America, real estate is a primary skill. The secondary skill would be to market your product or someone else's product. Let's start with real estate.

POSITIVE PROFITS FROM NEGATIVE HEADLINES

There are huge profits in solving people's real estate problems. The headlines are shouting these profit-generating words: foreclosures, delinquencies, defaults, bankruptcies, loan modifications, and repossessions. Don't let these words scare you away! In recent times, the value of real estate has been wildly fluctuating—from doubling in value in seven years to losing almost 20 percent of its value in less than a year. You might be nervous about the future of real estate. Not to worry. Real estate is not like the stock market, where a company stock can lose 100 percent of its value. Real estate *never* goes to zero. The land has value. The wood and roofing and paint and electrical wires—the stuff that makes the house—all costs money. Fortunes

Mr. Kim had lost his desire for life and quickly adopted a victim mentality. He was angry at life, and on some days he wished he had died on the battlefield. He was, at times, verbally abusive to Lei Kim. She knew he didn't mean some of the things he said, but she wondered how much more she could take.

Lei Kim was under emotional and financial pressure but managed to not let it show on the outside. She was strong-willed and always ready with a smile. This was something her mother had taught her at a very young age—that it was a wife and mother's job, if not her duty, to place the family first and herself second. This was probably why Lei Kim had waited to open the restaurant until her mother passed away five years ago.

Her son, Johnny, was now a college dropout, and was about to become more of a financial dependent than a financial asset to the family. This put a strain on Lei Kim. She wasn't sure how she was going to make it work. She wasn't sure if she could carry another full-time employee at the diner.

Although Lei Kim wanted him to make more of his life, Johnny was content to spend much of his time playing video games. Now that he had dropped out of school, Lei Kim wasn't sure what was going to happen. She'd suggested he look for a programming job within the video game industry, but ever since he'd dropped out, Johnny hadn't done much of anything. The truth was, Johnny lacked self-discipline. Overworked and underearning, Lei Kim was the sole breadwinner of the family.

Checking her watch, Lei Kim saw she had enough time to go home, cook dinner for her husband, take a shower, and be at the Heartlight in time for the meeting. It would be close, but she could fit everything in, so she folded her arms against the cold air and headed toward her 2003 Prius. Just as she was about to get in, she realized she'd left the light on near the bathrooms in the back of the diner. She

are made by finding and creating real estate value. No matter what the market is doing—rising or falling—you'll always be able to profit by buying right and selling right.

Real estate is the primary product because it's *real*! Buying and selling real property is a skill that *everyone* should learn. Why? You'll most likely buy and sell between three and ten houses in your lifetime. If you invest wisely, you could end up with a free and clear home of your dreams within ten years. How? By buying right and selling right at least every three years.

Suppose you buy your next home 20 percent below the market (today) and hang on to it long enough so that it increases in value within three years by an extra 10 percent. Then, just before you sell it, you improve it (fix it up) so that someone would be enticed to buy it at 10 percent above the market at that time. Here's what could happen in three years if we're talking about a $250,000 home.

Value	$250,000
Purchase price 20 percent below market	$200,000
Hold on to it for three years so it increases 10 percent	$275,000
Fix it up to sell for 10 percent above market	$300,000

Your purchase price is $200,000. Your sales price is $300,000. Your equity is now $100,000, Do this three more times ($100,000 profit minimum per flip) and within ten years you'll own your home free and clear. It might not be your dream home, but what a dream to own your home without monthly payments.

If you want to own a dream home that's twice as nice, just buy two bargain homes per year. If you buy, hold, fix up, and flip ten homes in ten years, you could move into a million-dollar home in ten years free and clear . . . or have a million dollars net worth. Just imagine, you're just ten deals away from that kind of freedom.

Real estate investing knowledge and skill are essential. Everybody should learn it—if you want to improve the roof over your head.

All around you there are real estate deals. You drive by millions of

checked her watch. "You don't have time," she said to herself. "You don't want to be late to the meeting. Just leave it, you'll get it tomorrow." Given her financial situation with the diner, though, every dollar counted, so with another check of her watch, she went back and unlocked the door of the diner.

Just as she stepped inside, Lei Kim suddenly felt dizzy, as she had the night of the hike. She tried to shake it off, but something was wrong. Her palms were clammy as her keys slipped from her hand. Her breath, moving quickly in and out, grew shallow, and she could feel her arms beginning to tingle. Bracing herself against the open door, she dug into her purse, frantically searching for her cell phone. She needed help, but it was too late—she was going down, and she knew it. Her vision began to kaleidoscope, twisting and turning out of focus until she finally fell. Her faced pressed into the cold tile floor of the diner.

She was dazed, but she wasn't unconscious. Lying on her side, her eyes focused into the hallway, where the light was still on. She'd never left the light on before; why tonight? And what was happening to her? Focusing, she saw the dustpan and broom that Johnny had forgotten to put into the closet. It was leaning in the corner where he'd left it, and somehow it was being framed by the overhead light. Suddenly, Johnny's voice began to echo inside her mind: *Stupid broom gave me no leverage.*

The words echoed again and again until they finally began to fade away because Lei Kim was now passing out. Just before her eyes closed, she saw the top end of the broom handle bend over on itself as her vision continued to play tricks on her. What was she seeing? Was this an idea for a new product? Before she could answer the questions rattling inside of her head, her eyelids began to flutter, and everything went black.

dollars of hidden profit every time you commute to and from a job you may not like. The profit from just one great real estate deal could exceed what you struggle to earn *in an entire year at your job.*

Why work on someone's mother ship when you can hit the mother lode in real estate? The last time we had a glut of foreclosures like we've been experiencing now was in the late 1980s. It was called the savings and loan crisis. Do you remember those times? Greedy bankers lent billions to developers with cheap money. These developers built apartment complexes, commercial buildings, and homes far in excess of the existing demand. The developers defaulted on the loans, the savings and loans were foreclosed by the government, and Uncle Sam became the owner of billions of dollars' worth of vacant property. They formed the Resolution Trust Corporation and liquidated *all* of it. Those who bought made billions in profits.

The same thing happened in the first five years of the new millennium. Interest rates were slashed and demand soared for residential real estate. Prices doubled in five years. Everyone thought that prices would never stop climbing. But the bubble burst. Prices began to drop. So the pendulum has swung back the other way *too far.*

Prices will stabilize. The supply will get absorbed. Maybe it will take another five years. Then prices will slowly continue to rise. Just like they have for the last hundred years. Real estate will continue to be the safest, surest, fastest, easiest way for an ordinary person to create a fortune. Someone will pick up this book ten years from now and read these words. They will seem like a prophecy.

The reason we can be so confident is that we know three obvious facts:

1. **America is a magnet for people all over the world.** As bad as the newspapers make it sound, the rest of the world wants to move here. We have to build fences to keep them out. The population projections with new births and immigration will grow from our current 300 million citizens to over 400 million citizens by 2040. Where will they put those extra hundred million people? In *your* rental houses and apartment buildings.

2. **Inflation will continue to be with us for as long as you live.** China

Down the street at the Heartlight, Michelle and Lisa were closing up shop and getting ready for tonight's meeting, which was a little over an hour away. Lisa finished counting the money in the cash drawer and Michelle turned off the lights to the sign outside. Checking her watch, she thought for a minute.

"Russell's at my house, right?" Michelle asked grabbing her keys.

"He better be," Lisa answered, counting the pennies in the drawer as the loud siren of a police car rose and fell outside. "Why? Whatcha thinking?"

"We have an hour before everyone gets here," Michelle said.

"Yeah? And?" Lisa asked.

"You feel like grabbing some dinner and surprising the kids?"

"How about pizza?" Lisa said like she was twelve again.

"Okay. I'll call Justine and have her hold off on the tacos," Michelle said, dialing her cell phone.

"Oh man, Taco Tuesday. I totally forgot. Tacos are cool with me," Lisa said.

"No, pizza's fine. The kids love it, plus it will give Justine a break."

"Let me put the cash drawer in the safe and I'm ready," Lisa answered as an ambulance raced by the front windows, sirens wailing and lights flashing. She and Michelle shared a quick look, but when the siren stopped just up the street, Lisa put the cash drawer back into the register and moved to the front doors to see what all the commotion was all about.

"Hey, Justine, it's me." Michelle spoke into her cell phone. "Lisa and I thought we'd grab a couple of pizzas and come home for dinner."

and India are right where America was twenty-five years ago. They are on a growth spurt that will consume basic commodities and force prices upward. The haven for devaluating currency is hard assets. Real estate is one of the hardest of assets. It will continue to increase in value simply because hard costs will increase along with continuing inflation. On top of this, we have massive government deficit spending. Our brilliant politicians are overprinting and overspending money by the trillion. Do you know how much a trillion is? It's like spending a million dollars a day for 2,700 years! One of these days, inflation will come roaring back. Hard assets are where you'll want to be.

3. **You don't have to have increasing prices in real estate to make immediate money.** You can always find a bargain, no matter what the current market prices are. You can always flip that bargain to someone at a below-market price and earn a profit. Always. That's what entrepreneurs do— they find value and they flip it to someone else for a profit. That will never change when it comes to real estate. Never.

Here's a quick story to highlight how entrepreneurs find seams of value where people have never thought to look. A student attended one of our real estate seminars. It was taught in San Francisco. Prices are always high in the immediate Bay Area.

He tried to find some bargains and found lots of competition. He was discouraged. He had a bright idea. He checked the real estate prices for properties in Reno, Nevada—a few hours' drive away in the neighboring state. Prices there are dramatically lower. Hmmmm. That's interesting. He found an eight-unit apartment building listed at $229,000. He made an offer to purchase it, with a minimum of earnest money, and locked in the price at $200,000. Now the property was legally his . . . until he closed on it. He then ran an ad in the San Francisco newspapers: eight-unit apartment building for $215,000.

This price appeared so cheap for a Bay Area property that his phone rang off the hook. Fifty calls later, he canceled the ad. He told the interested parties that his property was in a neighboring state. One person drove to look at it and made him a full-price offer.

Michelle paused when she glanced up and saw the look on Lisa's face. Something was wrong.

"Hold on," Michelle said, putting her hand over the cell phone. "What is it?" she asked Lisa, but Lisa didn't answer—she just took off running. To Justine, Michelle said, "I'll call you right back."

Just as Michelle stepped onto the sidewalk, she saw a crowd outside Lei Kim's diner. Someone was being loaded into the ambulance.

Michelle paced back and forth as Lisa sat slumped in a chair. Over an hour had passed since Lei Kim had been brought in. The doctors were running tests, but there was still no word on her condition.

Francie arrived in a rush, out of breath. "Where is she?"

"They have her upstairs," Michelle told her.

"And the doctors? What are they saying?" Francie wanted answers.

"Nothing," Lisa replied.

Francie didn't miss a beat. She marched out of the waiting room and directly to the nurses' station. She smiled as the young nurse looked up at the sound of her heels approaching.

"Hi there," Francie said in her nicest tone. "I have a friend who was brought in not too long ago. I'd like to talk to someone to see how she's doing."

"Name?" The nurse said, rolling her chair to a computer station.

"Lei Kim." Francie spelled it out.

"Your friend is . . . hmmm . . . let's see here." The nurse was reading through some notes on Lei Kim's file when Lisa and Michelle arrived.

"Anything?" Michelle asked.

"She's checking," Francie said.

Here are the interesting facts. The student had never physically seen the property himself. He found the property on the Internet and made an offer sight unseen, subject to his inspection. He never actually owned the property. He only had a signed offer. He "flipped" the contract to the new buyer for $15,000 cash.

All of this happened in two weeks, from start to finish.

Bargains are everywhere. They just take at least ninety days of persistent shopping to uncover them. Just buy one or two excellent real estate bargains each year for the next ten years and you'll be set for life. If you don't have any money to get started, check on our website, www.cashinaflashthebook.com/nothingdowntechniques, for a special report that will teach you the fifty nothing-down techniques. In addition, we'll include a powerful special report on the ten fastest ways to earn cash from real estate investments, especially in today's real estate market. Don't miss it! If you're still skeptical that profits can be earned during these slow times, go to www.millionairehalloffame.com and you can read more than seven thousand stories of our students who have earned over a *billion* dollars in profit.

Go out there and find some value and create your own success story.

PRODUCTS TWO AND THREE

So real estate is the primary product. It should be number one on your list of products to buy and sell. What are numbers two and three on the list?

Number two should consist of marketing products that someone else has perfected.

Number three should be marketing products that you create.

Real estate first. Others' products second. Your own products last. One, two, three, in that order.

That seems strange advice. Shouldn't we be marketing the products that *we* create from our purpose path? What if we don't like real estate? What if marketing someone else's product doesn't appeal to us? What if we have a strong urge to start something from scratch?

"Looks like they're going to hold your friend overnight for observation, but you can go up to the third floor and see her if you want," the nurse said.

Michelle about lost it. "Excuse me? I've been sitting over there for over an hour and not one word. 'Waiting room' means I'm waiting for you people to let us know something."

"Well, I'm sorry, ma'am, I just came on my shift."

"You're sorry? Don't you people talk to each other?" Michelle said, becoming uncorked. Francie put her hand on Michelle's arm to calm her down.

"Won't do you any good, dear. I learned my lesson when Christopher was sick. Let's just stay focused and go see how Lei Kim is doing, okay?" Francie said.

"Can you believe that?" Michelle grumbled as Lisa led her away.

"Yeah, as a matter of fact, I can," Lisa replied, looking back at Francie with a nod.

Francie stayed behind for a moment and leaned closer to the young nurse. "I'm not saying any of this was your fault, but for some of you, this is just a job. For the people on the other side of the counter, though, it's life and death, and it's not fun. And that is the tip of the day," Francie said with a compassionate smile. "Next one will cost ya."

Francie walked away, leaving the nurse with her mouth open. She might be only five-four, but Francie was a force to be reckoned with.

"Room three-oh-seven," Michelle said, as she, Lisa, and Francie walked along the third floor. "Here it is." Slowly Michelle opened the door to see Lei Kim sitting up in bed and watching television.

Each person's path to prodigious profit is different. Follow your heart. Yet the safest path in the risky world of business is to apprentice in the safest fields. Real estate is just flat out the fastest and safest way to chunks of cash and equity. Nothing touches it. Start one thousand people on a money marathon and more real estate millionaires will cross the finish line than all the other methods *combined*. Real estate wins. Every time. Hands down.

The second least risky way to earn profit is to hook onto some else's product as an independent marketer. Find a company that has a product that you love and that you believe in, and learn how to market it. The advantage is that the company has done all of the research, the production, the warehousing, and the creation of websites and training materials. All you need to do is to sell what they've created. You become a wholesaler for their existing product. You can be in business in minutes instead of months. You can learn almost immediately if anyone wants it . . . and if you have the desire and belief to convince yourself and others to buy it. If you can't sell someone else's product, what makes you think you could sell your own? Hooking up with someone else's company gets you in the game immediately and teaches you how to hone your selling skills. Like it or not, selling skills are critical. Learn how to sell. *Fast*.

How can you find a product to market? Go online and you'll find literally thousands of affiliate programs that will pay you affiliate commissions for every product you market online. Some of the affiliate programs will also pay you several levels of commissions. You can earn commissions if someone you enroll sells products. Therefore, you earn income off the efforts of others. It's a well-respected model online. If it works for Amazon.com, why can't it work for you? Since the world of the Internet is constantly changing, go to the website www.cashinaflashthebook.com/onlineprofits for the hottest new ways to profit online.

In the offline world, there are hundreds of respectable network marketing companies selling dozens of different kinds of products—from nutrition to skin care, household products, and success information. Check out several. Go to their marketing events. Find products that you believe in and can become passionate about. Network marketing is the elementary school of entrepreneurship. Once you've built a successful affiliate or

"Hey, great. You're here," Lei Kim said, flipping off the TV with the remote control.

Michelle was beside herself. "I'm going to go strangle that nurse."

Lisa held her back. "Easy, tiger."

"What's wrong?" Lei Kim asked.

"Nothing's wrong. Michelle's just a bit—" Francie began.

"Upset," Michelle said quickly, cutting Francie off. "Yes, I am upset. She's up here watching TV."

"Which is a good thing, isn't it?" Francie said with a smile.

"Yes, you're right. But still, somebody should . . ."

"Get a talking-to?" Francie finished the thought for her.

"Exactly," Michelle said, finding a smile through it all. "I'm sorry," she said, finally turning to Lei Kim. "What happened?"

"Yeah. Are you okay?" Lisa asked as they gathered around the hospital bed.

"Ah, just got myself a little tired, that's all."

"A little tired? Lei Kim, this isn't the Holiday Inn—you're in the hospital," Lisa said.

"What did the doctors say, dear?" Francie said, taking her hand.

"I'm fine. They just want to make me rest. My blood sugar got a little low, and I fell down and went boom," Lei Kim joked. "But I have to talk to you about the meeting," she added to Michelle.

"We can do that tomorrow. Is that okay with everyone? Meet at the store around seven?" Lisa and Francie both nodded. "You need to rest." Michelle told Lei Kim.

"Tomorrow can't wait. I'm fine. Please, I have an idea I need to tell someone about."

"An idea for what?" Lisa asked.

Lei Kim was talking in broken thoughts, her mind racing with excitement. "When I fell on the ground, the light by the bathroom . . .

networking business, you might be inspired to graduate to the university level of business.

The bachelor's, master's, and doctorate levels of business are to start your own company marketing your own PSIs. Maybe you have a brilliant widget that you've been inspired to bring to the world. Follow your heart. The marketing experience you've acquired in your successful networking business will save you years of mistakes.

THE SHOCKING SECRET TO YOUR SUCCESS

Just a final word about how you'll find your path to prosperity in the product world. We can teach you the fundamental ABCs of getting started. But sooner or later you'll discover something shocking.

There are thousands of how-to books, including this one. But there is only one how-to book that will actually work for you—the book you write for yourself. Why? Because, the how-to is unique for every single person. You have to create your own unique how-to method from the fundamental principles you read in books like this.

You can't learn all of it in a book. Ask successful people how they did it and they'll tell you a totally unique story. They followed some basics and then they had an *aha* moment that opened up a special method that seemed to work just for them. They might have tried a dozen different methods, and then something clicked.

When we talk about the Inner Winner, this is what we're referring to. Each person seems to have his or her own personal revelation that opens up a unique path. That's what happened for both of us. It's hard to describe. It's very spiritual.

Don't get too hung up on the how-to. Just follow your hunches . . . those whispers . . . those special insights.

It's our belief that there are invisible forces that guide us. They want you to win. They want you to prosper. They want you to tap into your own unique vein of gold. They want you to bless the world through your abundant giving.

Heaven knows, the world desperately needs it.

See, I left the light on, something I never do. But lying on the floor, I saw in the light . . . well, not in the light . . ."

"What did you see?" Michelle asked.

"I saw the broom handle," Lei Kim concluded.

"You saw the what?" Francie said, bewildered.

Lei Kim laughed as she realized how silly she sounded. "Johnny was cleaning up last week and he said something that came back to haunt me, but in a good way. When I fell to the floor, the light was shining on the broom he'd been using that day, the broom and dustpan. This sounds crazy, yes, but . . . it bent."

"What bent?"

"The light?" Lisa asked.

"Now that would be silly, wouldn't it? The broom handle bent."

"And that's not silly? A broom handle bending?" Lisa quipped, half joking.

Lei Kim saw her explanation wasn't quite hitting home, so she kept going. "Johnny swept over a piece of paper three, maybe four times, and nothing. The paper just stuck to the floor. When I told him he was lazy and he should bend over to pick it up, he said he wouldn't have to if he could get the right leverage from the broom. See, when you use the dustpan and broom, you're sweeping with the broom in one hand, the dustpan in the other. You don't have the right amount of leverage to efficiently do the job. But when I fell, I saw the broom handle bend over on itself."

"Did they put you on a morphine drip we don't know about?" Lisa teased. Francie looked at her and wondered if Lisa was ever serious about anything.

"Here, let me draw it for you," Lei Kim sighed, giving up. "Does anyone have a pencil?"

Digging in the drawer next to the bedside table, Michelle found a

17

THERE IS A BOOK IN YOU: FAST CASH IN INFORMATION MARKETING

If you believe it and desire it, you can acquire it.

—ROBERT G. ALLEN

There are at least three major paths to prosperity. Instead of salaries, you want to earn profits. Profits are earned by "selling stuff." Three kinds of stuff:

product

service

information

In our experience, one of the fastest paths to profit is by selling information. Read this next story to understand why.

small pad of notepaper. Francie looked in her purse and found a pen. Lei Kim drew the loop end of the handle just like the vision she saw when the broom handle bent back on itself before she passed out.

"This is what I saw," Lei Kim said, turning the pad of paper around for everyone to see.

"Looks like a broom with a large eye of a needle at the end of it," Lisa said.

"Yes, it's what gives you leverage," Lei Kim replied.

"How does it work?" Michelle inquired, looking closer.

"You put your arm through here." Lei Kim indicated the loop end of the broom. "And then you grab here," she said, indicating the straight part of the broom. "See, the loop hits your forearm and gives you the leverage you need to efficiently sweep the floor."

"That's your idea?" Lisa asked.

Lei Kim deflated a bit, because she couldn't understand why they weren't feeling the excitement she felt. "Well, yes."

"What's wrong, Lisa?" Michelle asked.

Lisa saw the look on Lei Kim's face. "Nothing. It's okay."

"Come on. If you have something to say, she needs to hear it. That's why we formed the group—to make our ideas invincible," Michelle said, coaching her.

"It's just . . . not very sexy," Lisa finally confessed.

"Neither was the zipper when it first came out, but look around, it's everywhere," Francie said in Lei Kim's defense.

"Some of the best ideas are simple," Michelle said before turning to Lei Kim. "Maybe if you can explain how it works again, we could get a clearer picture."

"Johnny puts the dustpan down, then sweeps the floor. He then goes back to the dustpan, then the back to the broom. All this back-and-forth is wasting time. This idea saves time because the sweeping and dustpanning are one motion, not five."

$137,000 IN FORTY-FIVE DAYS
STARTING FROM SCRATCH

Nicki sat in a seminar and was enamored by the numbers. It was a seminar we taught called "Cracking the Millionaire Code." And she cracked it. Here's how.

She was listening to our guest lecturer, the marketing guru Jay Abraham, talk about finding a product to market. You see, you don't even need your own product. There are millions of products out there already in some warehouse just waiting for you to come along and offer to help sell them. Talk about low-hanging fruit! It's hanging all around you.

Every business needs help selling. Some need it even worse than others. Some businesses are terrible at selling. They love to create products but they're lousy at marketing them. You can come to their rescue.

Jay Abraham suggested that you find a product category that matches your purpose—things that you love to sell because you believe in them. Enter a Google search using your purpose path.

Let's use Google. Everyone is fighting to have their products show up in the top 100 in a Google search. Let's do just the opposite in our Google search. Instead of going to the top of Google, go instead to the *bottom* of the Google search. (Or deeper than the top two or three hundred results . . . which is where few people ever go.)

What does this tell you? These companies don't know how to sell their products. They need help. Search through to find a hundred or so that have a PSI that you really connect with, that you'd actually love to sell. Contact them and ask them if they'd like to sell you a bunch of their products at a very wholesale price. Maybe they've got a warehouse full of older models that they'd love to get rid of. You're looking for products you can acquire for a super bargain—that you can almost steal. In economic times like these, there are thousands of companies with products they're dying to unload.

How many companies would you need to contact until you found a perfect product that fits your purpose at a bargain basement, below wholesale price?

"What about medical benefits?" Francie suggested.

"Medical benefits from a broom?" Lisa laughed. "You stealing her morphine?"

"Good idea, Francie. If you show how this ergonomic broom—" Michelle began, but Lei Kim cut her off.

"Ergonomic broom. Yes, that's good," Lei Kim said, writing it next to her drawing.

"If the broom provided safety benefits—protection from wrist injuries or carpal tunnel syndrome . . ."

"Don't forget about efficiency," Francie chimed in.

"The efficiency is a no-brainer, but this medical angle . . . that should be the focus." Michelle smiled.

"Because it's everywhere. Everywhere you look, this dustpan-broom combination is being used," Lei Kim said.

"So, why would they buy your broom with a bent handle?" Lisa challenged. When she saw the others' looks, she exclaimed, "What, I'm just asking."

"With this bent handle, the user can get the leverage needed to sweep more efficiently, and they never have to put either device down, which saves time. Isn't that clear?" Lei Kim said.

"It is. Lisa's just being difficult," Francie joked, as if to tell Lisa, *Lighten up, the woman's lying in a hospital bed.*

"No, this is good," Michelle spoke up. "We can't go into this with a Pollyannaish attitude. We have to ask and answer the tough questions. That's what makes the concept work. Teamwork."

Hearing this, Lisa fired off a new question. "Have you thought about what it's made out of?"

"Plastic?" Lei Kim said, more like a question than an answer. "I really haven't thought about it."

"You don't want it to break in the customer's hands, so it would have to be made of really durable plastic," Francie offered.

So you research a thousand companies to find a hundred possibilities to narrow down to ten possible products . . . or the best 1 percent.

Now, you don't have to warehouse it. It's already being warehoused. You don't have to ship it. They'll ship it for you as long as you pay for it. They've already created some marketing information that you can use. It's ready to go. You haven't spent a dime and you're in control of a million dollars' worth of product.

But you ask, "What if I don't have any money to buy these products at a wholesale price?" Well, why don't you just let them keep them and warehouse them for you until you bring them a buyer with cash to buy it? You could option the inventory at a fixed low price and flip it to the new buyer at your higher price—and you keep the difference as your profit. "But, you ask, "how do I find people to sell these products to?"

We're glad you asked.

Now it's time to find an appropriate database—people who are already looking for this kind of PSI.

In the world of the Internet, which reaches more than a billion people (and is growing hourly), how many databases are there? Millions of them. (A database, by the way, is just the contact information for a list of customers.) Some websites list the contact information of just the website owner. That's a database of one. Other databases gather the contact information of every customer. Some small online companies have only ten, a hundred, or a thousand customers.

You're searching for . . .

1,000,000 databases with 1 name = 1,000,000 customers
100,000 databases with 10 names = 1,000,000 customers
10,000 databases with 100 names = 1,000,000 customers
1,000 databases with 1000 names = 1,000,000 customers
100 databases with 10,000 names = 1,000,000 customers
10 databases with 100,000 names = 1,000,000 customers
1 database with 1,000,000 names = 1,000,000 customers

"Good thinking," Lei Kim said as she took notes.

"What would you call it?" Michelle asked.

"Ergo Broom? . . . Efficiency Broom?" Lei Kim tried.

"What if you just called it the E Broom?" Lisa said, thinking out loud. (Go to www.cashinaflashthebook.com to see an E Broom.)

They all liked the sound of it. The E Broom had a nice ring to it, Michelle thought. It sounded like a product you'd find at Wal-Mart or see an employee using at a baseball game to sweep up discarded peanut shells. Michelle smiled because they were holding a Mastermind Group meeting right there in the middle of Lei Kim's hospital room. It was perfect, she thought, but wished Kanisha could have been there for the experience.

After about fifteen minutes, the door to Lei Kim's room opened and her husband entered, followed by Johnny. Little did he know his fumbling with the dustpan and broom had caused his mother to get a million-dollar idea. And it was a million-dollar idea because of its simplicity. It took something in use virtually everywhere and made the function of that something better. A recipe for success, she thought.

After brief introductions around the room, the women excused themselves so the family could visit together.

Outside, Michelle, Lisa, and Francie continued to talk about Lei Kim's idea as they walked toward the elevators. A chime announced the arrival of the elevator, and the doors opened. The nurse from downstairs stepped from the elevator into the hallway, but when she saw Francie and Michelle walking toward her, she did an about-face and ducked through a door marked Authorized Personnel Only.

"Yeah, you better run." Michelle giggled, and Francie and Lisa joined in.

Bottom line? You're looking for at least 100 databases with 10,000 names or more.

Why would these database owners let you send an e-mail to their list of highly prized customers? If *you* sent it to their list, it would be spam. It has to come from *them*. Why would they let you do that? It would have to be some sort of profit split. You're looking for a widget that has a high profit margin—like something that costs you $1 and has a value of over $100.

This is exactly what Nicki did. She found a company with a CD that contained special software and hundreds of special reports for stay-at-home moms. It was extremely valuable. But it only cost $1 to reproduce. Nicki acquired the right to the unlimited, nonexclusive use of this CD for less than $1,000. This was her information product.

Then she searched high and low and stumbled upon two college students who had been studying database gathering in a computer class. They had been able to gather 700,000 opt-in e-mail addresses during the semester. (We assume they got an A in the class.) They also were unaware of just how valuable their database was. Nicki convinced them to let her send a message. But there was a twist. She explained in her e-mail that 100 percent of the profits—*all* of the money—would go to a cause Nicki feels strongly about—orphans and orphanages.

The e-mail went out. Here was the offer: *Send me $100 for this incredibly valuable CD. You get the CD and I'll give all of the money to charity. All of it. I won't keep a penny for myself.*

Guess how many people took her up on her offer? A total of 1,370 people. That was less than a third of 1 percent.

Total earnings were $137,000. Cash. Starting from nothing. In less than forty-five days after learning this concept. What an enlightened "profitable servant" project!

Starting with this initial success, she and her new partners have since generated over $1 million in profit for themselves in addition to the orphan project from this same database. How do they do it? They find profitable PSIs to offer to their database.

12

Who's Next?

Knowing When to Speak Up

Michelle pulled to the curb in front of the Heartlight. Across the street, she saw Francie on the steps of the bank, talking with a young couple. The young woman hugged Francie as they said their good-byes. When Michelle shut off the engine of the Range Rover, Nicky and Hannah jumped out of the backseat and rushed inside the store to meet Russell, who was eagerly awaiting their arrival.

Locking her car, Michelle waited on the curb for Francie to arrive.

"Your new tenants?" Michelle asked.

"Yes. My new tenants," Francie said with a smile.

"You did it. You're officially now the owner of an income-producing property. Congratulations, Francie. How does it feel?"

"Let's just hope the PayPal account doesn't dry up anytime soon."

"It's okay to feel nervous. You already did the hard part—you pulled the trigger. Now you have to learn how to trust that everything is going to be okay."

As they went inside, Francie thought how Michelle always had a great way of making you feel at ease, no matter what you were going through.

Inside the store, everyone assumed the same positions they'd had last night. Nicky flipped open his video camera and pressed

You now have just learned this concept. How soon can you earn your first dollar?

The goal is to eventually be selling thousands of units per day without having to spend more than a few hours a month to cash the checks.

THE INFORMATION BUSINESS

Now, let's explore the secret to why this approach works so well with information products. With most product products—that is, hard lumpy objects—the cost of producing that product is at least 10 percent of the price of the product. Often, it's much more than that. For example, how much does it cost General Motors to produce a car? The hard costs of metal and plastic are very expensive, plus all of the labor and shipping. The profit margin per car is low. But with information products, the profit margin is extremely high. Why? Because it's so inexpensive to produce it.

In the previous example, Nicki was able to find an information product that someone else had produced. It was a CD that was jammed with valuable information. To the right customer, this organized information was valued at over $1,000, so the purchase price of $100 seemed like a bargain. Yet the cost to duplicate the CD was less than a dollar. The profit margin was 99 percent.

In many cases, this information can be digitized and sent over the Internet at lightning speed for free. If people have a serious problem and need specific information yesterday, they'll pay a premium for immediate delivery.

Of all the products you could sell, information is the ultimate product.

record. Lisa removed Russell's iPod ear buds from his ears and put the iPod in her purse. He didn't object, but slid from the couch and joined Nicky on the beanbag.

"Okay. Where were we?" Michelle asked, setting up the whiteboard.

"I think you were asking a question," Kanisha said. She was holding the baby walkie-talkie in case Faith woke up from her nap in the office and started to cry.

"You're right. I think it was, 'Who's next?'"

"Who's next?" Lisa asked

"Yes." Michelle waited for Lisa to speak up, but she didn't. "Remember, the only thing that separates *creative* people"—she used her fingers to make quotation marks in the air—"and *noncreative* people is that creative people find a way to express the message they receive. As businesswomen—and little men," she said, nodding to Russell and Nicky behind the camera, "we have a fiduciary responsibility to the ideas we have. Lei Kim, if you hadn't fainted, do you think you would've come up with your broom idea?"

"No," Lei Kim said with a smile.

"Where are you with it?"

"I met with the patent attorney you referred me to. He's helping me find a fabrication company to make the prototype. It's going to take some time—maybe even eighteen months for the official patent—but I'll have a patent pending in three to four weeks."

"And that's okay. Good ideas come in all forms. Some take a while to come about, and some arrive in an instant. The key is to never talk yourself out of an idea until you've really given it a chance. What is the wow you want to bring into the now? Remember, the wow comes from accessing the Inner Winner." Michelle waited to see if anyone spoke up, but the group was again silent.

"So, I'll ask again. Who's next?"

INTELLECTUAL PROPERTY IS THE REAL ESTATE OF THE TWENTY-FIRST CENTURY

Another term for information is *intellectual property*. It's the real estate of the twenty-first century. It's so easy to create and sell. It's the ultimate wealth creation vehicle. That's why we say the information business is the best business in the world.

THE BENEFITS OF INFORMATION MARKETING

- Easy to research
- Easy to create
- Easy and cheap to test
- Easy and cheap to produce, inventory, and correct
- Low-cost start-up
- High perceived value
- High markup
- Income while you sleep
- Unlimited worldwide market
- Mobility: operate from any mailbox in the world
- Copyright protection from competitors

"Very well. I'll go," Francie said, standing. Smiling at Kanisha, she began. "During our little adventure the other night, Kanisha and I had some . . . actually we had a lot of quality time together thanks to your little stunt. And I must say there was a point after you pulled away that I swore I'd come back here and give you what-for. But that was before everything changed and we came up with a few ideas together."

"You ain't gonna talk about the bear?" Kanisha stopped, shook her head, and restated her sentence in perfect diction and grammar. "You must tell them about the bear, Francie," she said with a smile. Francie was the only one who caught the correction, because everyone else instantly had questions about the bear.

"Bear?"

"What bear?"

"Goodness, what happened?"

Francie hugged Kanisha and said, "What happened was this little girl here probably saved my life."

"Little? Who you callin' little, shorty?" Kanisha added with a smile.

"I'm sorry, but I doubt you would like me to call you 'this large woman,' would you?" Francie replied.

"Careful," Kanisha said, protecting her belly.

"As you wish," Francie said, bowing. "This young lady here saved my life." And with that, she began to tell the story of their adventure. The kids' eyes grew wide with excitement. It was like Francie was telling them a campfire story. This was precisely the kind of cinematic energy Nicky had been looking for, and his camera captured every dangerous detail.

After about fifteen minutes, Francie began to talk about the idea she and Kanisha had come up with on their long walk home.

"While we are so very different in many ways, we found we were

- Prestigious, impressive career: "I'm an author."
- Satisfying: a permanent record for future generations
- Make a difference

There as so many ways to create information products.

51 WAYS TO PROFIT FROM INTELLECTUAL PROPERTY

Books

E-books

Audio books

Audio programs

Single audio cassettes

Video trainings

Multimedia systems

Workbooks

Coaching programs

Mentoring and apprenticeship
programs

Speaking internationally

Speaking in breakout sessions

Speaking representing your
employer

Train-the-trainer programs

Public seminars

Corporate training programs

Presenter-at-large events

Boot camps

Tele-boot camps

Hourly consulting

Long-term consulting

Subscription consulting

Spokesperson contracts

Licensing

Infomercial products

Home-study courses

Tele-seminars

Weekend retreats

Subscription audio CD series

Ghostwriting and coauthoring

Branded retail products

Mini-books

Trade associations

Conventions and trade shows

Agenting and information arbitrage

Seminar company workshops

Business-building systems

Practice-management tools

Newsletters

Radio or TV show

Philanthropic foundation

Media expert

Syndicated column

Private-label magazine

Rights—yours

Rights—other people's

Special reports and white papers

CD-ROM and DVD training

Counseling services

Adult professional education

Reference guides and
directories software

both looking for the same thing in life—to be part of something that matters, which I guess is the Inner Winner you were talking about." Michelle smiled encouragingly at Francie. "And when we were doing research online this morning, we ran across a website that got us . . ."

"Fired up," Kanisha said, helping Francie find the words of enthusiasm.

"Yes, fired up." Francie chuckled. "Kanisha is helping me work on my cool."

"It's a tall order, but she's learning," Kanisha joked.

"So what's the website?" Lisa had grown tired of all the cuteness.

"The website is to teach people to remember that anything is possible in life. Here, let me show you," Francie said as everyone gathered around one of the twenty-four-inch iMac computers. Francie typed in the web address, www.iwillremember.com. The images loaded, and a Flash presentation began. Set over stunning photography shots, an inspirational message began, talking about the quiet moments of inspiration and the belief that *you* are the celebration *you've* been looking for. As they watched, Nicky circled the group in a slow-moving shot.

The whole thing was perfect, Michelle thought. Looking over, she shared a smile with Francie as the others continued to watch. Yes, Francie had become an invaluable source of inspiration to the group, and it was at this moment, Michelle was grateful she'd listened to her Inner Winner and gotten Francie in the group.

As it ended, the group moved back to the couches and Francie continued. "And after we saw that, we began to brainstorm different ideas for websites."

"And we ate ice cream. An important ingredient for any brainstorming session, I must say," Kanisha added with a smile.

Learning to Sell a Billion Books

STARTING WITH NOTHING, FROM NOWHERE, AND WITH NO REASON TO BELIEVE THAT I COULD DO IT

MARK VICTOR HANSEN

When I was bankrupt and upside down financially in 1974, I felt hopeless and helpless. Fortunately, several years earlier I had sold my way through Southern Illinois University. I won a little telephone selling contest and had been given an audiotape by Cavett Robert, the dean of speakers, founder of the National Speakers Association, and the man who invented selling books and products from the platform. His tape was called *Are You the Cause or the Effect?*

It was the message of this simple tape that came to my rescue when I was so low that I had to reach up to touch bottom. I listened to that great and inspiring tape 287 times. Like the gunslingers of old, who scratched notches into the side of their guns, I made a mark on the tape after every listening. I could repeat the entire talk perfectly, word for word, and thought about offering to do Cavett's talk for him if ever he couldn't show up.

Deeply inspired, I wrote Cavett. To my astonishment, he hand-wrote me a letter and told me to send $35 and join his newly founded organization, the National Speakers Association. I didn't have the $35 to join or the airfare to get from New York to Phoenix to attend the first convention. I wanted to be there so badly, I borrowed the money to go.

At this meeting that wowed my soul, spirit, and desire to become a giant in the speaking business, Cavett planted in my mind the idea that would change my life. He said, "As a public speaker, you need to write a book. If you personally cannot write an entire book from your own experience today, do a multiauthored book."

The thought captured my mind and heart and illuminated an immediate possibility that I had never heard, thought about, or even considered. I could do this and make it manifest in almost no

"Now *that* I can agree with," Lisa told her.

"We wanted to create something where we could work once, like you talked about, and be paid multiple times," Francie noted.

"So the wow we came up with, which we'd like to be now, is the idea of creating social networking sites," Kanisha began. "One site will help pregnant teens, because before I met all of you, the books over there on the shelves were . . ." She searched for the right words. "Well, they sucked."

"They were inadequate," Francie said, correcting her.

"Yeah, that too," Kanisha said playfully. "I wanted someone I could talk to about what I was going through when I was pregnant. And then I thought, duh, chat rooms."

"Why chat rooms?" Michelle asked.

"Do you realize how many people are out there, searching around online?" Kanisha asked.

"Actually, yes, I do," Michelle replied.

"Then you know when you're inside a chat room, you can talk with anyone about anything without feeling . . ."

"Vulnerable," Francie said, finishing her thought. "After hearing her talk about that . . ."

Francie's words stalled as she saw Kanisha quietly talking to herself. It was clear Kanisha was working something out. An idea was forming.

"What is it?" Francie asked.

"Chat rooms. Online. Oh my God, the phone. We use the *phone*!" Kanisha said, standing up. "This is huge."

"What's huge? Why am I always missing everything?" Lisa was upset.

Kanisha stood up, oblivious to Lisa's chatter. "I got it. We find a way to end illiteracy. Not online, but through the phone. Cell

time at all. Cavett had done it himself and showed the book that he had created, of which he had sold hundreds of thousands of copies from the platform.

I leaned over to my seatmate, Keith DeGreen, and asked, "Are you a good editor?"

Keith said, "I was head of the law school journal."

"Great. Let's do a multiauthored book. I am a great salesman and I will sell eighteen people in this room, at $2,000 each, to write a chapter of our book. For that, each person would receive one thousand books fully paid for, since the book costs $2 to print, that they can sell at $10 and turn it into $10,000, plus have the calling card of a book with their name on it." For Keith and me, it became a self-funding deal. As a child selling greeting cards and now as a young adult, I had found a formula to pre-sell my dream and have what I wanted in the shortest time possible. Most readers could do something like this to fund their future enterprises.

Eighteen people paid us $2,000 apiece. We took in $36,000 before we had even written a single word. Then we used that money to get the book printed. The book became *Stand Up, Speak Out and Win!*

I sold twenty thousand copies of that book, at $10 each, in one year from the platform—signing each and every one of them. I jokingly told every audience that this was my bestselling book—and it was at the time. I earned about $200,000 doing basically free talks and selling one book. I thought I had died and gone to heaven. I was thoroughly enjoying myself, doing what I totally loved—helping people decide to make an ever greater difference—and traveling and getting clients to underwrite that and my lodging costs.

I had sold myself out of my financial disaster and sold myself into a brand-new life.

Let's jump forward fifteen years in time.

Jack Canfield and I had been public speakers for several years. We knew the power of a goose-bump story to transform a speech. Once day, we brainstormed the idea of putting together a book of

phones." Kanisha was on a roll. "We get Apple to donate iPhones. Hundreds of them. Wait, thousands, we'll need thousands. Yes, and kids could—"

"What about adults?" Francie asked.

"Good instincts, Francie," Michelle put in. "No matter what the product is, it's important to always find a way to expand the market. If it can work for kids, there's got to be a market for adults too."

The interruption didn't matter. Kanisha was in her own world. Nothing could derail her inspiration—nothing, that is, but the baby waking up from all the commotion. Kanisha didn't miss a beat. She went and got Faith, and came back talking.

"We get Apple to donate these iPhones and we put content on the phones that prepare kids . . . people . . . to take the GED. It's like having school in the palm of your hand."

"Okay, you're offering convenience. Great. I understand that, but why wouldn't someone just go to a night school program for the very same thing?"

"Chat rooms," Francie said.

"Chat rooms?" Michelle asked.

"Yes. Chat rooms are popular because they provide anonymity," Francie explained.

Kanisha kept going. "And the idea of the phone takes away the embarrassment of not having a high school education. You don't ever have to register in person—you could do it totally under the radar and not have to worry about anyone finding out or recognizing you. That could be a great motivator."

"Great. Now how do you monetize the idea?" Michelle asked.

Silence. Kanisha was stumped. She paced back and forth, bouncing Faith in her arms.

"I don't know," Kanisha finally said, deflated that her idea had stalled.

our best stories, plus dozens of other goose-bump-type stories. We called it *Chicken Soup for the Soul*.

Unfortunately, no publisher wanted anything to do with a book of short stories, but we were convinced that this book was a winner. Hundreds of rejections later, we finally found a publisher who would give us a shot if we guaranteed to buy the first 20,000 copies. We agreed. At every one of our speeches, we sold the unpublished book to our audiences. When the book was finally published, we had thousands of buyers waiting to buy the book.

It wasn't an instant hit, but by the end of the first year, the book took off and has been selling millions of copies every year since. From the first Chicken Soup book in 1994, we have now over two hundred different titles, like *Chicken Soup for Teens*, for moms, for golfers, and so on.

(Go to www.markvictorhansen.com and get a free audio, video, and text download from several of our books.)

Early on, we told our skeptical publisher that we wanted to sell a billion books by the year 2020. He just laughed at us. But we were going to have the last laugh. To date, we have sold over 112 million books; that includes all the titles that my name graces, many of which are specialty books and electronic books. We're well on the way to our billion books!

The question is, did we know we could do these phenomenal numbers and make it into the Guinness Book of World Records as the world's bestselling nonfiction authors? We did not. We pinch ourselves that it has happened and is still happening.

Recently, our former publisher informed us that he thought the Chicken Soup idea was tapped out. So we found a new partner who was passionately convinced otherwise. We sold Chicken Soup for the Soul Enterprises and the trademark. Our new owners got us lots of big-time opportunities, one of which is IMG (International Management Group)—they have Tiger Woods, Emmitt Smith, the Vatican, Rolex watches, and a thousand other giant brand names.

When I met Tim Rothwell, executive vice president of IMG, his

"These people have little money," Lei Kim spoke up. "The program must be cheap."

"*Accessible*, not *cheap*. We want words that buzz," Francie pointed out.

"Do they have to buy the phone?" Lei Kim asked.

"No." Kanisha was back. "But we have them sign a financial contract to help teach responsibility. You know, help them become accountable for stuff."

"What about Muhammad Yunus?" Lei Kim said quietly.

"Microlending. Perfect! You don't have them pay for the GED out of their own pocket. You loan them the money to get their education and they have a certain amount of time to pay the loan back. You could make your money off the interest from the loans. How much will you charge?" Michelle asked.

"Three hundred bucks," Lisa said, eager to contribute something.

"Three hundred bucks?" Kanisha balked. "For an education?"

"It's for a diploma. There's a big difference," Lisa explained. "When you go to school, you get more than just a diploma, you get life experience *and* a diploma. Big difference."

"Yeah, okay. Whatever. This is huge!" Kanisha continued.

It went on like this for over an hour. Flip charts were filled and strategies were formed around the program, which consisted of eighty hours of digital content, preloaded onto each iPhone. Hinging off Francie's statement that "we want words that buzz," they came up with the name for the website, www.globalGEDchallenge.com. It was the perfect enlightened idea, Michelle realized. Not only was this a way to make money, but it was also providing a service to the planet. "Could it really end illiteracy as we know it?" Michelle mused. "Why not? Crazier things have happened, and that's how it starts . . . from someone with a little idea."

first line to me was "As a brand, Chicken Soup is totally untapped! We are going to do . . ." And he mentioned the roll-out of more greeting cards, games, pet foods, women's fashion, and other joint ventures with IMGers. One man thought we had tapped the market and another thought it was untapped.

May we suggest (and give you permission to believe) your future earning power is vast and untapped? We give you permission to have a billion-dollar idea and to execute it. If you can make a million, you can make a thousand times that, a billion. We want you to do it. Give yourself a gift by downloading the free e-book *Chronic Profitability* at www.cashinaflashthebook.com/gift.

A Billion in Specialized Knowledge
ROBERT G. ALLEN

I discovered my scalable profit project by teaching a small seminar on real estate investing. I had knowledge, skill, expertise, and a passion for real estate, and I loved to teach. I began teaching an evening course at a local hotel in Provo, Utah. The year was 1978. As I remember, it was $75 for a four-week class. There were about twenty students a month—an extra $1,500 in revenue. The hotel room was cheap. The manual was collated by me and my wife in our master bedroom. It was high-profit.

Then one day I had a bright idea. I wondered if someone would pay $100 for a full-day seminar. Rather than four weekly sessions, we could get it all done in one Saturday. I ran a simple ad in the newspaper for a free seminar on how to buy real estate with little or no money down. A lot of people attended. We held more free events. Eventually, I held a full-day seminar filled with about a hundred people who enrolled for $100. A hundred people times $100 is . . . *ka-ching* . . . $10,000 for a single day of teaching. (Of course, it took several days of planning and marketing.) Still,

"Another idea we had," Francie resumed after they came back from the break, "was a networking website designed specifically for widows and widowers."

"You mean like a dating site?" Lisa asked.

"Oh no. Not a dating site."

"Why not?" Lisa prodded.

"Because dating is a little different when you're my age. There aren't too many single men running around looking for dates with older women."

Kanisha spoke up. "I'm almost eighteen and I'm single with a daughter. It's not like the boys will be beating down my door to spend time with me either. So how's it different for you?"

"For one, your body is going to snap back in a few months. My body's done all the snappin' it's going to do. In fact, I need a few zippers here and there, if you know what I mean," Francie joked. "A dating site for seniors. That's just what I need in my life, a bunch of old guys hopped up on Viagra knockin' on my door." Laughter rippled through the group. "But, if that's what comes out of the experience for someone, fine—it's just not for me. The idea Kanisha and I had was more of a place where widows and widowers could go to talk about loss, and help each other through those moments when you feel really alone. I was locked in fear of meeting anyone new because I was now a widow. It sounds silly, but talking with Kanisha, I realized I've been wasting my time by being afraid. I was running out of money. Running out of money? Hell, I was flat broke." She chuckled.

"I know it's not funny," she went on. "In fact, it got downright scary there for a while. But my fear was actually keeping me from asking for help, or doing something that might get me out of trouble.

$10,000 was a lot of money thirty years ago. That's a lot of money today! I had found a vein of pure gold.

I wondered how much someone would pay for a *two*-day seminar. Would they pay $195? I ran a full-page ad in the newspaper. Two hundred people ended up coming at about $200 per person. That was $40,000 for a single weekend. We're talking serious money. I decided to scale up some more.

Of course, this sounds too easy. I've left out the hard parts—the times when *nobody* paid for the seminar. There were dozens of hard knocks and disappointments—like the time when my wife's purse was stolen when she was registering people at one of our seminars in Baltimore. Or the time when I invested a lot of advertising in Denver, Colorado, for a seminar when the Denver Broncos were playing a key football game. Money down the drain.

Still, we kept scaling things up. We eventually charged $500 for a weekend seminar. Ultimately, I licensed the seminar to a nationwide outfit and scaled down my payout to a net royalty of $58.50 per student. Each week there would be hundreds of students nationwide. I collected weekly checks for $20,000, $30,000, sometimes $50,000. And I didn't even need to be there to teach the seminar. They eventually taught 103,000 people at about $500 per person. I just cashed the checks. Millions of dollars' worth.

During this time, I released the book *Nothing Down: A Proven Program That Shows You How to Buy Real Estate with Little or No Money Down.* Fueled by the advertising from the seminars, the book took off. It spent fifty-eight weeks on the *New York Times* best-seller list.

But good things often come to an end. The seminar outfit stopped earning profit during a down time in the real estate market. They closed their doors. That major source of income dried up. Then a freak avalanche destroyed our mountain home at the Sundance ski resort. When the insurance company balked at paying the insurance, our banker demanded immediate payment on a large loan I had borrowed on a speculative real estate project. We went

I now realize that we have two choices; do more of the same, or do something different."

"And all this happened because of your encounter with the bear?" Lisa wondered aloud.

"Yes," Francie replied. "It was dangerous, but that danger pushed me into a place I had not thought of before."

"What place was that?" Michelle said.

"Forgiveness. Before Kanisha started throwing rocks at that bear, I saw my life flash before my eyes and all I could think about were the things I didn't do because I was afraid. It was like all of a sudden I flipped a switch." She snapped her fingers. "In an instance, I forgave my parents. I forgave Christopher for dying—like he had a choice in the matter—and I forgave myself. Instantly, my eyes opened to what is really important in life. Even though I'd made all that money before we ran into the bear, I still had felt emotionally bankrupt. That bear made me realize what mattered most in my life, which is . . . all of you." Francie paused, tears in her eyes. Then a wicked gleam joined them. "Oh, yes, and my black Prada heels with the gold buckle, too."

The other women began to laugh together through their own tears. Hannah and Russell shared a look as if to say, *You think we should cry too?*

"Okay," Michelle said at last, "why don't we take another fifteen-minute break? We'll meet back on the couches at eight-thirty."

into a full financial avalanche. We lost everything . . . and eventually declared bankruptcy.

From nothing to everything to nothing again in seven short years. Scaling up to 100 percent and then scaling back down to zero. About a year after this financial collapse began, one of my previous employees, Thomas R. Painter, tracked me down and convinced me to scale things back up again. Our first seminar was taught to ninety-three people at $1,000 per person. We scaled up our prices over the next five years and scaled up the number of people we taught. We eventually went on to teach twenty thousand people during a weeklong Wealth Training at $5,000 per person. Do the math. It's breathtaking.

Then Saddam Hussein invaded Kuwait. The United States launched Desert Storm on January 17, 1991. People started watching the bombs drop and stopped attending seminars. Our business dried up. It was time to scale things back down to zero. We closed the doors for the next seven years.

When the conditions were right, we started to scale things back up. As a test, Tom Painter and I started a financial tele-coaching business in 1999. Tele-coaching was just in its infancy. Our first online class had eight people who paid $1,000 for a series of live weekly teleconferences with me. From that small re-beginning, we have grown into one of the largest training operations for real estate investment education in the world. We have hundreds of thousands of students who have attended our one-day to three-day free events. Tens of thousands more are protégés who have paid up to $5,000.

But only a few qualify for our intense, yearlong Mastery Program. It includes one-on-one coaching. Live field training in various cities. Several powerful three-day bootcamps. The Harvard of Wealth. The Stanford of Profit. We work with our students until the money starts to flow. But we charge a Harvard/Stanford–type tuition. Price tag: $29,900. That's a hefty tuition. But our Mastery Students often go from learning to earning real profit in ninety days or less. In fact, the success of our students is staggering (check out MillionaireHallOf

13

Finding Closure

In the Wow of Their Now

As the rain continued to fall outside, the mood inside the Heartlight was raw, as was evident on the footage from Nicky's camera. Hannah and Russell huddled around the zebra print beanbag where Nicky sat watching the playback of Francie's story. "Watch this," Nicky said as the shot pushed in close on Francie as she began to cry. Nicky smiled because he knew he finally had filmed something really dramatic.

When the session resumed, Michelle emerged from the office, scrolling through a playlist on her iPod.

"Everybody ready? Kids? Ready to get back to it?" Michelle asked, not waiting for an answer as she moved to the stereo cabinet behind the front counter. "Watching that little video presentation on the Internet made me think about a song I've been listening to. So, in the spirit of show-and-tell," she said, smiling at the children, "I want to play a song that I think is perfect for what we're talking about here." When she finally looked up to make sure they were ready, she noticed Lisa was missing.

"Wait. Where's Lisa?" she asked, looking around the store.

"She walked up to Starbucks to get coffee," Lei Kim answered.

"The girl went up there to get cookies, don't kid yourself," Kanisha said with a grin.

Before Michelle could react, Lisa knocked on the front door.

Fame.com). With our coaching, our students have earned over a billion dollars in actual profits and have donated over $30 million to various charities of their choice.

Each ninety days we have a new challenge patterned after my famous real estate challenges.

In our various challenges, over $100 million in profit has been logged. What kind of income is generated from only one hundred Mastery students? Once again, do the math.

It's taken me over thirty years—through several incarnations—to create programs with enough excellence to be worth that kind of tuition. At times, it's a very lucrative business. Other times, it's very, very difficult. Through it all, the scaling up and down, I keep pursuing my purpose path with my various partners.

SO HOW DO *YOU* EARN YOUR FORTUNE WITH INTELLECTUAL PROPERTY?

Both of us have gone from bankruptcy to billions. If you're struggling through bleak financial times, all we can say is, we totally understand! We've earned the right to tell you that you can survive and prosper . . . starting right now with what you already have.

The money can start to flow into your life in as little as twenty-four hours from this very minute. What? Twenty-four hours from now? Yup. Look at a clock. Log in the time. Your twenty-four hours just started.

Rich in Six
ROBERT G. ALLEN

That's the name of a new information product I just launched and marketed through an infomercial, Rich in Six. The product offering is a book, some CDs, special reports, et cetera. By the time this book is published the Rich in Six program will hopefully have already

Balancing a cup carrier with coffee for everyone, a chocolate chip cookie wedged in her mouth, Lisa fought with the storm's howling wind, which was a losing battle at this point. Her flimsy umbrella popped inside out and Lisa almost dropped the coffee. Francie quickly unlocked the door and Lisa stepped in from the pouring rain. Despite having an umbrella, she was drenched.

"You're all wet, sweetie," Francie said as Lisa handed her the coffee.

"That's because this umbrella is terrible," Lisa groused, holding up the rickety contraption. "Why can't someone make an umbrella that won't turn inside out like a sock every damn time a storm moves into town? I mean, honestly, isn't that what they're made to do, keep you dry?" she asked, not really looking for an answer. She swung open the door and threw the broken umbrella onto the sidewalk.

"Attagirl—you show that umbrella who's boss," Michelle said.

"Stupid thing," Lisa said, finding a smile as she took one of the cups of coffee from Francie. "I tell you what, this better be the best coffee I've ever had, because I worked hard for it."

"Okay, we ready?" Michelle asked.

"What're we doing?" Lisa whispered over to Francie as they sat down.

"I don't know, she's going to play a song for us."

"If it's 'Raindrops Keep Falling on My Head,' I'm outta here." Grabbing one of the quilts draped over the back of the couches, Lisa wrapped herself up before plopping back into place.

"This CD came in the mail last week," Michelle explained. "We get all sorts of demos from the record companies as samples. I'm not sure why this one made its way into my car, but when I heard this song, I thought . . . wow. Everyone close their eyes and we'll get started," Michelle said, ready to hit the play button.

been on TV for several months. The success rate of infomercials is about one in twenty-five. But those that hit are extremely profitable. Let's just say my fingers are crossed.

Here is the story of a student of the Rich in Six program and exactly how she earned her first profit in twenty-four hours. One of her hobbies is painting. She's been painting for years but has sold few paintings. It was more of a hobby than a profession. I challenged her on a live conference call to turn professional and start selling her paintings. She created a nice e-mail message and sent it out to about 150 of her friends and family. On the PSI scale, she was selling paintings . . . products. She got some interest and sold a painting or two. Then I enlightened her to the possibility that one of her other PSIs was her skill as a painter. She could sell this know-how to others and earn even more profit. I challenged her to create a sixteen-week painting seminar and to sell her knowledge. She had never done anything like this before. As soon as she heard the idea, she almost went into a panic. The *how* word started to attack her. "How will I sell it? How will I deliver it? How can I find people who might want it? How? How? How?"

She beat back her uncertainties and put together an e-mail to the same people to whom she had offered her paintings. I had coached her to create scarcity by saying in her e-mail that she had only one spot available. She offered to coach one student how to paint over the Internet using a live webinar with sound and visuals. She reasoned she would be able to teach basic painting skills one-on-one to a student.

How was she going do this over the Internet? She didn't know. How was she actually going to teach successfully? She didn't know. She just knew that somehow she'd be able to figure it out.

My challenge came to her on a Monday afternoon at about five o'clock. She spent the rest of the day wondering and worrying. Then she got clear in her mind and heart exactly what she would do. She would send another e-mail to her current database. Twenty-two hours after she had been challenged, she sent the

"Can I ask a question?" Kanisha said, raising her hand. "What's with all the eye closing?"

"Because it enables you to become single-minded. When you have your eyes open, you're looking around at other people, worried about them looking at you, both wondering if you look okay; 'How's my hair? Oh, is that a new dress she's wearing? I think I have something in my teeth.'"

Everyone giggled. Michelle wasn't just about business all the time; she did have a playful side, and when she showed it, she really shone. "Just trust me—you'll see what I mean. Close your eyes." Michelle pressed play and sat down as the song began to play over the sound system. Gentle piano chords started softly, and a movement of harmonic progressions slowly built into a crescendo. Then a man's soft voice began to sing:

Get ready. My soul. I'm diving in.
Get ready. My soul. I'm diving in.
To the deepest kind of love.
To the sweetest kind of life.
Get ready. Get ready. My soul.

Everything I've ever done. Everything I've ever seen.
Everything I lost or won. Everything I've ever dreamed.
Has brought me here. To the present moment.
Here. To a new beginning.
Here. And I'm seeing life so clearly . . . now.

Get ready. My soul. I'm diving in.
Get ready. My soul. I'm diving in.
To the deepest kind of love.
To the sweetest kind of life.
Get ready. Get ready. My soul.

e-mail. It offered to mentor someone to paint in a sixteen-week course for $1,000 tuition, payable immediately.

Exactly two hours later she received the following email:

> Hi, Linda:
>
> Are you sure you can teach me to paint over the phone?
>
> If so—I always felt we had a connection ever since we met at that seminar . . .
>
> I would love to be your sixteen-week student and I have the $1,000!
>
> Debra Jo

Following is the e-mail that Linda sent me after she had just made a thousand dollars in a single day from idea to cash.

> Hi, Bob:
>
> I felt a little shaken up on Monday after the Rich in Six teleconference. :-) When your mentor tells you exactly what you can do, I figure you'd better do it. So I did—I pushed away any fears and spent the rest of Monday thinking about how I would structure my offer. And Tuesday morning I wrote out my e-mail.
>
> I checked and Debra Jo's e-mail is marked as arriving at 5:06 Tuesday. Exactly twenty-four hours after the call ended the day before! She and I are both excited! Thank you for your great mentoring!
>
> Linda

She turned her knowledge, skill, and passion into $1,000 cash in twenty-four hours. That may not seem like much to you. But I had launched my training business almost exactly the same way nearly thirty years before—an eight-week course for $75.

Let's just dream for a minute. How could Linda turn this simple success into a million-dollar-a-year empire using this simple idea? Well, we already know that someone is willing to invest $1,000 for a sixteen-week course. How many more people does she need to attract? One million dollars is generated from only a thousand students. Do you think there might be another thousand

'Cause here I go. Deeper. Deeper. Deeper than I've ever been before.

Here I go. Closer. Closer. Closer to my sacred source.

Here I go. Deeper. Deeper. Deeper than I've ever been before.

Here I go. Closer. Closer. Closer to my sacred source.

Here I go. Deeper. Deeper. Deeper than I've ever been before.

Here I go Closer. Closer. Closer to my sacred source.

Get ready. My soul. I'm diving in.

Get ready. My soul. I'm diving in.

To the deepest kind of love.

To the sweetest kind of life.

Get ready. Get ready. My soul.

From the CD *Sacred Love* by Daniel Nahmod, copyright Nahmod Music Co. (ASCAP). (Download a free copy of this song at www.cashinaflashthebook.com.)

The women's eyes slowly opened as the song ended, and they wiped away tears. The song spoke directly to their hearts, and even though she'd heard it many times before, Michelle had tears in her eyes as well. Each one was filled with a silent desire to live life from a deeper place. Of all creative expressions, Michelle thought music was the most powerful. It was poetry with musical notes. Could a painting cause such emotions? A photograph? Perhaps, Michelle thought, but music somehow spoke to a deeper place in the heart. It was a place most people would talk about only when life became difficult or when tragedy struck. Right now, however, the group was active in the pursuit of a more abundant life.

Rising amidst the silence, Michelle moved to the whiteboard and wrote down the most powerful line in the song. They were all powerful, she thought, but the line "Get ready. My soul. I'm diving in" was perfect. She stood back and looked at the line as if they were

people somewhere in the world who might want the same experience? Absolutely!

Here's the problem: she is only one person and she can't teach a thousand people a one-on-one course. She has to scale things up. First, she needs to perfect her system by teaching twenty, thirty, fifty people until she has individual success stories. She needs to show proof that her system works. Then she turns on the marketing machines.

She makes herself available for a class three times a week. She increases the class size to ten students. As a bonus, she offers them archives of her most successful classes online for advanced study. So now her student base is thirty students at $1,000 per student. That's $30,000 per "semester." She can do three semesters per year . . . or close to the $100,000-a-year figure.

Let's scale this up. She can either increase her class size or find other artists in her city whom she can train to teach her system. Each trainee needs to attend her $5,000 train-the-trainer course. She finds ten people in her city who are willing to pay her $5,000 for the privilege of earning nice incomes teaching art students. Of course, they earn half of the $1,000 tuition. So their $5,000 tuition turns into a $15,000-per-semester income. Not bad for a $5,000 investment!

Now Linda has ten people each teaching thirty students per semester. That's three hundred students, for which she earns $500 per student or $150,000 per semester. That's close to half a million dollars a year. And she doesn't have to teach any of those classes.

But we're not done. By this time, she's learned not only how to market her painting programs to individual art students but also how to market train-the-trainer programs. Her total income is over $500,000 a year. Of course, this is not all net profit. There would be marketing costs, Web fees, and the like. But there would still be a very, very nice profit left over.

Let's scale this up some more. She thinks that there are other people who would like to earn half a million dollars a year selling

admiring an artwork hanging in a museum. What Michelle loved most about the lyric, and the song in general, was the simplicity of it. "Get ready. My soul. I'm diving in" meant life was ready to be lived, and before you could go confidently in the directions of your dreams, your soul had to be in play.

Snapping the marker's cap back on, Michelle turned to Lisa and asked, "So, are you ready?"

"You expect me to talk after a song like that?" Lisa answered, dabbing the tears from her eyes with a Starbucks napkin.

"It's beautiful, Michelle," Francie added.

"Hits me deep inside every time." Michelle smiled, then turned to Lisa. "Are you ready?"

Sensing something was about to happen, Nicky turned on his camera from the zebra beanbag and panned over to Lisa, framing her in a tight close-up. Not wanting to call attention to himself, Nicky rested the camera on his lap and used the small monitor on the side of the camera to frame his shot. Hannah joined him on the beanbag. He gave her a look but made room. She watched as Nicky zoomed in close; when Lisa's tears started again, Nicky zoomed in even tighter. Lisa's attention swung to the front door, where the tattered umbrella was being jostled about by the wind. Nicky panned over and captured the umbrella as it danced against the glass of the front doors like a fly looking for a way in. Lisa took a deep breath and turned back to the group.

"I'm sorry, but I'm not like you guys. This stuff about the Inner Winner and this Now Wow or whatever . . ."

Hannah giggled.

"Hannah." Michelle quickly spoke up.

"Mommy, it sounded like she said 'bow wow,'" Hannah said innocently.

Even Lisa had to laugh. The mood quickly lightened in the group,

art training. So she launches her advanced business-building program. How much should she charge someone? We're going for the big bucks because it's worth it. It's $10,000. She will only allow one advanced business builder in each city in the world. She gives them exclusive territory. There are a thousand big cities in the world in which she could sell her $10,000 business-building experience. This would require some serious marketing. But is there enough margin to hire a whole team of people to carry it out? Let's do the numbers: 1,000 ABB students times $10,000 equals (drum roll, please): $10 million.

Of course, each of these 1,000 students would have to buy the art training materials for each of their students. It's only $50 per kit, and she only earns $20 profit per kit, but since there are a thousand business-building students who market nine hundred students per year at $20 profit to her, that equals (drum roll, please): $18 million per year.

Do the math. You get the picture? Information products can become *very, very* exciting *very, very* quickly.

Earlier we shared Mark's story of how he sold a multiauthored book to eighteen people for $2,000 a person. In other words, each person received his or her own chapter in the book. That gave Mark and his partner, Keith, instant cash to create the book. Each author could buy extra copies at a low price to resell for a profit.

Let's go in the opposite direction. Let's get multiple sponsors for a single-authored book.

$62,000 OUT OF THIN AIR
THE BERNICE WINTER STORY

When we talk to multimillionaires who have amazing success stories, we ask them what got them started, what was the catalyst for

and Lisa shifted in her seat, still struggling with the spotlight. She took a sip of her coffee and took another deep breath before she continued.

"Ideas like you guys are having, they just don't come to me, okay? I'm sorry, but I've never been one to think that way. It's not how I'm built."

"Why do you keep apologizing?" Francie asked.

"What?" Lisa asked.

"You've said 'I'm sorry' twice in the last ten seconds."

"It's just a word, Francie." Lisa huffed.

"Yes, it is," Michelle said, "but I think Francie might be on to something."

"You know what, Michelle? Let's not make something out of nothing. It's just a word. That's it. Nothing more. I'm not sorry for my life. I'm not sorry for the way I am, either. Not everyone's an entrepreneur like you. I like to leave work behind and go home. And hey, if that's where the phrase 'ignorance is bliss" comes from, then I guess I'm ignorant. But I will not sit here and act like something I'm not."

"And that's a good thing, but just like anything, you can learn to see opportunity in your daily life. You never know where the fish are going to bite," Michelle offered.

"*I'm sorry,* I don't know what you mean." Lisa emphasized the words "I'm sorry" in Francie's direction to make a point. "Or should I say, 'Excuse me, I don't know what you mean'?"

"It's how Gideon would talk about his inventions, in metaphors. It used to drive me crazy, but they help sometimes. The kids will tell you, their father loved to go fishing. He'd wake up three hours before sunrise just to spend five hours on the lake. He said it helped him think, and because he had so many ideas and projects going on at the same time, he'd say, 'You gotta keep as many lines in the

their action, and what was the creativity that led to their extraordinary results. We have found that most often it was an unwanted and unwelcome event, an exigent circumstance, that yielded the extraordinary results.

Bernice Winter grew up the oldest of five children in a dysfunctional family. Hers was a life way too full of drama for a little girl. In her young life, the police came and took her and her siblings to shelters time after time after time. Consequently, she attended several different schools while living in shelters. Some of the schools were located in wealthy neighborhoods and others in poor districts.

Bernice noticed some profound differences between the rich kids from the wealthy-neighborhood schools and the poor kids. The rich kids didn't worry about money. Their parents took care of the basic necessities of life for them. The rich kids talked about the activities they had planned for the weekend, fun stuff. The poor kids didn't talk about having fun; instead they had responsibilities such as how to put food on the table, how to keep a roof over their heads, and who would be there for their siblings. They didn't have to worry about weekend activities. There were none.

At a young age, Bernice had seen enough contrasts in life to determine that she would not just accept what life had dealt her. Bernice decided that if she had a choice to worry about money or not to worry about money, she would choose not to have to worry about money when she grew up. She was a dreamer. She told her mother, "I will never work for money when I grow up. I will have money work for me."

Bernice said, "I was a thinker. My mother would laugh at me and lock me in the closet, telling me to think. That's what I did in the dark closet. I would dream and I never let go of my dreams and I let them be huge. I believe in fairy tales."

By the time Bernice was eight, she was knocking on doors to find cleaning jobs to earn money to put food on the table so she and her younger brothers and sisters could eat. By the time

water as you can, baby. You never know where the fish are going to bite.' He looked at ideas like fish bait. If one thing didn't work, he would try something else. The more ideas you have going, the better chance you have to see one of those ideas become a reality. Without ideas, he used to say, you're just spinning your wheels, punching a clock making money for someone else."

"Okay, now I'm the one who's sorry," Francie said, smiling at Lisa. "I'm not sure *I* understand."

Michelle stood up and went to the whiteboard again.

"There's no *one* thing that will cause you to have a financial awakening, spiritual insight, or revelation. Whatever you want to call it, the process of becoming an enlightened entrepreneur is a combination of all things." Michelle wrote the word *entrepreneur* on the board. The erasable marker squeaked with every stroke.

"What does this mean?" she asked the group.

"Daddy," Hannah said.

Michelle smiled at Hannah. "Yes, honey, that's how Daddy described himself."

"Independence?" Lei Kim offered.

"Exactly. Willing to take on greater than normal financial risks." Then Michelle wrote the word *enlightened* in front of *entrepreneur.*

"Now, what does this mean?"

"Daddy," Hannah said again.

"Yes, honey. That was Daddy too." She turned her attention back to the women and answered the question herself. "An enlightened entrepreneur operates from a place of abundance, creates massive value for everyone, in every way, and learns and leaves a legacy of abundance." She paused for a second. "Sounds exciting, don't you think?"

"It sounds kinda scary, is what I think," Kanisha said, speaking up.

she was fifteen she was out on her own trying to create her own fairy tale.

Eventually Bernice got into the condo business and stayed there for fourteen years before venturing out into a new career. Within a short period of time, this new venture failed and she lost everything—her home, her bank account, and her car—and ended up homeless and on the street.

It was a long way back up from the bottom. During this tough time she picked up a copy of our first book, *The One Minute Millionaire.* It caught her eye because of the purple and yellow book cover with the butterfly.

Reading *The One Minute Millionaire* transformed her mind-set about money. She began to reconnect to her dreams. With each new bit of information she learned and applied, Bernice's level of success increased. Within one short year she was back on her feet. Her confidence was back. That year she received an award from the Canadian Condominium Institute for her contribution to the condominium industry in Canada.

Bernice's most brilliant lesson was to turn her existing knowledge into a book. She wrote *Ten Secrets to Surviving Life in a Condominium.* The book was written as a guidebook, resource book, and fictional story meant to educate anyone who is or wants to be a condo owner and for anyone who has to deal with one.

In the story, a couple by the name of Bob and Betty decide to sell their house and buy a condo. The reader then travels on an educational journey about life in a condominium while encountering problems and learning how to solve them from experts in the field.

After coming up with the idea, Bernice needed to consider how she was going to produce the book and get it published. She knew that her printing cost would be $7,000. Artwork and other costs associated with publishing the book would run the overall costs up to $13,000. By then, Bernice was a true protégé. Bernice decided to apply Robert Allen's Nothing-down or OPM (Other People's Money) principle to publish her book.

"Only if you think of it that way. Financial freedom rarely comes from living a linear-income life. Working nine to five is like being on a treadmill—you never really get anywhere, but the activity tricks you into thinking that you're making progress when actually, you aren't. Corporate raises barely keep you up to speed with inflation. That's not progress, that's treading water, and that's where companies want you. Stuck on a treadmill, in debt, so you have to stay at the desk, working to make them more money. I'm not anti-corporate or anti-nine-to-five in general; I'm simply pro-financial-freedom."

"That's easy for you to say. You're already rich," Lisa quipped.

"And you think that makes me different from you, because of my bank account? Wealth isn't defined by your bank records. Wealth is defined as courage. Commitment. You mustn't forget, I was beyond broke before I became rich. But I don't want to talk about me, I want to get back to this," she said, underlining the word *ent-epreneur*. "Can anyone think of some examples that might fall under the definition of what it is to be an entrepreneur?

"Franchise?"

"Writers?"

"Product inventions?"

"Maybe eBay?" Lisa finally added her two cents.

"Great, Lisa. Let's look at the eBay business model, which is the buying and selling of items. The great thing about doing this kind of work is that you don't have to wait to create a product or file for a patent, which can take up to eighteen months. You don't have to write the book, shoot the infomercial, or produce anything in any way. You can start making money by selling someone else's inventory, and get this—you don't even need a license to do it. The reason eBay's business model works is that it's very simple. They connect those who *don't want* with those who *want*. How do they make their money? They charge a percentage on the deal."

She approached vendors on her trade list (Realtors, contractors, service companies, advertisers—companies that did business with the condo trade) and pitched them with the idea of buying into the book. She told them it was worth spending bigger dollar amounts because newspaper and magazine advertisements were expensive but they didn't stay on the shelf. Within a day, a week, or a month, all the advertising money spent on these forms of advertising went into the trash can. She compared that to a book. Books don't go off the shelf. They reside in homes and in libraries and their message remains over time.

Bernice contacted the vendors on her trade and referral lists and offered to write them into her story and give them a full-page exclusive advertisement (in their vendor category) in her book for $7,000. She also offered a lesser advertising package where they could buy a half-page ad for $5,000 but they wouldn't be in the story and they wouldn't get an exclusive ad in their vendor category. The first advertisement she sold paid for printing her book. The second advertisement paid for all other publishing costs. She made approximately $62,000 from advertising before she sold the first copy.

Bernice sold three thousand copies of her book in hardback for $19. When she ran out of books she sold another two thousand e-book copies for $15 each. Bernice then decided to edit and rename her book and do a second printing. She went back to the vendors and asked if they wanted to be in the next edition. The vendors had had such great results with the first book that they jumped at the chance and paid another $7,000.

Bernice said that it is a really neat feeling to see her book in a library or to have someone bring the book to a meeting and ask for her autograph. And this is only the beginning.

A lesson that Bernice has learned along the way: If you're lying in a hospital bed looking at the monitor that is recording your vital signs, you want to see peaks and valleys, not a flat line. Get excited

"Want? Don't want?" Francie asked.

"You have someone who doesn't want an item anymore and you connect them with a person who wants that item. Everything you see in life was bought and sold, and someone made money on the transaction. A car. A boat. Jewelry. Sports equipment. Shoes. Trinkets. You name it, and someone's made money on the sale of that item. That's what I want you to start thinking about, Lisa. I'm not looking for you to quit your job and put all your eggs in one basket, so to speak. What I want you to think about, what I want everyone to think about, is creating chunks of money. Fast money. A fast nickel is better than a slow dime. The eBay model invites everyone to the opportunity to make money. Anyone can do it. While these ideas up here on the whiteboard are great, it's not the end . . . it's only the beginning. There are infinite ways to make money."

"I'm not going to get into the garage sale business, Michelle," Lisa said.

"Stop getting hung up on the details, Lisa. It's just an example. Stay focused on the principle that there are infinite ways to make money. I don't care if you're selling tables and chairs, making computers in China, or flipping Prada shoes on the Internet—the lesson here is the endless streams of income are out there, waiting for us to secure them. Life is abundant. There are always ways to make money, regardless of the economy or whether or not Mercury is in retrograde. Business is always going to be there. It's our time. Say that with me. 'It's my time.'" The group repeated the phrase with a blasé tone.

"Oh, come on. *It's my time.*" She repeated it with the enthusiasm she was looking for.

"It's my time," the group said in unison, smiling at each other.

"So, how do we do it?" Michelle said, directing her attention to Lisa, who at the moment was becoming more and more annoyed by

about those curves that life throws you—those peaks and valleys. It means you're alive and still in the game!

THERE'S A BOOK IN YOU

You also have a story that's worth writing about. When it comes to the information business, your story is the most important story. Writing your book about your experience is your most important product. So scan through your cache of problems, fears, or failures that have occurred in your life. Make a decision to solve or resolve them one by one. Everyone likes a survivor. But everyone *loves* a winner!

That's your richest vein of gold. Your story is easy for you to sell. Why? Because it's true for you. It's comes from your own experience—from your own heart and your own mind. Therefore, as you share your testimony about what happened for you, it's real. It's authentic. It's enlightened selling because you passionately believe it. It's your lowest-hanging fruit.

Both of us have programs where we show would-be authors how to become *New York Times* bestselling authors like we are. Check it out at www.cashinaflashthebook.com/author.

Could you become a bestselling author? If Linda can do it, so can you. If Bernice can do it, so can you. If Mark and Bob can do it, so can you.

the tapping sound her umbrella was making on the glass of the front doors. The wind was really beginning to kick up outside, and the tattered umbrella was thrashing about. Lisa turned to Michelle and challenged her again.

"Okay, Michelle, what *are* we talking about?"

"Everybody wants to make money, but nobody wants to talk about the consciousness of money."

"The consciousness of money?" Lei Kim asked, leaning forward.

"Are you aware of how many people go broke after winning millions in the lottery?"

Nobody answered, so Michelle continued.

"Well, the number is staggering. It happens because the people who win the lottery aren't at the same vibrational level as the money they win."

"Vibrational what?" Kanisha asked.

"Vibrational level. Everything we do, everything we are, comes from our vibrational frequency. Energy. It's this energy that enables us or disables us to do what we want to do in life." Michelle was met with blank stares from the group.

"Let me put it another way," she said, thinking for a second. "Here's a question. Can a bird fly backward?"

"No," Lisa said immediately. The others simply shook their heads like they didn't know or agreed with Lisa.

Hannah's hand quickly shot up like she was in class.

"Hannah?" Michelle said with a nod to her daughter.

"The hummingbird can fly backward," she said proudly.

"That's right, baby. The hummingbird is the only bird able to fly backward."

Lisa scoffed, not happy at being shown up by a seven-year-old. "Why are we talking about hummingbirds?"

18

THE ONLY WAY OUT IS TO SELL YOUR WAY OUT

The one key talent of the entrepreneur is to see profit and to have the desire to create a solution. The one key skill that you *must* possess (or acquire) is the ability to sell. If you can't persuade people to buy into your project, then it won't get off the ground. For an entrepreneur, there are a host of different people who need to be sold: partners, customers, employees, bankers, suppliers. As soon as your PSI (product/service/information) is ready to market to the world, if you can't sell it, your business will shrivel up and die. If you can sell it, your business with survive and flourish. You've got to be able to sell.

Most people hate to sell.

A woman once complained to her friend how much she hated selling.

"What don't you like about selling?" her friend asked.

"Everything! The rejection! The pushy people. It's a low-class profession. It's a job that I would *never* do. I mean. . . . *never!*"

Her friend listened and then said, "I agree. You sure sold me!"

Without realizing it, the woman who hated selling was selling passionately the whole time. She just didn't call it selling. She would probably call it "sincere sharing of my true, passionate beliefs."

No matter what you think about selling, everyone sells! Whether you're an employee or the owner, you're constantly selling. If you need a job, you have to sell yourself to your employer to get hired. Then you need to constantly sell your value to your employer to keep from being fired. If your company is downsizing, why should they keep you? If you haven't sold them on the value of keeping you, you'll be on the pink slip list.

"Can you imagine how fast the wings of a hummingbird have to move in order for it to fly backward, or stop on a dime to hover in front of a flower?" Michelle said. "And further imagine if that bird stopped in front of a flower that was without any nectar. Do you think it would sit around and complain, 'Oh, poor me, there's no more nectar here'?" She leaned forward like she was telling them a secret. "Of course not. They are always on the move, from one flower to the next flower. And why, you ask?" Her voice began to boom with excitement. "Because, other than an insect, the hummingbird has the highest metabolism of all animals on the planet."

"Have you seen Paris Hilton lately?" Lisa said, joking. "Girl's metabolism is workin' overtime."

Michelle ignored Lisa's comment. "They need to stay busy. If they don't, they die. A hummingbird needs to drink its body weight in nectar every day, or it will die. The wings of a hummingbird flap something like eighty times per second, and its heart can beat up to twelve hundred times a minute. The high metabolism and heart rate are all needed to accommodate the high vibrational frequency their bodies create, which enables them to, yes, fly backward. Those lottery winners we were talking about? Bad decisions and overspending sends them right back to the poorhouse. Why? Because at the end of the day, they chose a vibrational frequency that is lower than the money they won. They believe that they aren't worth the money they won," Michelle said, satisfied at her explanation. By the looks on everyone's faces, everyone was satisfied by Michelle's explanation—everyone but Lisa.

"And this brings us back to the Inner Winner and the Wow Now philosophy. It's fine to have your mind invested in something, but without your heart—the wow now, as it were—you simply remain the same as you were before the idea arrived." Michelle set the pen in the tray of the easel and joined everyone on the couches.

Sir Richard Branson learned how to sell as a teenager, as he explains in his book *Screw It, Let's Do It*:

I have spent much of my life being happy about promoting myself and Virgin. Advertising, publicity, promotion—call it what you will—works. Even nature puts on a show—flowers, birds, even beetles display themselves. There is so much competition in the world that if you have something to sell, no matter what, you have to get it noticed. Those early days of hard sell were to stand me in good stead. I learned that we all have something to sell, whether it's a tangible object like a car or a box of Girl Scout cookies or offering our talents for hire. It's no use producing goods or having the best ideas in the universe if they just stay in your head or stacked up in a corner of your bedroom.

You see, you're always selling—whether you like it or not. Let's assume that you're one of those people who is not good at selling. You don't want to sell. You don't believe in selling. As a matter of fact, you *hate* selling. How do you behave when you try to sell anything? You stumble over your words. Your body language shows that you're uncomfortable. You act embarrassed when you ask for the money. The result? You don't get the sale. You get rejected. You don't make any money.

But the whole time you were selling. What were you selling? You were selling the fact that you hated selling. And your customer bought your sales pitch. He bought that you didn't believe in your product. He bought that you didn't enjoy selling it. He bought that you hated to sell it. He bought that you were embarrassed trying to sell it. You convinced him. So he did exactly what you sold him to do—he rejected your sales pitch. He didn't buy.

In *every* interaction, there is a buyer and a seller. What are you selling? You are selling what you passionately, congruently believe. If you passionately, congruently believe that you don't like selling, that's exactly what gets bought.

LIFE IS 100 PERCENT SELLING

There is no way around this fact. Life isn't 37 percent selling or 60 percent selling or 92 percent selling. Life is 100 percent selling.

"So, where does that leave us?" She looked around the room, which was again silent. There were no quick answers. Sensing the silence wasn't going to end anytime soon, Michelle continued.

"Lisa, you say you're not like the rest of us, but that's just your opinion at this particular moment in time. Your perception of a thing doesn't make that thing true. We aren't dealing in absolutes here. When we talk about consciousness, the sky's the limit. Opinions—"

"It's not my opinion, Michelle," Lisa snapped. She was annoyed that she was the center of debate again, and the damn tapping of the umbrella was driving her crazy. It was as if she was the only one who heard the sound, which at this point was like a jackhammer going off inside her head.

Michelle gently corrected her. "By developing this Inner Winner philosophy, you have a better understanding of the truth about yourself, rather than the lies and deception you've carried up to this point, which have told you, 'I'm not like that.' You are more than you think you are. Stop believing the opinions you've formed about yourself."

Still there was nothing from Lisa. Michelle was challenging her, but Lisa wasn't taking the bait because the umbrella had her full attention now. *Tap. Tap. Tap.* The wind outside whipped down Main Street with gale force. *Tap. Tap. Tap.* She couldn't stand it anymore, but Michelle kept going, only adding to the chaos growing inside Lisa's head.

"Focused intention can actually change the object focused on. The same can be said for insight and revelation. The message is being sent out, and the signal might come in the form of a billboard along the highway that speaks directly to your desired intention."

Tap. Tap. Tap.

"How about a line in a song?" Francie volunteered.

If you try to sell us on the fact that your life sucks and life isn't fair, we believe you. You sold us. We buy that you believe that. Why do we buy it? Because consciously or unconsciously, we notice the subtle sales clues that you give off—slumped shoulders, sallow face, dejected language.

If you try to sell us on the fact that life is great, we believe you. You sold us. Why do we buy it? Because consciously or unconsciously, we notice the subtle sales clues that you give off—good posture, glowing face, uplifting language.

The first sale you make is to yourself. In fact, whatever you believe is the pitch you make to yourself. If you believe that you can change your life in the next ninety days, then you've sold yourself that message. Then, having sold yourself, you now reorder your life to bring in the evidence to prove the sales pitch you made to yourself. Everyone around you picks up your sales pitch by the way you talk, the way you dress, the way you move, the little and big decisions you make. You are a walking sales pitch for what you've sold yourself.

A BELIEF IS JUST ANOTHER WAY OF SAYING A SALES PITCH

You might say, "My dad told me constantly that I was worthless." Let's put that same sentence into sales language. Your dad sold you on the fact that you are worthless. You bought it. And you've been selling yourself on that belief ever since. Are you really worthless? Of course not! You're a child of God! At least, that's what we've been selling ourselves since we were little kids. It's a good sales pitch. You should try it sometime.

You are on the front line of the sales force of the company called You. You're not selling PSIs. You're selling yourself. *You* are the product on sale. People don't buy things, they buy people. Why would someone buy you? Do you think you are valuable enough? Whatever you believe, they will buy.

Are you selling yourself short? Are you selling what you want to be selling? Do you want to be selling your time an hour at a time? Or do you

Tap. Tap. Tap.

"Perfect, Francie," Michelle said.

"Like the song we just listened to. Those lyrics felt like it was written for me," Lei Kim added.

Tap. Tap. Tap.

Just as Kanisha was about to add to the conversation, Lisa sprang to her feet. "Doesn't anyone hear that?" she said, stomping to the door.

Tap! Tap! Tap!

Swinging the door open, Lisa grabbed the umbrella and pulled it inside. When she did, however, one of the broken ribs caught on the door jamb, which only seemed to fuel her anger with the device. She tugged on it again and again until the rib finally snapped off. Holding up the mangled device, which no longer resembled an umbrella, she said, "See? Why can't they make an umbrella that's worth anything?" She tossed it into the garbage can in disgust.

As she took a step back toward the group, she froze. It was like a bolt of lightning hit her directly in the soul. Suddenly, everything for her moved in slow motion. The sounds of the room drifted away and she could feel her heart beating like a bass drum. Her breath echoed in her head. It was happening. Right there, standing in the middle of Heartlight Bookstore, Lisa finally got it. She was becoming aware that she was aware. While it seemed to her like the moment lasted an eternity, it passed in a blink of an eye for everyone else. Slowly, the sounds of the room returned as Lisa began to hear a faint voice asking her a question.

"Lisa? What is it?" Michelle was asking.

"The umbrella," Lisa muttered, more to herself than anyone else.

"Girl, I'm not sure you can call it an umbrella anymore," Kanisha said. A ripple of laughter filled the room, but Lisa remained single-minded and laser-focused.

want to shift to a new way of thinking—from selling your time for dollars to selling your time for profits?

When beliefs are wrapped in strong desire, they are even more persuasive.

To find out how we learned to sell, visit www.cashinaflashthebook.com.

When you're selling something you believe in from your heart, you're not selling. You're sharing your truth.

What does your truth consist of?

Your mind and your heart. That is the essence of you. What do you believe? What do you truly desire? That's the truth of you.

ENLIGHTENED SELLING
AND ENDARKENED SELLING

When most people think about selling, they're usually referring to endarkened selling. That's when people don't believe in what they're selling and don't really want to sell it. But they try to sell it anyway because they need money to survive. That's insincere selling. It lacks belief and passion. It leaves most people cold.

Enlightened selling is when you *sincerely believe* in what you are selling. You have a conviction that it's the right thing for your customer *and* for you.

Enlightened selling is when you have an innate passion for what you are selling. You actually enjoy talking about your PSI. You use it yourself. You have experienced the benefits of it. It's true for you . . . so why wouldn't it be true for someone else?

Belief and desire. Mix those two together and there is an explosion of results.

The best salespeople are passionately convinced.

> *You can't sell what you're not proud of.*
> —GARY HALBERT

"Why doesn't someone make an umbrella that's worth any-thing?" she said slowly, turning to the group. It was less a question than a statement of intention.

"Can you unwrap that?" Nicky asked. Michelle loved the way her children thought.

For the first time, Lisa was eager to unwrap something in the group discussion.

"I make a great umbrella. Not just a great umbrella—the best umbrella ever made. I'm sure I'm not the only one who's complained about flimsy umbrellas. Yes. That's it. You're right, Michelle. You're right!"

"About what?" Michelle loved the moment unfolding before her.

"Your problem is your solution. You know how many umbrellas I've gone through this last year? It's like those stupid things kept breaking so I'd come to this—I can't believe I'm about to say this, but—this *now* moment."

"What are you feeling right now, Lisa?" Michelle asked, hoping to harvest more of Lisa's revelation.

"It's going to sound crazy, I know, but . . . I used to think stuff like this happened to other people. Like somehow I wasn't deserving enough—which makes your lottery comment ring so true. But the sky didn't part and I didn't hear the Mormon Tabernacle Choir begin to sing."

"Were they supposed to?" Michelle said, smiling at the others.

"That's what I used to think. I thought angels were supposed to sing and the sea would part. I was looking for miracles."

"And now?"

"I don't know what to call it, but . . . now that I think about it, this kind of thing has been happening my whole life—I just wasn't listening. I'm blown away right now. *Finally!*"

Bursting the bubble, Francie said, "I don't think it's that great.

I remember a friend of mine, Collette, trying to sell me on belonging to a network marketing company in the nutrition field. It was totally off purpose for me. Health and nutrition were at the bottom of my list. I took no vitamins. I almost laughed when she told me that I should join her. By the way, she was my secretary. I was the money guru. I wasn't about to listen to her. Especially about expensive vitamins!

You see, my beliefs were 180 degrees opposite of hers. I didn't believe my health was in danger. (As evidenced by my being fifty pounds overweight.) I didn't believe in nutrition. I didn't believe that any vitamins were necessary. I didn't believe in network marketing. There was no way you could get me to sell it. It would have been endarkened selling.

For her, however, it was enlightened selling. She had two children with cystic fibrosis, and the nutritional products had helped them dramatically. She also had a deep need to earn income because her husband had just abandoned her with five children. She was passionately convinced.

But she didn't try to convince me. She knew I was a money guy. So the next week she showed me her first $100 check. "That's nice," I thought. "Good for her." A month or so later, it was a $1,000 check. "Interesting," I thought. "Good for her." A few weeks later she told me that she was earning $1,000 a week.

Now, *this* got my attention. That was certainly more than I was paying her as my secretary. "Hmmmm. A thousand bucks a week. Residual. How did she do that?" My purpose path is to research and teach people how to earn multiple streams of income. I thought there was no way that anyone could earn that kind of residual income that quickly—especially not her. But when she showed me her check, I had to believe it. My belief went from "Network marketing is a scam" to "By golly, this works. My secretary is really making a thousand dollars a week!"

Then she quit and went to do it full-time. "Good for her," I thought. "But never for me. I'm never going to get involved in one of those MLM thingies selling nutrition. I don't take nutritional products myself and I doubt I ever will."

You just want to make a great umbrella? Buy a more expensive umbrella. You're not thinking of something original." She looked sympathetically at Lisa. "Sorry. I just don't think it's a very special idea."

"Good point," Kanisha said.

"How can we make this different from anything you have ever seen from an umbrella?" Michelle asked.

There were no quick answers. The idea was stalled. Lisa slowly sank back into her seat on the couch. She was so close to something great, but it didn't seem meant to be. Another minute passed and it felt like the longest minute of Lisa's life.

Finally Russell spoke up. "Hey, Mom, could you put a flashlight in the umbrella so you could see at night?" Looks shot around the room because Russell had just added a great idea. Lisa kissed him on the head.

"I don't care what you guys think, but that is a great idea It could be like a glow-light umbrella."

"Dark cloudy nights . . . walking your dog," Francie put in.

"I love it," Kanisha said.

"Lei Kim?" Michelle asked.

"Yes. I love it too," she offered with a smile.

"Me too. So let's keep going here. Other than the obvious, how can this idea for a better umbrella be of service to others?" Michelle asked, leading Lisa.

She thought for a minute. "We could call it the Love Umbrella . . . and 10 percent of the profits could be given to the kids' school. We could create an after-school program for kids. Or maybe for single mothers?"

"Just here in Idyllwild?" Kanisha asked.

"Why not?"

"Wow Now," Kanisha replied.

"Why not take the program national? That way, you have more

Collette was one of my wife's best friends. They went to lunch. My wife wasn't skeptical like me. She thought it was great and tried to get me to sign up with this nutrition company called USANA. "No thanks," I said. "Honey, you can keep all the money." In retrospect, those were the seven dumbest words I've ever uttered. She launched her network marketing business and the money started to roll in.

But I still wanted nothing to do with it. Okay, people could make money, but I still didn't believe in vitamins. So I wasn't going to try to sell something I didn't believe in. That's endarkened selling. My wife shared it with some people at one of my seminars. I was so embarrassed; I sat at the back of the room. People rushed to sign up. After all, it was Robert Allen's wife, even after I had told them that I wasn't convinced myself. Then people started calling me to say that the product my wife had sold them was incredible. It made them feel like a million bucks. "Hmmmmm," I thought as the testimonials started flowing back. "Maybe this stuff really is worth it. Maybe the doctor who invented it really did know what he was doing. Maybe I should be trying it."

And so I did. I began taking the product and noticed an amazing difference. More energy. Less aches and pains. Less fatigue. Less colds and laryngitis. As they say, the rest is history. I've been taking it every day for the last fifteen years and I will for the rest of my (I hope) longer life. I believe in it *that* much.

As for the money, well, my wife has deposited over $3 million into her bank account. Sometimes she even shares some of it with me. By the way, my former secretary now earns over a million dollars a year! I'm not skeptical anymore.

Did you notice how I transitioned from someone who was anti- to someone who is extremely pro-? At first, I thought the money was a joke and the product was a rip-off. Now, after cashing millions in checks, we're laughing all the way to the bank. And I've never felt better or healthier.

When you believe something this strongly, it affects your desire. You start to *want* to talk about it. You're less afraid to talk about it. Because no matter what they say, it still works for you.

exposure for the umbrellas," Francie said, picking up on Kanisha's response.

"And mothers could buy their daughters a dirt bike, too," Hannah added in all seriousness. The women laughed.

"If people know your product is giving money to kids, single mothers, or something like education, they'll want to buy it over the competition because of the intention behind the product," Francie pointed out.

"Do you think this would work for the E Broom?" Lei Kim asked.

"Of course," Michelle answered.

"And we could create programs with our websites that do something like this, right? Maybe offer the mothers some kind of financial grant or scholarship," Kanisha said, adding her two cents.

The ideas were flowing within the group and Michelle could barely get a word in edgewise. And that was okay. The teacher was sitting back and watching her students learn what it meant to really fly in life. She looked around the room. She smiled fondly at the children, because she knew this was something that would prove to be invaluable for them later in life. She gazed at the women and thought about how different they were now compared to just a month ago. She herself was happy, but she couldn't help feeling like something was missing. Slowly, she stood up and went toward her office. The only one to notice was Hannah, who just smiled briefly as she returned to watch the viewfinder on Nicky's camera, as he captured the entire mastermind process.

Sitting behind her desk, Michelle smiled at the energy coming from the other room. She picked up the phone and dialed the mayor's cell phone. After a few rings, he picked up.

"How's it going?" he asked.

"Amazing. Lisa finally had a breakthrough."

If your belief is weak and your desire is tepid, then when someone challenges you, you feel like a fraud. Like a phony. That's endarkened selling. If someone asks you, "Is this network marketing?" you cower behind your fear and give some excuse about how *your* network marketing thingy is different from and better than all the other network marketing thingies.

But if you have strong belief and true passion, when they ask the question "Is this network marketing?" you reply, "Absolutely! I don't know what your experience has been, but my experience with my MLM thingy has been fantastic."

You're probably already involved with some form of network marketing. Isn't everyone? (Mark and I think everyone should be. It's a great training ground for beginning entrepreneurs.) The purpose of this story is to highlight for you that your belief and your desire must be calibrated at liftoff intensity or you'll never get off the ground.

You have to find something that you believe in until it becomes a passion for you. When your passion kicks in, you're not selling anymore. You're just sharing what you believe is true.

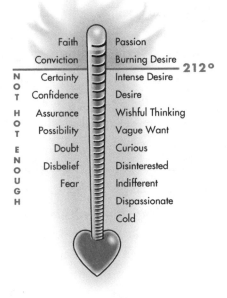

"And now?"

"They're still at it, but I'm in the office, talking to you. Where are you, by the way?"

"In my car—I was running a quick errand. Is everything okay?"

"Everything's fine." Michelle took a deep breath. "Well, I'm stalling, and I probably should get right to the reason I called. I want to say something, but I don't want to scare you off, because . . . well, shoot. I guess I'll just say it . . . and you don't have to like it . . . and I don't know if you—"

"Michelle?" Brady said, cutting her off.

"Yes?"

"I love you."

Michelle was crying before the words finished leaving his mouth.

"Can you come down to the store?" she asked. Just then there was a knock on the back door of the store.

"I'm sorry, what did you say?" he asked.

"Can you—"

The knocking on the back door cut her off in midsentence again.

"What's wrong?" he asked.

"Can you hold on a second?"

"Of course," he said, forever the gentleman.

Michelle came out of her office just as Lisa appeared in the hallway, reacting to the knocking.

"There you are," Lisa said. "Someone's at the back door. Please tell me you ordered takeout, because I'm starving."

Michelle unbolted the back door and opened it. There, in the dark alley, illuminated by the light from the store's hallway, stood Brady Wilson, holding a bouquet of flowers.

What is true for you? What do you believe in and desire so strongly that even rejection will not deter you? That's the secret to selling.

Which comes first, belief or desire? It depends. Sometimes one triggers the other. But your belief or desire must reach a high enough intensity or nothing happens. Belief must reach the level of conviction. Desire must reach the level of burning desire or passion.

This is the description of someone who is passionately convinced! That's when your intensity reaches the success threshold. This threshold is represented many ways.

- Threshold speed is called escape velocity. It's the speed at which an airplane leaves the runway and rises into the air. It's the speed at which rockets escape the earth's gravitational attraction.

- Threshold temperature is called the boiling point—212 degrees. It's the temperature at which water boils. A degree below this boiling point and you just have very hot water.

- Threshold pressure is when temperature and force are applied for the right length of time to transform ordinary carbon into diamonds. This is how synthetic diamonds are actually produced today. Believe it or not, ordinary cow manure (carbon) can be turned into diamond in a few hours with the correct pressure and temperature.

Sometimes we want things but don't believe we can get them.

ROBERT ALLEN: I wanted to lose fifty pounds. I'd tried a hundred times and had finally given up. Then my doctor informed me that my genetic disposition to diabetes had manifested.—I had the disease. My belief that my health was in danger went from zero to 100 percent in sixty seconds. My desire for ice cream and cookies went from 100 percent to zero in sixty seconds. Conviction and burning desire combined. I dropped fifty pounds in the next fifty days. And I've not gained it back.

14

Your Abundant Life
Are You Ready?

Winter raced by with a series of storms that brought record snow-fall, but it left as fast as it arrived. Spring's warm weather made the kids restless for summer vacation, which was still a whole month away. Life for the women of the Heartlight Broad Squad would never be the same. Their meetings went from once a week to once a month because of the workload their ideas carried, but this was a good thing.

Kanisha moved into Francie's house, and together they formed their own company, called the Unusual Suspects. The name was their way of showcasing that you never know where your true friends will come from. While the social networking idea for widows and widowers fell apart, the GED Challenge to end illiteracy secured a deal with Apple for its iPhones, and the program awarded over twenty-five thousand GEDs diplomas across the country in its first year alone. The teen pregnancy network idea took off as well. Kanisha and Francie's success was a testament to the power of the TEAM concept (Together, Everyone Achieves Miracles) for the Broad Squad. By working together, Kanisha and Francie were able to find solutions inside the problems that seemingly were roadblocks in both of their lives. Instead of complaining about the roadblocks, they provided a way through. Their website, www.teenmomworld.com, had become something of an Internet phenomenon,

When your desire and belief get in synch, the results are almost immediate. What do you call it when your desire and belief are in synch and have reached the threshold? Burning desire.

One day a dispassionate young man approached the Greek philosopher and casually said, "O great Socrates, I come to you for knowledge."

The philosopher took the young man down to the sea, waded in with him, and then dunked him under the water for thirty seconds. When he let the young man up for air, Socrates asked him to repeat what he wanted. "Knowledge, O great one," he sputtered.

Socrates put him under the water again, only this time a little longer.

After repeated dunkings and responses, the philosopher asked, "What do you want?" The young man finally gasped, "Air. I want air!" "Good," answered Socrates. "Now, when you want knowledge as much as you wanted air, you shall have it."

Success is not the result of spontaneous combustion.
You just set yourself on fire.
—REGGIE LEACH

So what do you want? What is your burning desire? What do you *really, really, really* want? What do you want more than air, more than any other thing? Why do we ask you this question?

Because when you set a goal, there will be a million distractions between now and your achieving of that goal. Each distraction is disguised as an immediate want, a pressing want, an urgent want. Do you want that immediate want? Or do you want your ultimate want? Hold both of them in your hands—your immediate want in your left hand and your ultimate want in your right hand.

Left hand: Do you want that doughnut?
Right hand: Or do you want to see yourself reaching your goal
             weight?

with five thousand new users each month. The site, while focusing on teen pregnancy, was also a daily stop for teenage girls who weren't pregnant and boys as well. Kids joined Teen Mom World because they were curious about the topic of pregnancy. Reading the first-person stories posted on the website about teenage pregnancy seemed to help kids answer the many questions filling their minds about what to do and what not to do where sex was concerned. Here they could ask questions without being judged by parents or peers.

Initially, Kanisha's idea set out to capture a niche of the teen pregnancy market, but it ended up as a major player in the social networking market for kids under the age of eighteen. It was a huge success, both financially and morally, for Francie and Kanisha, who were speaking around the country to teenagers. Within the first year, the foundation arm of their business, the Teen Mom Foundation, provided fifty grants at $2,000 each as well as online training to teen mothers to help with their pregnancy. Together, they were not only making a financial difference in their own lives, they were making a difference in the lives of others.

Out of all the Broad Squad students, Lei Kim turned out to be the most successful. Her situation was a perfect example of living in sync with the enlightened energy current behind money. When her Meal in a Bar was featured on a Food Network show, Lei Kim was quickly offered *Raw Cooking with Lei Kim,* a weekly show to air nationally on the network. The only problem was she would need to commute to Denver twice a week, which she didn't want to do. Lei Kim found the solution when Dogma, the pet food store located right next to Lei Kim's diner, decided to move across town. She got the idea of taking over the space to open a second restaurant that would offer a completely organic raw food menu. This second restaurant would be called Raw, and it would offer Idyllwild an alternative to the normal

If you choose the immediate want, you get the consequences that go with it. Your ultimate want must be so burning, so important, of such a high priority that *nothing* distracts you from it. *Nothing* tempts you away from it. *Nothing* diverts or delays you. You want it as badly as you want air. Just try holding your breath for sixty seconds right now. Bet you can't do it. Come on. Try it.

As the sixtieth second approached, did you want to take a breath? Did you? *Nothing* could stop you, could it? You had to have it, didn't you? *Nothing* could distract you, could it? You wanted to breathe, and you did.

This is the urgency you need to feel for your ultimate want. You want it urgently. Immediately. Right now. Nothing else takes precedence. You *must* have it. Even if it is a month, six months, a year, two years, or more in the future. Since it's such an important part of your *why*, you keep thinking about it, wanting, hoping for it, expecting it, moving toward it. Relentlessly. Unstoppably.

When you want it and believe it this much, you won't have trouble selling it. By the way, you won't call it selling. Just like the woman who hated selling, you'll call it sincere sharing of your true, passionate beliefs.

What do you want to sell?

diner food as well as a place for Lei Kim to shoot the weekly episodes of *Raw Cooking with Lei Kim*. Lei Kim's husband and son took over duties at the diner full time.

Raw food restaurants were already widely popular in California, but the trend was rapidly moving across the country and Lei Kim knew she was way ahead of the curve. Somehow, through her own enlightenment and success, she caused her family and those around her to rise in consciousness by example, not by the drama of confrontation or force.

But everything didn't go as smoothly as initially planned because the owner of the building didn't approve of the idea of having two restaurants located side by side; he told Lei Kim he wanted more diversity. Lei Kim knew what she wanted, so she made him an offer and bought the entire building, which in addition to five retail shops had three large offices on the second floor. It wasn't a power move as much as it was a need for office space. Project Education Sweep and the associated website were no longer a dream but a reality, a result of the overwhelming success of the E Broom.

Funded with 10 percent of the E Broom's profits, Project Education Sweep provided grants to educators around the world. Lei Kim believed if you have a teacher who isn't worried about having enough money, you'd have a teacher more focused on providing quality education. As soon as corporations discovered they could help education around the world by purchasing a more efficient version of a product they were already buying, not to mention the preventive effects on wrist injuries and carpal tunnel syndrome, orders for the E Broom/dustpan combination began to flood in.

While the largest sales numbers came from commercial markets, which included sports arenas and stadiums, parks and recreation centers, subways, and fast-food and hotel chains, the consumer market was beyond impressive for a new product venture. Within a year

Sell the low-hanging fruit on the tree of you. That's the best stuff that you have to offer. The stuff in your own backyard. Your acres of diamonds. That's your money tree.

Here is your wax on/wax off assignment. Look through the following list of things to sell and find one PSI that you'll commit to selling successfully in the next ninety days.

WHAT PRODUCTS DO YOU HAVE TO SELL?

Sell your used products. Put it up on eBay. Get rid of it.

Sell a bargain property. Find and flip a bargain piece of real estate.

Sell someone a product-selling business. Find a network marketing company that you believe in.

Sell your own new product. Create a new product that solves a world problem.

Sell other people's new products. Buy wholesale and market someone else's product solution.

Sell others' used products. Learn how to sell on eBay. It's working for millions. Why not you?

WHAT SERVICES DO YOU HAVE TO SELL?

Sell an existing service based on an old skill. What do you know how to do, that people need done?

Sell a new service based on your new skill. What do you want to learn how to do for people?

Sell someone else on learning and selling a new skill. You take a piece of the deal.

Sell someone else on learning how to sell an old skill. You take a piece of the deal.

Sell someone's skill or service.

Sell someone on how to get into business selling services.

her E Broom had captured 1 percent of the entire U.S. consumer broom market when an infomercial ran on the Home Shopping Network. One percent didn't sound like much, but 1 percent of 105 million households meant Lei Kim sold over a million E Brooms to American households alone. The rapid success landed Lei Kim on the cover of *Entrepreneur* magazine.

True to her word, Lisa continued to live her life in a simple fashion. When the Love Umbrella was licensed by a major retailer, Lisa gladly took a minor position in the company to focus on the nonprofit foundation she created, and this was still only part-time. The Foundation of Love, as she named it, provided scholarships to children of single mothers around the country and helped single mothers with the rising costs of education, summer camp tuition, and entrepreneurial ventures. When the umbrella continued to bring in record profits, Lisa expanded the reach of the foundation to include a new idea. Because she'd never finished college herself, Lisa came up with the idea for CollegeTracks.org. College Track was the catalyst for change for underresourced high school students who were motivated to earn a college degree. During its first year, College Track strengthened its services and expanded its program to support more students. Through the center-based approach and core service areas, College Track created a culture of high expectations and success. Lisa wanted to ensure that each student was college-ready and to provide support that many students did not have at home or school. Together, the components made a powerful, comprehensive program that empowered students to achieve their dream of a college education. While the Foundation of Love and CollegeTracks.org were a success, Lisa continued to work at Heartlight twice a week simply because she loved the fellowship of the store and felt indebted to Michelle for helping her change her life.

Michelle married Brady Wilson in an intimate Christmas Eve ceremony. After a honeymoon in Aspen, they moved into a new house

WHAT INFORMATION DO YOU HAVE TO SELL?

Sell your knowledge. What do you know that others need to know?

Sell your skill. What do you know how to do that others need to learn how to do?

Sell other people's knowledge. Who has knowledge that other people need to know?

Sell other people's skill. Whom do you know that has skill that other people need to learn?

Find something you passionately believe it. Get passionately convinced. And then start selling it.

In Danish the word *selji* is the original word for "selling," and it means "to serve." One of the greatest salesmen in the world, Jesus Christ, said, "The greatest among you is the servant of all." So if you serve greatly with passion and share your PSI with a lot of people on the front end, you'll be paid enormous amounts on the back end. You have to share your message with a whole lot of people with a positive mental attitude and ask for the business, and ultimately and inevitably you'll earn a fortune.

on the east side of town near the lake. The day they moved in, Michelle brought home a golden retriever puppy. The house was a four-bedroom Craftsman gem, which the mayor snapped up out of foreclosure, surprising Michelle with the purchase. Hannah got the dirt bike she'd been dreaming about, and Nicky had become something of a famous filmmaker in town. As a result of the Broad Squad success, Nicky set out to make a real movie. His film, *Richest Kids in America—How They Got That Way and You Can Too,* won the documentary prize for first-time filmmakers at the Denver International Film Festival, and Hannah got her producer credit. Nicky was the youngest filmmaker to ever win the Maverick Award. While he entered into a distribution deal with a U.S. distributor, which gave him a $40,000 advance against the film's profits, Nicky told his mom to negotiate to keep all Internet rights for the film. Selling downloads on his website, www.richestkidsinamerica.com, Nicky became an entrepreneur at the ripe old age of twelve. The attention surrounding the film also spawned a new business idea for Michelle. The website www.mastermindsrevealed.com became a moderate Internet coaching success at first, but it wasn't until Michelle wrote an e-book on the subject that the business really took off. At $3.99 for each download at www.youpublish.com, the book was selling more than a thousand copies a week.

On top of her duties at the Heartlight, Michelle was performing ten coaching calls a week and had to spend one week a month traveling around the country speaking. Her latest stop was in Los Angeles, California.

It was seven-thirty in the morning on September 7, almost a year to the day she started the Broad Squad. Sitting behind the mike in the

⑲

THE DASH TO CASH!

Throughout this book we've used several metaphors to illustrate the process of creating wealth, from the recipe metaphor to the hummingbird, the Wish-Fulfilling Tree, the path, low-hanging fruit, and the ladder. We hope at least a few of these images have resonated with you, to help you remember the lessons we are trying to teach.

As you scan back over what you've read, we hope you've internalized the importance of finding a "profitable servant" project about which you are passionately convinced. We hope you've attracted a team of like-minded and like-hearted winners who will support you on your journey.

As a final metaphor to send you off, here is the dash to cash.

When people think about money they usually think about the bottom line, the cold hard facts, the nitty-gritty details. That's the end result of the race to money—the finish line.

The beginning of money is the "soft stuff," the internal stuff, the heart and mind stuff. This is the starting line.

Turn the page for a test to determine if you're ready to take action.

studio of a local drive-time morning show, Michelle was giving her second interview of the day.

"The spiritual truth of the universe. That's how great ideas work," she said. "When you are single-minded in your intention, which essentially means your attention is on your intention, the universe responds in kind. This is one of the laws of the universe. The more we are able to stand in the truth of who we are, the more we are becoming aware of the great power within. With our Broad Squad, the name we gave our Mastermind Group, we are held accountable for our thoughts, words, and actions. Basically, when you have a TEAM, it teaches you to remember the truth about yourself and that you are indeed creative, abundant, and special."

"What *is* the truth?" the interviewer asked.

"The truth is simply a reminder of what you already know," Michelle explained. "When we are born, we aren't judgmental of others, or ourselves, for that matter. We trust that we are special. We celebrate it, but somehow, during the course of growing up, where life and society kick us around more than a few times, we forget that simple truth."

The interviewer smiled. "I'll ask you again: what is the truth?"

"The truth is like an electrical outlet in your house. It's always there, on the wall, waiting for you to plug something into it. A lamp doesn't work unless you plug it in, right? A toaster can't toast bread unless it's plugged in. It might sit there and try really hard to toast the bread, but unless it's plugged in, it's fighting an impossible battle. The same can be said for life. While I don't mean to blaspheme the life I had with my late husband, I was living life in wait. I was waiting for something to happen in my life. That's the secret behind the concept of a mastermind. The one mind created by the group is more powerful than the lies we perpetuate by our single mind. It's

THE WINNER'S TEST

Answer the following questions on a scale of 1 to 10—where 1 is frozen cold and 10 is boiling hot.

- ✦ M I am committed to a clear and measurable objective. ____
- ✦ I I virtualize myself having accomplished it. ____
- ✦ N I bring the confidence of my many past successes. ____
- ✦ D I bring the wisdom learned from my many challenges. ____
- ✦ & My critical voice does not affect my effectiveness at all. ____
- ✦ H I am passionate about achieving my objective. ____
- ✦ E My objective is in alignment with my purpose. ____
- ✦ A My intuition is congruent with me accomplishing it. ____
- ✦ R I feel that Higher Power approves and is cheering me on. ____
- ✦ T I am determined and unstoppable. I never give in. ____

If you score 50 or less, you're cold. Are you sure you want to do this?
If you scored 51–80, you're warm. Reconsider your plans.
If you scored 81–90, you're getting hotter. You'll probably make it.
If you scored 91–100, you're passionately convinced. Watch out, world!

When your mind is clear and your heart is right, you're ready for the hundred-yard dash to cash.

Can you imagine a sprinter in the blocks, ready for the sound of the starter's pistol, being focused on anything other than the finish line a hundred yards away? Would it be useful for that sprinter to harbor any doubtful thoughts? Any fearful thoughts? Any distracting thoughts, such as a relationship problem, a financial challenge, or the need to make travel arrangements for an upcoming vacation? Nope. Any other thought besides winning deducts precious milliseconds off the final result. And only the top three finishers advance. You miss by a millisecond and you're going home without a medal.

Yet, how do ordinary people start their day in the blocks of life? They're not focused on the finish line. They don't even know what or

not what other people say about you, either. It's what you say about yourself in those quiet moments when you're all alone. That's what life is about. Knowing the truth of who you are."

Michelle sat back and smiled at the interviewer as if to say, *Take that.*

"We've been talking to Michelle Erickson-Wilson, author and creator of the wildly successful e-book *Masterminds Revealed.* Before you go, Michelle, one last question."

"Sure."

"What's next for you?"

"Who knows? The world is full of possibilities."

"Thank you, Michelle."

"You're welcome."

where it is! They're distracted with a million thoughts—a cauldron of conflicting visions, voices, and vibrations. *They turn an ordinary hundred-yard dash into a difficult twenty-six-mile marathon.* They spend precious time and money on doubts and fears. They write down goals and surge off to get them, then get distracted by off-purpose opportunities. They have false starts and outright failures.

If any of that describes you, it's time to follow our recipe:

1. **Wow Now:** Focus your mind and its visions, voices, and vibrations.
2. **Inner Winner:** Listen to your intuitions. Pursue your passions.
3. **Dream Team:** Engage your Dream Team. Explore with them your plan. Let them improve it. Determine what you are going to have to sell. Get ready to sell it.
4. Check your fuel gauges.

   Mind: Are you convinced that you will do whatever it takes to get what you want?

   Heart: What do you really, passionately want? What is your burning desire?

   Team: Are your teammates as convinced and passionate as you are?

5. Set a start date and a finish date, no matter what.
6. Get in the starter's blocks.

ON YOUR MARK.

GET SET

SELL!

CASH IN A FLASH

ACKNOWLEDGMENTS

Awareness is the key to freeing everyone. This book is about expanding and improving everyone's awareness financially, mentally, heartfully, and experientially. Our hearts are overflowing with appreciation and rampaging gratitude for those who contributed to our deepening awareness, so we could serve greatly our ever-increasing number of readers.

We simply want to help every reader become abundant and enjoy greater freedoms. We acknowledge that these folks served us brilliantly in our quest; we are profoundly thankful for them and want you to know it.

Our agent, Jillian Manus, is the "go the extra *ten* miles" person. She has tirelessly worked with us, our ideas, our manuscript, our marketing ideas, and our publisher to create the greatest product ever. Theresa Van Eeghen is Jillian's right and left hand and makes the impossible look effortless.

Shaye Areheart is our publisher at Harmony Books. Shaye loves books, writers, and especially us. We totally and absolutely love her and her care and consideration for the most important profession in the world, writing. Julia Pastore is the finest and most loving editor in the world. She has done an extraordinary job working with us and we lovingly thank her.

Eric DelaBarre, a writer for the TV show *Law & Order*, brilliantly helped us make the story side of our book read like a page-turning novel, for which we are deeply thankful and appreciative.

Daryl Allen, Bob's wife, is forever cheering Bob on to the successful and happy conclusion of his great writing and thinking. He is eternally grateful to the wealth lessons that his three wonderful children have taught him: Amae, Aaron, and Hunter.

Bob's right hand, Justine Painter, is indispensable at doing everything she can to keep Bob free to write. Bob's business partners in his various businesses have taught him priceless lessons: Thomas R. Painter, president of the Enlightened Wealth Institute and all the excellent, enlightened visionary leaders of EWI; Steve Carlson; Jan Stephan; Sharm Smith; and Ron and Sue McMillan. Many thanks also to Richard Paul Evans, Meagen Bunten, Dave Wentz, Nick Essayian, and Ari Wasserman.

Mark is endlessly thankful to his entire team: Debbie Lefever, Mark's executive assistant, who kept Mark free to pursue his endless efforts to make a bestselling book look like it was effortless ease, and kept away the endless parade of people who want to talk to Mark; Patti Coffey, his chief of staff, a Dream Team leader of leaders and a godsend who makes things happen; Stephanie DeMizio, head of clear thinking, editing, syntax, and writing of this book; Lauren Mastrodonato and Gina-Rose Kimball, working marvelously in marketing; Liora Mendeloff, courageously reading every word and commenting on how to make it ever better; Karen Schoenfeld, accounting; Connie Simoni, customer service; Josh Escamilla, the man who keeps our warehouse operation flowing with grace and ease; and Jeff Cohen, our abundantly wise and able attorney.

Mark's daughters, who grew up reading and love the entire book process, are Melanie Hansen and Elisabeth Hansen Delgesso.

Chaz DeSimone is our accomplished and brilliant graphic designer and artist.

We offer our sincere thanks to our hand-selected support team of marketing and Internet experts: Rick Dearr, Simon Leung, Lee Collins, Robin Collins, Andy Huang, James D. Lee, and Alicia Ashley.

To all of these, and the hundreds of others not mentioned, *thanks a million*!

We also want to give thanks to each of our "Screaming Eagles" who helped us research the concepts in this book, and they are: Dave Aiken, Saquina Akanni, Giovanni Amadeo, David Anderson, Linda Anderson, Ross Arntson, Gaye Barker, Neil Basford, Rob Baxter, Brady Bradley, Tony Carino, James Christmas, Eileen Colony, Cherie Duncan, Sue Elliott, Cristy Emerson, Laszlo Fekete, Jonathan Freeman, Joanna Garzilli, Dorie Geniesse, David Gilman, Julie Gordon White, Heidi Hanseen DeRoest,

Sonny Harrison, Bunny Hodas, Joan Kappes, Katie Krim, Sandi L'Amie, Kim Law, Mary Elizabeth Lenahan, Wendell MacRae, Carol Marturano-Becker, David Masters, Ann McIndoo, Pat McKelvey, David Mease, Cecile Miranda, Linda Moy, Ellen Myers, August Roberson, Kim Roman Corle, Kimball Roundy, Leila Samoodi, Albert Steven, Zoltan Vincze, Elizabeth Zachariah.

INDEX

Right-side pages, "Michelle's Story," are not included in the index.

Matthew, 188
Maximum Achievement (Tracy), 132–34
megasizing goals, 112–18, 122
memories:
    future, 100–106, 134
    of past, transforming, 96–102,
        134, 136
    of special moments in past, 12
Mendez, Lester, 148
microcredit movement, 24, 194–98,
    210–12, 214, 266–68
Millionaire Matrix, 316–20
mind, 34–36, 44–48, 76–78, 110
    Cache Scan of, 182–88, 358
    see also Wow Now
mobility, 260
    measuring, 264–66
money, 262–64
    chunks and streams of, 4–7
    linear and residual income and,
        4–5; *see also* residual income
    measuring, 264–66
Money Soup, 222–24
multiauthored books, 300–4, 320

N
National Speakers Association, 300
negative emotions:
    critical inner voice and, 66
    see also fear
negative thoughts:
    envisioning consequences of,
        124–26, 136
    refusing to think, 86, 104
    see also critical inner voice
negativity, in world, 114, 120
network marketing, 242, 284,
    338–42
9 Steps to Financial Freedom, The
    (Orman), 2
Nothing Down (Allen), 308
now, empowering, 132–44
    Secret Spot and, 138–44
    vision of past and future and, 132,
        134–36

O
obvious, starting with, 168–70
One Minute Manicure, 256
One Minute Millionaire, The (Hansen
    and Allen), 4, 114–18, 206, 324

Orman, Suze, 2
Oswald, Yvonne, 82

P
Painter, Thomas R., 310
Parable of the Talents, 188
past, 132, 134
    handling of problems in, 254
    now affected by, 132, 134–36
    remembering special moments in,
        12
    transforming memories of,
        96–102, 134, 136
pattern integrity, 172
Peale, Norman Vincent, 246
positive thinking, 76–94
    empowering questions and, 76–82,
        88, 90–92, 94, 104–6
    high-energy words and, 82–86,
        90–92
    ka-ching thinking and, 124–28,
        136
    setbacks and, 104
    wax on/wax off assignment for, 94
problems, 248–68
    bigger, 256–58
    future, avoiding or navigating,
        258–64
    getting stuck in, 248
    other people's, solving, 270–86
    turning into profits, 244, 246–68,
        322–28
    virtualization technique and,
        252–54
    in world at large, 266–68
    your own, creating solutions to,
        248–50, 252–54, 256–58
procrastination, 30, 36, 62, 104, 156
Proctor, Bob, 86–87
products, selling, 234, 238–44,
    270–328
    Google searches and, 288
    information, 286–328; *see also*
        information, selling
    others' products and, 280–84,
        288–94
    production costs and, 294
    real estate, 270–78, 280–82; *see
        also* real estate
    wax on/wax off assignment for,
        350

ABOUT THE AUTHORS

You can easily create the life you deserve.
—MARK VICTOR HANSEN

MARK VICTOR HANSEN

Focused solely on helping people from all walks of life reshape their vision of what's possible, no one is better respected in the area of human potential than Mark Victor Hansen. Creating powerful change in thousands of organizations and millions of individuals worldwide for over thirty years, Mark delivers proven messages of possibility, opportunity, and action.

You May Know Mark as "That *Chicken Soup for the Soul* Guy"

Established as a cultural icon in 1990, Mark and his business partner Jack Canfield created what *Time* magazine called "the publishing phenomenon of the decade," with over 112 million *Chicken Soup for the Soul* books sold worldwide—one of the most successful publishing franchises of all time.

Internationally Known Keynote Speaker and Personality

With his one-of-a-kind technique and masterful authority of his work, time and again he receives high accolades from his audiences as one of the most dynamic and compelling speakers of our time. Having spoken in more than sixty countries, Mark has shared his powerful transformations with thousands of organizations and millions of individuals worldwide.

Bestsellers

Mark's other bestselling books include *The One Minute Millionaire, Cracking the Millionaire Code, How to Make the Rest of Your Life the Best of Your Life, The Aladdin Factor, Dare to Win,* and *The Power of Focus.*

Media

His endearing and charismatic style captures audiences' hearts as well as their attention in person, on television or radio, and in print. He has appeared on *Oprah*, CNN, the *Today* show, and has taken part in countless television, print, and radio interviews. He has been quoted in *Time*, *U.S. News & World Report*, *USA Today*, the *New York Times*, and *Entrepreneur*.

Entrepreneur

Expanding his business ventures and leading by example, Mark launched Hansen House publishing in 2008, bringing the most compelling ideas from the world's greatest thinkers to print.

Further, he has targeted the realms of television and feature film for his next steps in his own journey.

Through his library of audio recordings, videos, and articles in the areas of big thinking, sales achievement, wealth building, publishing success, and personal and professional development, Mark continues to create a profound influence.

Coaching and teaching aspiring authors, speakers, and experts on building lucrative publishing and speaking careers through his MEGA seminar series, Mark produces top-notch, results-oriented annual conferences.

Recipient of numerous awards honoring his entrepreneurial spirit, philanthropic heart, and business acumen, Mark was inducted into the Sales & Marketing Executives International Hall of Fame and accepted the Horatio Alger Award for extraordinary life achievement in the area of free enterprise leadership.

Philanthropist and Humanitarian

Working tirelessly for organizations such as Habitat for Humanity, American Red Cross, March of Dimes, and Childhelp USA, and establishing his own foundation dedicated to literacy as a means to end poverty, Mark firmly believes that giving back is paramount to his own personal happiness and success. He is proud to be the recipient of the Visional Philanthropist for Youth Award by Covenant House of California (2004) among others.

To book Mark for a speaking engagement, contact Debbie Lefever at (949) 764–2640 ext. 105 or e-mail debbie@markvictorhansen.com.

ARE YOU NEXT?

Are you the next bestselling author? The next highly paid speaker? Or the next entrepreneur who strikes it rich with your idea?

Achieve success faster with an expert to mentor you! Mark Victor Hansen Coaching was designed to help people who are committed to achieving the goals of becoming a successful entrepreneur, book author, or public speaker by giving them access to an expert personal coach. **This is your year to succeed**—pursue the Mega Success you desire when you work one-on-one with a certified coach and apply Mark Victor Hansen's principles of accomplishment.

The difference between someone who has achieved success and someone who just dreams about it is usually who they have on their team. Mark Victor Hansen developed a coaching program that will give you access to Mark's expert coaches. Don't go it alone, you'll get there faster when you have experience and support on your side. Call 1–800–207–6249 Ext. 506 for a FREE introduction to Mark Victor Hansen's coaching program.

Your Mark Victor Hansen Coach will help you:
- Implement strategies and best practices from Mark Victor Hansen
- Take action and receive measurable results
- Learn how to sell your vision and ideas
- Identify the strengths you possess and leverage them for success
- Cultivate a positive outlook and overcome limiting beliefs
- Develop the essential habits for maximizing success
- And much more!

What is your dream? Do you wish to write a book? Market your book to the bestseller list? Are you trying to take your talents to a speaking career? Are you an entrepreneur craving success at another level? Achieve success faster with an elite coach on your side. Mark Victor Hansen Coaching is now accepting new clients, so call **1–800–207–6249 Ext. 506 TODAY!**

ROBERT G. ALLEN

Robert G. Allen has been teaching ordinary people how to achieve extraordinary success and financial freedom for over thirty years. He is the author of some of the most influential financial books of all time, including the *New York Times* bestsellers *Creating Wealth, Nothing Down, Multiple Streams of Income,* and *The One Minute Millionaire,* which he coauthored with Mark Victor Hansen.

Today there are literally thousands of millionaires who attribute their success to Mr. Allen's systems and strategies. The National Speakers Association has named him America's Top Millionaire Maker.

He is a popular television and radio guest, appearing on hundreds of radio and television programs, including *Good Morning America, Live! with Regis and Kelly,* and *Larry King Live.* He has been the subject in numerous international publications including the *Wall Street Journal,* the *Los Angeles Times,* the *Washington Post, Newsweek, Barron's, Money* magazine, and *Reader's Digest* to name just a few.

Robert Allen believes that part of his purpose in life is to teach people how to achieve financial success—even starting from nothing. As proof, he once said, "Send me to any city. Take away my wallet. Give me $100 for living expenses. And in seventy-two hours, I'll buy an excellent piece of real estate using none of my own money."

Challenged by the *Los Angeles Times* to live up to his claim, he flew to San Francisco and proceeded to buy six properties in fifty-seven hours. The *L.A. Times* headline proclaimed, "Buying Home Without Cash— Boastful Investor Accepts *Times'* Challenge and Wins."

Most people assume that "it takes money to make money." Mr. Allen demonstrated that the source of true wealth is an internal reservoir of passion, courage, and persistence.

On the home front, Robert and his wife, Daryl, just celebrated thirty-two years of marriage and are the proud parents of three children, Amae, Aaron, and Hunter.

THE ENLIGHTENED WEALTH INSTITUTE

For over thirty years, graduates of Robert Allen's popular seminars and trainings have successfully applied his techniques to earn multiple streams of income. You can read thousands of these success stories at www .millionairehalloffame.com.

Robert Allen's Enlightened Wealth Institute conducts basic and advanced programs in real estate, the stock market, information marketing, and entrepreneurship. If you want more information about these programs, click on the link for EWI at www.robertallen.com. If financial success is your goal, Robert Allen and his team of trainers and coaches can get you there.